1.20/1.05

JOHN L. DUNLAP, JR.

KERYGMA AND MYTH
A Theological Debate

hARPER ✦ TORChBOOKS

*A reference-list of Harper Torchbooks, classified
by subjects, is printed at the end of this volume.*

KERYGMA AND MYTH

A Theological Debate

by
RUDOLF BULTMANN
and
Ernst Lohmeyer, Julius Schniewind,
Helmut Thielicke, and Austin Farrer

Edited by Hans Werner Bartsch
Revised edition of this translation by Reginald H. Fuller

HARPER TORCHBOOKS / **The Cloister Library**
HARPER & ROW, PUBLISHERS
NEW YORK

KERYGMA AND MYTH

Printed in the United States of America

This book, with the exception of the Austin
Farrer article, was first published in German by
Herbert Reich of Hamburg-Volksdorf, Germany;
the English edition, including the Austin Farrer
article, was first published in 1953 by S.P.C.K.,
London, and is here reprinted by arrangement.
The English translation has been revised for the
Torchbook edition.

First HARPER TORCHBOOK edition published 1961

CONTENTS

v

FOREWORD

NO single work which has appeared in the field of New Testament scholarship during the war years has evoked such a lively discussion as Bultmann's original manifesto, _New Testament and Mythology_ (p. 1ff. in the present volume). Unless we are prepared to rule out any advance in New Testament scholarship in Germany since the outbreak of the war, like Ethelbert Stauffer in the preface to the third edition of his _Theologie des Neuen Testaments_ (Stuttgart, 1947, p. v) we must surely recognize such an advance in this debate. Since the relevant material has hitherto been almost inaccessible, or available only to a very limited circle in cyclostyled form, it has seemed all the more urgent to place the discussion as a whole before the theological public. It will at once be seen that there is no question of our being able to present a series of assured results. There is that much truth in Stauffer's contention so far as this particular debate is concerned. Yet even Sir Edwyn Hoskyns in his review of New Testament studies in the years between the wars[1] was equally unable to present a series of "assured results". Even for him the only result was an open question. All the same Hoskyns's work itself appeared to many to be a particularly important result in New Testament scholarship. The New Testament is the Word of God spoken through the words of men, and since the proclamation of the act of God as the incarnate word confronts us in this particular form, it can never be spoken of in direct, straightforward language, and therefore there cannot be in the strictest sense any "assured results". Yet it would not necessarily be wrong to see in the debate on "demythologizing" both a real "result", a positive contribution made to New Testament studies by German theologians during the second World War, and also a factor which is bound to have a profound effect on the study of the New Testament in the future.

[1] _The Riddle of the New Testament_, 1931, German trans. 1938.

This problem of the interpretation of the mythological elements in the New Testament is not in itself a new one. It was raised as soon as the world view which lay behind the New Testament began to change. The most recent attempt to grapple with the problem was that of liberal theology, so called. We may leave out of account the "supernaturalistic" answer, which sought to retain the New Testament view of the world as it stood. The liberal answer consisted in the elimination of all mythology from the New Testament. In course of time, however, this particular answer was shown to be untenable, so the problem presented itself anew and in a far more inexorable form than ever before. For now it was realized that what was needed was not elimination but interpretation. The recognition of the kerygmatic character of the gospels, and of the fact that the kerygma was not confined to the historical narratives of the gospels, made the right interpretation of the mythology of the New Testament more urgent than it had ever been before. So the relation between kerygma and myth came to be the crucial problem in the interpretation of the New Testament writings. It is the merit of Bultmann that in trying to solve this problem by demythologizing the New Testament he has called our attention to the problem in all its inexorability. It should be noted, however, that this problem has been the driving force behind the study of the New Testament for many years. It has been constantly recurring ever since Martin Kähler's equally novel manifesto, *Der sogennante historische Jesus und der biblische Christus* (new impression, Leipzig, 1928). Indeed, it may be traced back as far as William Wrede in the identical form in which Bultmann has raised it. In our own time we meet it when we compare Bultmann's own commentary on the Fourth Gospel in the Meyer series (1941) with Ernst Pery's examination of the sources of the Johannine theology (Lund, 1939). We meet it again in all the recent commentaries on the synoptic gospels, and also in Martin Dibelius's *Jesus* (1939). The prominence of this subject in both the earlier and the more recent work on the New Testament suggests that it is the fundamental problem of all New Testament exposition. It faces both the theologian in the lecture room and the parish priest in the preparation of his sermons.

All that the present volume seeks to do is to indicate the lines

on which the debate has been carried on by both sides. No attempt
is made to take sides in the controversy, except on one particular
point—viz., in the essays which have been selected for inclusion.
Space was not the only determining factor. There has been no
lack of critics who have denied the problem altogether. It has
been contended that "there is no need to demythologize the
New Testament, because it does not contain any myth".[1] What
Bultmann and his school are trying to remove, according to Sasse,
is not myth but dogma ("dedogmatizing, not demythologizing"). It would be agreed on all sides that no theology speaking
for the church could have a hand in that. By the omission of
essays which take Sasse's line we are *ipso facto* adopting a positive
attitude to the debate. We believe that there is a real issue at
stake.

Similarly, the actual choice of essays is intended to suggest
the lines on which an answer to the question and a solution of
the problem are to be sought. Most of the contributions we
have selected come from those who are engaged in New Testament exegesis. But it must not therefore be concluded that this
question is of no interest to systematic theology. Indeed, the
systematic theologian must be interested in it if he is to take
account of modern philosophy. So must the student of comparative religion when he compares modern religious movements
with those of ancient times. That is why we include contributions
from these fields as well. But as this is a matter of the interpretation of the New Testament documents, the solution must come
from the exegesis of the New Testament. We must hearken to
the testimony of the New Testament itself. That is why the
discussion between Bultmann and Schniewind occupies the
centre of the stage, for the criticisms of New Testament scholars
are obviously the most important. In this problem we are
concerned with the right hearing of the New Testament message,
of the kerygma of Jesus Christ the Son of God. This right hearing
is the decisive presupposition for every interpretation. This
therefore must be the hidden centre of the discussion, and it is
with this that all the other contributions are also concerned.

If that be the direction and aim of this volume, we cannot do
more than offer an introduction to the debate. That debate is
carried on in every exegesis of a New Testament document, for

[1] H. Sasse, *Flucht vorm Dogma*, Luthertum, 1942, p. 161ff.

every exegesis involves taking up a definite position with regard to this problem. The debate is not therefore limited to essays written specifically on the subject. In order, however, to recognize the problem even where it is only latent, we must know what it really is, and that is what Bultmann's essay and the discussion it evoked enable us to do. Such is the service which the present volume would hope to perform.

SAHMS,   H. W. BARTSCH.
13 *September* 1948.

TRANSLATOR'S PREFACE

AS Ian Henderson has pointed out in his *Myth in the New Testament* (S.C.M. Press, 1952), the translation of some of the words in Bultmann's essay presents certain difficulties, difficulties which also occur in the subsequent discussion. As Henderson says, "In some important points, Bultmann and the existentialists mint their verbal coinage and use words in a sense which is not necessarily contained in other German writing." While Heidegger's *Sein und Zeit* has not yet been translated, there is a valuable exposition of its thought and a discussion of its terminology in the prefatory essay to a collection of essays by Martin Heidegger published under the title of *Existence and Being*. This prefatory essay is by Dr Werner Brock, and the reader is referred to it for an elucidation of some of the terms mentioned below, as well as to Henderson's work mentioned above.

As yet, no one has ventured to translate *Dasein* or *Vorhanden*, but in order not to disfigure the English translation by the frequent use of German words, I have rendered *Dasein* as "human life", "human Being", or even "Being" where its human character is made clear by the context. *Vorhanden*, which Heidegger uses of the peculiar mode of being characteristic of inanimate objects, as contrasted with responsible human *Dasein*, I have translated by "tangible", as in Bultmann the antithesis is not so much between *Vorhandensein* and *Dasein* as between the tangible realities of the visible world and eternal realities, very much like the Pauline contrast of *kata sarka* and *kata pneuma*. I have followed Brock in rendering *Geworfenheit* by "thrownness". The distinction between *existentiell* and *existential*, the first meaning that which belongs to existence as such, the second that which belongs to the particular philosophical system called existentialism, is expressed by the use of "existential" for the former, and "existentialist" for the latter. The distinction Bultmann makes between *geschichtlich* and *historisch* I have endeavoured to observe by the use of "historic" for the former and "historical" or, sometimes, "past-historical" for the latter. By *historisch* Bultmann means that which can be established by the historian's criticism of the past; by *geschichtlich* he means that which, although occurring in past history, has a vital existential reference to our life today.

REGINALD H. FULLER.

KERYGMA AND MYTH
A Theological Debate

RUDOLF BULTMANN

NEW TESTAMENT AND MYTHOLOGY

The Mythological Element in the Message of the New Testament and the Problem of its Re-interpretation

I

THE TASK OF DEMYTHOLOGIZING THE NEW TESTAMENT PROCLAMATION

A. The Problem

1. The Mythical View of the World and the Mythical Event of Redemption

THE cosmology of the New Testament is essentially mythical in character. The world is viewed as a three-storied structure, with the earth in the centre, the heaven above, and the underworld beneath. Heaven is the abode of God and of celestial beings—the angels. The underworld is hell, the place of torment. Even the earth is more than the scene of natural, everyday events, of the trivial round and common task. It is the scene of the supernatural activity of God and his angels on the one hand, and of Satan and his daemons on the other. These supernatural forces intervene in the course of nature and in all that men think and will and do. Miracles are by no means rare. Man is not in control of his own life. Evil spirits may take possession of him. Satan may inspire him with evil thoughts. Alternatively, God may inspire his thought and guide his purposes. He may grant him heavenly visions. He may allow him to hear his word of succour or demand. He may give him the supernatural power of his Spirit. History does not follow a smooth unbroken course; it is set in motion and controlled by these supernatural powers. This aeon is held in bondage by

Satan, sin, and death (for "powers" is precisely what they are),
and hastens towards its end. That end will come very soon, and
will take the form of a cosmic catastrophe. It will be inaugurated
by the "woes" of the last time. Then the Judge will come from
heaven, the dead will rise, the last judgement will take place,
and men will enter into eternal salvation or damnation.

*This then is the mythical view of the world which the New Testament
presupposes when it presents the event of redemption which is the subject
of its preaching.* It proclaims in the language of mythology that
the last time has now come. "In the fulness of time" God sent
forth his Son, a pre-existent divine Being, who appears on earth
as a man.[1] He dies the death of a sinner[2] on the cross and makes
atonement for the sins of men.[3] His resurrection marks the
beginning of the cosmic catastrophe. Death, the consequence of
Adam's sin, is abolished,[4] and the daemonic forces are deprived
of their power.[5] The risen Christ is exalted to the right hand of
God in heaven[6] and made "Lord" and "King".[7] He will come
again on the clouds of heaven to complete the work of redemption,
and the resurrection and judgement of men will follow.[8] Sin,
suffering and death will then be finally abolished.[9] All this is to
happen very soon; indeed, St Paul thinks that he himself will live
to see it.[10]

All who belong to Christ's Church and are joined to the Lord
by Baptism and the Eucharist are certain of resurrection to
salvation,[11] unless they forfeit it by unworthy behaviour.
Christian believers already enjoy the first instalment of salvation,
for the Spirit[12] is at work within them, bearing witness to their
adoption as sons of God,[13] and guaranteeing their final resurrection.[14]

[1] Gal. 4. 4; Phil. 2. 6ff.; 2 Cor. 8. 9; John 1. 14, etc.
[2] 2 Cor. 5. 21; Rom. 8. 3.
[3] Rom. 3. 23–26; 4. 25; 8. 3; 2 Cor. 5. 14, 19; John 1. 29; 1 John 2. 2, etc.
[4] 1 Cor. 15. 21f.; Rom. 5. 12ff.
[5] 1 Cor. 2. 6; Col. 2. 15; Rev. 12. 7ff., etc.
[6] Acts 1. 6f.; 2. 33; Rom. 8. 34, etc.　　　[7] Phil. 2. 9–11; 1 Cor. 15. 25.
[8] 1 Cor. 15. 23f., 50ff., etc.　　　[9] Rev. 21. 4, etc.
[10] 1 Thess. 4. 15ff.; 1 Cor. 15. 51f.; cf. Mark 9. 1.
[11] Rom. 5. 12ff.; 1 Cor. 15. 21ff., 44b, ff.
[12] Ἀπαρχή: Rom. 8. 23, ἀρραβών: 2 Cor. 1. 22; 5. 5.
[13] Rom. 8. 15; Gal. 4. 6.　　　[14] Rom. 8. 11.

2. *The Mythological View of the World Obsolete*

All this is the language of mythology, and the origin of the various themes can be easily traced in the contemporary mythology of Jewish Apocalyptic and in the redemption myths of Gnosticism. To this extent *the kerygma is incredible to modern man, for he is convinced that the mythical view of the world is obsolete.* We are therefore bound to ask whether, when we preach the Gospel to-day, we expect our converts to accept not only the Gospel message, but also the mythical view of the world in which it is set. If not, does the New Testament embody a truth which is quite independent of its mythical setting? If it does, theology must undertake the task of stripping the Kerygma from its mythical framework, of "demythologizing" it.

Can Christian preaching expect modern man *to accept the mythical view of the world as true?* To do so would be both senseless and impossible. It would be senseless, because there is nothing specifically Christian in the mythical view of the world as such. It is simply the cosmology of a pre-scientific age. Again, it would be impossible, because no man can adopt a view of the world by his own volition—it is already determined for him by his place in history. Of course such a view is not absolutely unalterable, and the individual may even contribute to its change. But he can do so only when he is faced by a new set of facts so compelling as to make his previous view of the world untenable. He has then no alternative but to modify his view of the world or produce a new one. The discoveries of Copernicus and the atomic theory are instances of this, and so was romanticism, with its discovery that the human subject is richer and more complex than enlightenment or idealism had allowed, and nationalism, with its new realization of the importance of history and the tradition of peoples.

It may equally well happen that truths which a shallow enlightenment had failed to perceive are later rediscovered in ancient myths. Theologians are perfectly justified in asking whether this is not exactly what has happened with the New Testament. At the same time it is impossible to revive an obsolete view of the world by a mere fiat, and certainly not a mythical view. For all our thinking to-day is shaped irrevocably by modern science. A blind acceptance of the New Testament mythology would be arbitrary, and to press for its acceptance as an article of faith would be to reduce faith to works. Wilhelm Herrmann pointed this out, and one would have thought that his demonstration was conclusive. It would involve a sacrifice of the intellect which could have only one result—a curious form of schizophrenia and insincerity. It would mean accepting a view of the world in our faith and religion which we should deny in our everyday life. Modern thought as we have inherited it brings with it criticism of *the New Testament view of the world*.

Man's knowledge and mastery of the world have advanced to such an extent through science and technology that it is no longer possible for anyone seriously to hold the New Testament view of the world—in fact, there is no one who does. What meaning, for instance, can we attach to such phrases in the creed as "descended into hell" or "ascended into heaven"? We no longer believe in the three-storied universe which the creeds take for granted. The only honest way of reciting the creeds is to strip the mythological framework from the truth they enshrine—that is, assuming that they contain any truth at all, which is just the question that theology has to ask. No one who is old enough to think for himself supposes that God lives in a local heaven. There is no longer any heaven in the traditional sense of the word. The same applies to hell in the sense of a mythical underworld beneath our feet. And if this is so, the story of Christ's descent into hell and of his Ascension into heaven is done with. We can no longer look for the return of the Son of Man on the clouds of heaven or hope that the faithful will meet him in the air (1 Thess. 4. 15ff.).

Now that the forces and the laws of nature have been discovered, we can no longer believe in *spirits, whether good or evil*. We know that the stars are physical bodies whose motions are controlled by the laws of the universe, and not daemonic beings which enslave mankind to their service. Any influence they may have over human life must be explicable in terms of the ordinary laws of nature; it cannot in any way be attributed to their malevolence. Sickness and the cure of disease are likewise attributable to natural causation; they are not the result of daemonic activity or of evil spells.[1] The *miracles of the New Testament* have ceased to be miraculous, and to defend their historicity by recourse to nervous disorders or hypnotic effects only serves to underline the fact. And if we are still left with certain physiological and psychological phenomena which we can only assign to mysterious and enigmatic causes, we are still assigning them to causes, and thus far are trying to make them scientifically intelligible. Even occultism pretends to be a science.

It is impossible to use electric light and the wireless and to avail ourselves of modern medical and surgical discoveries, and at the same time to believe in the New Testament world of spirits and miracles.[2] We may think we can manage it in our own lives, but to expect others to do so is to make the Christian faith unintelligible and unacceptable to the modern world.

The mythical eschatology is untenable for the simple reason that the parousia of Christ never took place as the New Testament expected. History did not come to an end, and, as every schoolboy knows, it will continue to run its course. Even if we believe that the world as we know it will come to an end in time, we expect the end to take the form of a natural catastrophe, not of a mythical event such as the New Testament expects. And if we explain the parousia in terms of modern scientific theory, we are applying criticism to the New Testament, albeit unconsciously.

But natural science is not the only challenge which the mythology of the New Testament has to face. There is the still

---

[1] It may of course be argued that there are people alive to-day whose confidence in the traditional scientific view of the world has been shaken, and others who are primitive enough to qualify for an age of mythical thought. And there are also many varieties of superstition. But when belief in spirits and miracles has degenerated into superstition, it has become something entirely different from what it was when it was genuine faith. The various impressions and speculations which influence credulous people here and there are of little importance, nor does it matter to what extent cheap slogans have spread an atmosphere inimical to science. What matters is the world view which men imbibe from their environment, and it is science which determines that view of the world through the school, the press, the wireless, the cinema, and all the other fruits of technical progress.

[2] Cp. the observations of Paul Schütz on the decay of mythical religion in the East through the introduction of modern hygiene and medicine.

more serious challenge presented by *modern man's understanding of himself.*

Modern man is confronted by a curious dilemma. He may regard himself as pure nature, or as pure spirit. In the latter case he distinguishes the essential part of his being from nature. In either case, however, *man is essentially a unity.* He bears the sole responsibility for his own feeling, thinking, and willing.[1] He is not, as the New Testament regards him, the victim of a strange dichotomy which exposes him to the interference of powers outside himself. If his exterior behaviour and his interior condition are in perfect harmony, it is something he has achieved himself, and if other people think their interior unity is torn asunder by daemonic or divine interference, he calls it schizophrenia.

Although biology and psychology recognize that man is a highly dependent being, that does not mean that he has been handed over to powers outside of and distinct from himself. This dependence is inseparable from human nature, and he needs only to understand it in order to recover his self-mastery and organize his life on a rational basis. If he regards himself as spirit, he knows that he is permanently conditioned by the physical, bodily part of his being, but he distinguishes his true self from it, and knows that he is independent and responsible for his mastery over nature.

In either case he finds *what the New Testament has to say about the "Spirit"* (πνεῦμα) *and the sacraments utterly strange and incomprehensible.* Biological man cannot see how a supernatural entity like the πνεῦμα can penetrate within the close texture of his natural powers and set to work within him. Nor can the idealist understand how a πνεῦμα working like a natural power can touch and influence his mind and spirit. Conscious as he is of his own moral responsibility, he cannot conceive how baptism in water can convey a mysterious something which is henceforth the agent of all his decisions and actions. He cannot see how physical food can convey spiritual strength, and how the unworthy receiving of the Eucharist can result in physical sickness and death (1 Cor. 11. 30). The only possible explanation is that it is

[1] Cp. Gerhardt Krüger, *Einsicht und Leidenschaft, Das Wesen des platonischen Denkens,* Frankfort, 1939, p. 11 f.

due to suggestion. He cannot understand how anyone can be baptized for the dead (1 Cor. 15. 29).

We need not examine in detail the various forms of modern *Weltanschauung*, whether idealist or naturalist. For the only criticism of the New Testament which is theologically relevant is that which arises *necessarily* out of the situation of modern man. The biological *Weltanschauung* does not, for instance, arise necessarily out of the contemporary situation. We are still free to adopt it or not as we choose. The only relevant question for the theologian is the basic assumption on which the adoption of a biological as of every other *Weltanschauung* rests, and that assumption is the view of the world which has been moulded by modern science and the modern conception of human nature as a self-subsistent unity immune from the interference of supernatural powers.

Again, the biblical doctrine that *death is the punishment of sin* is equally abhorrent to naturalism and idealism, since they both regard death as a simple and necessary process of nature. To the naturalist death is no problem at all, and to the idealist it is a problem for that very reason, for so far from arising out of man's essential spiritual being it actually destroys it. The idealist is faced with a paradox. On the one hand man is a spiritual being, and therefore essentially different from plants and animals, and on the other hand he is the prisoner of nature, whose birth, life, and death are just the same as those of the animals. Death may present him with a problem, but he cannot see how it can be a punishment for sin. Human beings are subject to death even before they have committed any sin. And to attribute human mortality to the fall of Adam is sheer nonsense, for guilt implies personal responsibility, and the idea of original sin as an inherited infection is sub-ethical, irrational, and absurd.

The same objections apply to *the doctrine of the atonement*. How can the guilt of one man be expiated by the death of another who is sinless—if indeed one may speak of a sinless man at all? What primitive notions of guilt and righteousness does this imply? And what primitive idea of God? The rationale of sacrifice in general may of course throw some light on the theory of the atonement, but even so, what a primitive mythology it is, that a divine Being should become incarnate, and atone for the sins of men through his own blood! Or again, one might adopt an analogy from the law courts, and explain the death of Christ as a transaction between God and man through which God's claims on man were satisfied. But that would make sin a juridical matter; it would be no more than an external transgression of a commandment, and it would make nonsense of all our ethical standards. Moreover, if the Christ who died such a death was the pre-existent Son of God, what could death mean for him? Obviously very little, if he knew that he would rise again in three days!

The *resurrection of Jesus* is just as difficult for modern man, if it means an event whereby a living supernatural power is released which can henceforth be appropriated through the sacraments. To the biologist such language is meaningless, for he does not regard death as a problem at all. The idealist would not object to the idea of a life immune from death, but he could not believe that such a life is made available by the resuscitation of a dead person. If that is the way God makes life available for man, his action is inextricably involved in a nature miracle. Such a notion he finds incomprehensible, for he can see God at work only in the reality of his personal life and in his transformation. But, quite apart from the incredibility of such a miracle, he cannot see how an event like this could be the act of God, or how it could affect his own life.

Gnostic influence suggests that this Christ, who died and rose again, was not a mere human being but a God-man. His death and resurrection were not isolated facts which concerned him alone, but a cosmic event in which we are all involved.[1] It is only with effort that modern man can think himself back into such an intellectual atmosphere, and even then he could never accept it himself, because it regards man's essential being as nature and redemption as a process of nature. And as for the pre-existence of Christ, with its corollary of man's translation into a celestial realm of light, and the clothing of the human personality in heavenly robes and a spiritual body—all this is not only irrational but utterly meaningless. Why should salvation take this particular form? Why should this be the fulfilment of human life and the realization of man's true being?

[1] Rom. 5. 12ff.; 1 Cor. 15. 21ff., 44b.

B. *The Task before Us*

1. *Not Selection or Subtraction*

Does this drastic criticism of the New Testament mythology mean the complete elimination of the kerygma?

Whatever else may be true, we cannot save the kerygma by selecting some of its features and subtracting others, and thus reduce the amount of mythology in it. For instance, it is impossible to dismiss St Paul's teaching about the unworthy reception of Holy Communion or about baptism for the dead, and yet cling to the belief that physical eating and drinking can have a spiritual effect. If we accept *one* idea, we must accept everything which the New Testament has to say about Baptism and Holy Communion, and it is just this one idea which we cannot accept.

It may of course be argued that some features of the New Testament mythology are given greater prominence than others: not all of them appear with the same regularity in the various books. There is for example only one occurrence of the legends of the Virgin birth and the Ascension; St Paul and St John appear to be totally unaware of them. But, even if we take them to be later accretions, it does not affect the mythical character of the event of redemption as a whole. And if we once start subtracting from the kerygma, where are we to draw the line? The mythical view of the world must be accepted or rejected in its entirety.

At this point absolute clarity and ruthless honesty are essential both for the academic theologian and for the parish priest. It is a duty they owe to themselves, to the Church they serve, and to those whom they seek to win for the Church. They must make it quite clear what their hearers are expected to accept and what they are not. At all costs the preacher must not leave his people in the dark about what he secretly eliminates, nor must he be in the dark about it himself. In Karl Barth's book *The Resurrection of the Dead* the cosmic eschatology in the sense of "chronologically final history" is eliminated in favour of what he intends to be a non-mythological "ultimate history". He is able to delude himself into thinking that this is exegesis of St Paul and of the New Testament generally only because he gets rid of everything mythological in 1 Corinthians by subjecting it to an interpretation which does violence to its meaning. But that is an impossible procedure.

If the truth of the New Testament proclamation is to be preserved, the only way is to demythologize it. But our motive in so doing must not be to make the New Testament relevant to the modern world at all costs. The question is simply whether the New Testament message consists exclusively of mythology, or whether it actually demands the elimination of myth if it is to be understood as it is meant to be. This question is forced upon us from two sides. First there is the nature of myth in general, and then there is the New Testament itself.

2. The Nature of Myth

The real purpose of myth is not to present an objective picture of the world as it is, but to express man's understanding of himself in the world in which he lives. Myth should be interpreted not cosmologically, but anthropologically, or better still, existentially.[1] Myth speaks of the power or the powers which man supposes he experiences as the ground and limit of his world and of his own activity and suffering. He describes these powers in terms derived from the visible world, with its tangible objects and forces, and from human life, with its feelings, motives, and potentialities. He may, for instance, explain the origin of the world by speaking of a world egg or a world tree. Similarly he may account for the present state and order of the world by speaking of a primeval war between the gods. He speaks of the other world in terms of this world, and of the gods in terms derived from human life.[2]

Myth is an expression of man's conviction that the origin and purpose of the world in which he lives are to be sought not within it but beyond it—that is, beyond the realm of known and tangiblereality —and that this realm is perpetually dominated

[1] Cp. Gerhardt Krüger, Einsicht und Leidenschaft, esp. p. 17f., 56f.

[2] Myth is here used in the sense popularized by the 'History of Religions' school. Mythology is the use of imagery to express the other worldly in terms of this world and the divine in terms of human life, the other side in terms of this side. For instance, divine transcendence is expressed as spatial distance. It is a mode of expression which makes it easy to understand the cultus as an action in which material means are used to convey immaterial power. Myth is not used in that modern sense, according to which it is practically equivalent to ideology.

and menaced by those mysterious powers which are its source and limit. Myth is also an expression of man's awareness that he is not lord of his own being. It expresses his sense of dependence not only within the visible world, but more especially on those forces which hold sway beyond the confines of the known. Finally, myth expresses man's belief that in this state of dependence he can be delivered from the forces within the visible world.

Thus myth contains elements which demand its own criticism —namely, its imagery with its apparent claim to objective validity. The real purpose of myth is to speak of a transcendent power which controls the world and man, but that purpose is impeded and obscured by the terms in which it is expressed.

Hence the importance of the New Testament mythology lies not in its imagery but in the understanding of existence which it enshrines. The real question is whether this understanding of existence is true. Faith claims that it is, and faith ought not to be tied down to the imagery of New Testament mythology.

3. *The New Testament Itself*

The New Testament itself invites this kind of criticism. Not only are there rough edges in its mythology, but some of its features are actually contradictory. For example, the death of Christ is sometimes a sacrifice and sometimes a cosmic event. Sometimes his person is interpreted as the Messiah and sometimes as the Second Adam. The kenosis of the pre-existent Son (Phil. 2. 6ff.) is incompatible with the miracle narratives as proofs of his messianic claims. The Virgin birth is inconsistent with the assertion of his pre-existence. The doctrine of the Creation is incompatible with the conception of the "rulers of this world" (1 Cor. 2. 6ff.), the "god of this world" (2 Cor. 4. 4) and the "elements of this world" στοιχεῖα τοῦ κόσμου, Gal. 4. 3). It is impossible to square the belief that the law was given by God with the theory that it comes from the angels (Gal. 3. 19f.).

But the principal demand for the criticism of mythology comes from a curious contradiction which runs right through the New Testament. Sometimes we are told that human life is determined by cosmic forces, at others we are challenged to a decision. Side by side with the Pauline indicative stands the Pauline imperative. In short, man is sometimes regarded as a

cosmic being, sometimes as an independent "I" for whom
decision is a matter of life or death. Incidentally, this explains
why so many sayings in the New Testament speak directly to
modern man's condition while others remain enigmatic and
obscure. Finally, attempts at demythologization are sometimes
made even within the New Testament itself. But more will be
said on this point later.

4. Previous Attempts at Demythologizing

How then is the mythology of the New Testament to be re-
interpreted? This is not the first time that theologians have
approached this task. Indeed, all we have said so far might have
been said in much the same way thirty or forty years ago, and it
is a sign of the bankruptcy of contemporary theology that it has
been necessary to go all over the same ground again. The reason
for this is not far to seek. The liberal theologians of the last
century were working on the wrong lines. They threw away not
only the mythology but also the kerygma itself. Were they
right? Is that the treatment the New Testament itself required?
That is the question we must face to-day. The last twenty years
have witnessed a movement away from criticism and a return to
a naïve acceptance of the kerygma. The danger both for theological scholarship and for the Church is that this uncritical
resuscitation of the New Testament mythology may make the
Gospel message unintelligible to the modern world. We cannot
dismiss the critical labours of earlier generations without further
ado. We must take them up and put them to constructive use.
Failure to do so will mean that the old battles between orthodoxy
and liberalism will have to be fought out all over again, that is
assuming that there will be any Church or any theologians to
fight them at all! Perhaps we may put it schematically like this:
whereas the older liberals used criticism to *eliminate* the mythology of the New Testament, our task to-day is to use criticism
to *interpret* it. Of course it may still be necessary to eliminate
mythology here and there. But the criterion adopted must be
taken not from modern thought, but from the understanding of
human existence which the New Testament itself enshrines.[1]

To begin with, let us review some of these earlier attempts

[1] As an illustration of this critical re-interpretation of myth cf. Hans Jonas,
Augustin und das paulinische Freiheitsproblem, 1930, pp. 66–76.

at demythologizing. We need only mention briefly the allegorical interpretation of the New Testament which has dogged the Church throughout its history. This method spiritualizes the mythical events so that they become symbols of processes going on in the soul. This is certainly the most comfortable way of avoiding the critical question. The literal meaning is allowed to stand and is dispensed with only for the individual believer, who can escape into the realm of the soul.

It was characteristic of the older liberal theologians that they regarded mythology as relative and temporary. Hence they thought they could safely eliminate it altogether, and retain only the broad, basic principles of religion and ethics. They distinguished between what they took to be the essence of religion and the temporary garb which it assumed. Listen to what Harnack has to say about the essence of Jesus' preaching of the Kingdom of God and its coming: "The kingdom has a triple meaning. Firstly, it is something supernatural, a gift from above, not a product of ordinary life. Secondly, it is a purely religious blessing, the inner link with the living God; thirdly, it is the most important experience that a man can have, that on which everything else depends; it permeates and dominates his whole existence, because sin is forgiven and misery banished." Note how completely the mythology is eliminated: "The kingdom of God comes by coming to the individual, by entering into his *soul* and laying hold of it."[1]

It will be noticed how Harnack reduces the kerygma to a few basic principles of religion and ethics. Unfortunately this means that *the kerygma has ceased to be kerygma*: it is no longer the proclamation of the decisive act of God in Christ. For the liberals the great truths of religion and ethics are timeless and eternal, though it is only within human history that they are realized, and only in concrete historical processes that they are given clear expression. But the apprehension and acceptance of these principles does not depend on the knowledge and acceptance of the age in which they first took shape, or of the historical persons who first discovered them. We are all capable of verifying them in our own experience at whatever period we happen to live. History may be of academic interest, but never of paramount importance for religion.

[1] *What is Christianity?* Williams and Norgate, 1904, pp. 63–4 and 57.

But the New Testament speaks of an *event* through which God has wrought man's redemption. For it, Jesus is not primarily the teacher, who certainly had extremely important things to say and will always be honoured for saying them, but whose person in the last analysis is immaterial for those who have assimilated his teaching. On the contrary, his person is just what the New Testament proclaims as the decisive event of redemption. It speaks of this person in mythological terms, but does this mean that we can reject the kerygma altogether on the ground that it is nothing more than mythology? That is the question.

Next came the History of Religions school. Its representatives were the first to discover the extent to which the New Testament is permeated by mythology. The importance of the New Testament, they saw, lay not in its teaching about religion and ethics but in its actual religion and piety; in comparison with that all the dogma it contains, and therefore all the mythological imagery with its apparent objectivity, was of secondary importance or completely negligible. The essence of the New Testament lay in the religious life it portrayed; its high-watermark was the experience of mystical union with Christ, in whom God took symbolic form.

These critics grasped one important truth. Christian faith is not the same as religious idealism; the Christian life does not consist in developing the individual personality, in the improvement of society, or in making the world a better place. The Christian life means a turning away from the world, a detachment from it. But the critics of the History of Religions school failed to see that in the New Testament this detachment is essentially eschatological and not mystical. Religion for them was an expression of the human yearning to rise above the world and transcend it: it was the discovery of a supramundane sphere where the soul could detach itself from all earthly care and find its rest. Hence the supreme manifestation of religion was to be found not in personal ethics or in social idealism but in the cultus regarded as an end in itself. This was just the kind of religious life portrayed in the New Testament, not only as a model and pattern, but as a challenge and inspiration. The New Testament was thus the abiding source of power which enabled man to realize the true life of religion, and Christ was the eternal symbol for the cultus of the Christian Church.[1] It will be noticed how the Church is here defined exclusively as a worshipping community, and this represents a great advance on the older liberalism. This school rediscovered the Church as a *religious* institution. For the idealist there was really no place for the Church at all. But did they succeed in recovering the meaning of the Ecclesia in the full, New Testament sense of the word? For in the New Testament the Ecclesia is invariably a phenomenon of salvation history and eschatology.

Moreover, if the History of Religions school is right, the kerygma has once more ceased to be kerygma. Like the liberals, they are silent about a decisive act of God in Christ proclaimed as the event of redemption. So we are still left with the question whether this event and the person of Jesus, both of which are described in the New Testament in mythological terms, are nothing more than mythology. Can the kerygma be interpreted apart from mythology? Can we recover the truth of the kerygma for men who do not think in mythological terms without forfeiting its character as kerygma?

5. An Existentialist Interpretation the Only Solution

The theological work which such an interpretation involves can be sketched only in the broadest outline and with only a few examples. We must avoid the impression that this is a light and easy task, as if all we have to do is to discover the right formula and finish the job on the spot. It is much more formidable than that. It cannot be done single-handed. It will tax the time and strength of a whole theological generation.

The mythology of the New Testament is in essence that of Jewish apocalyptic and the Gnostic redemption myths. A common feature of them both is their basic dualism, according to which the present world and its human inhabitants are under the control of daemonic, satanic powers, and stand in need of redemption. Man cannot achieve this redemption by his own efforts; it must come as a gift through a divine intervention. Both types of mythology speak of such an intervention: Jewish apocalyptic of an imminent world crisis in which this present aeon will be

---

[1] Cp. e.g. Troeltsch, *Die Bedeutung der Geschichtlichkeit Jesu für den Glauben*, Tübingen, 1911.

brought to an end and the new aeon ushered in by the coming
of the Messiah, and Gnosticism of a Son of God sent down from
the realm of light, entering into this world in the guise of a man,
and by his fate and teaching delivering the elect and opening up
the way for their return to their heavenly home.

The meaning of these two types of mythology lies once more
not in their imagery with its apparent objectivity but in the
understanding of human existence which both are trying to
express. In other words, they need to be interpreted existentially.
A good example of such treatment is to be found in Hans Jonas's
book on Gnosticism.[1]

Our task is to produce an existentialist interpretation of the
dualistic mythology of the New Testament along similar lines.
When, for instance, we read of daemonic powers ruling the
world and holding mankind in bondage, does the understanding
of human existence which underlies such language offer a
solution to the riddle of human life which will be acceptable even
to the non-mythological mind of to-day? Of course we must not
take this to imply that the New Testament presents us with
an anthropology like that which modern science can give us.
It cannot be proved by logic or demonstrated by an appeal to
factual evidence. Scientific anthropologies always take for
granted a definite understanding of existence, which is invariably
the consequence of a deliberate decision of the scientist, whether
he makes it consciously or not. And that is why we have to discover whether the New Testament offers man an understanding
of himself which will challenge him to a genuine existential
decision.

[1] *Gnosis und spätantiker Geist*. I. *Die mythologische Gnosis*, 1934.

II

DEMYTHOLOGIZING IN OUTLINE

A. The Christian Interpretation of Being

1. Human Existence apart from Faith

WHAT does the New Testament mean when it talks of the "world", of "this world" (ὁ κόσμος οὗτος), or of "this aeon" (οὗτος ὁ αἰών)? In speaking thus, the New Testament is in agreement with the Gnostics, for they too speak of "this world", and of the princes, prince, or god of this world; and moreover they both regard man as the slave of the world and its powers. But there is one significant difference. In the New Testament one of these powers in conspicuously absent —viz., *matter*, the physical, sensual part of man's constitution. Never does the New Testament complain that the soul of man, his authentic self, is imprisoned in a material body: never does it complain of the power of sensuality over the spirit. That is why it never doubts the responsibility of man for his sin. God is always the Creator of the world, including human life in the body. He is also the Judge before whom man must give account. The part played by Satan as the Lord of this world must therefore be limited in a peculiar way, or else, if he is the lord or god of world, "this world" must stand in a peculiar dialectical relation to the world as the creation of God.

"This world" is the world of corruption and death. Clearly, it was not so when it left the hands of the Creator, for it was only in consequence of the fall of Adam that death entered into the world (Rom. 5. 12). Hence it is sin, rather than matter as such, which is the cause of corruption and death. The Gnostic conception of the soul as a pure, celestial element imprisoned by some tragic fate in a material body is entirely absent. Death is the wages of sin (Rom. 6. 23; cf. 1 Cor. 15. 56). True, St Paul seems to agree with the Gnostics as regards the effects which he ascribes to the fall of Adam as the ancestor of the human race.

But it is clear that he later returns to the idea of individual responsibility when he says that since Adam death came to all men "for that all sinned" (Rom. 5. 12), a statement which stands in formal contradiction to the Adam theory. Perhaps he means to say that with Adam death became possible rather than inevitable. However that may be, there is another idea which St Paul is constantly repeating and which is equally incompatible with the Adam theory, and that is the theory that sin, including death, is derived from the flesh (σάρξ, Rom. 8. 13; Gal. 6. 8, etc.). But what does he mean by "flesh"? Not the bodily or physical side of human nature, but the sphere of visible, concrete, tangible, and measurable reality, which as such is also the sphere of corruption and death. When a man chooses to live entirely in and for this sphere, or, as St Paul puts it, when he "lives after the flesh", it assumes the shape of a "power". There are indeed many different ways of living after the flesh. There is the crude life of sensual pleasure and there is the refined way of basing one's life on the pride of achievement, on the "works of the law" as St Paul would say. But these distinctions are ultimately immaterial. For "flesh" embraces not only the material things of life, but all human creation and achievement pursued for the sake of some tangible reward, such as for example the fulfilling of the law (Gal. 3. 3). It includes every passive quality, and every advantage a man can have, in the sphere of visible, tangible reality (Phil. 3. 4ff.).

St Paul sees that the life of man is weighed down by anxiety (μεριμνᾶν, 1 Cor. 7. 32ff.). Every man focuses his anxiety upon some particular object. The natural man focuses it upon security, and in proportion to his opportunities and his success in the visible sphere he places his "confidence" in the "flesh" (Phil. 3. 3f.), and the consciousness of security finds its expression in "glorying" (καυχᾶσθαι).

Such a pursuit is, however, incongruous with man's real situation, for the fact is that he is not secure at all. Indeed, this is the way in which he loses his true life and becomes the slave of that very sphere which he had hoped to master, and which he hoped would give him security. Whereas hitherto he might have enjoyed the world as God's creation, it has now become "this world", the world in revolt against God. This is the way in which the "powers" which dominate human life come into being, and as such they acquire the character of mythical entities.[1] Since the visible and tangible sphere is essentially transitory, the man who bases his life on it becomes the prisoner and slave of corruption. An illustration of this may be seen in the way our attempts to secure visible security for ourselves bring us into collision with others; we can seek security for ourselves only at their expense. Thus on the one hand we get envy, anger, jealousy, and the like, and on the other compromise, bargainings, and adjustments of conflicting interests. This creates an all-pervasive atmosphere which controls all our judgements; we all pay homage to it and take it for granted. Thus man becomes the slave of anxiety (Rom. 8. 15). Everybody tries to hold fast to his own life and property, because he has a secret feeling that it is all slipping away from him.

The Life of Faith

The authentic life, on the other hand, would be a life based on unseen, intangible realities. Such a life means the abandonment of all self-contrived security. This is what the New Testament means by "life after the Spirit" or "life in faith".

For this life we must have faith in the grace of God. It means faith that the unseen, intangible reality actually confronts us as love, opening up our future and signifying not death but life.

The grace of God means the forgiveness of sin, and brings deliverance from the bondage of the past. The old quest for visible security, the hankering after tangible realities, and the clinging to transitory objects, is sin, for by it we shut out invisible reality from our lives and refuse God's future which comes to us as a gift. But once we open our hearts to the grace of God, our sins are forgiven; we are released from the past. This is what is meant by "faith": to open ourselves freely to the future. But at the same time faith involves obedience, for faith means turning our backs on self and abandoning all security. It means giving up every attempt to carve out a niche in life for ourselves, surrendering all our self-confidence, and resolving to trust in God alone, in the God who raises the dead (2 Cor. 1. 9) and who calls the things that are not into being (Rom. 4. 17). It

[1] Terms like "the spirit of the age" or "the spirit of technology" provide some sort of modern analogy.

means radical self-commitment to God in the expectation that everything will come from him and nothing from ourselves. Such a life spells deliverance from all worldly, tangible objects, leading to complete detachment from the world and thus to freedom.

This detachment from the world is something quite different from asceticism. It means preserving a distance from the world and dealing with it in a spirit of "as if not" (ὡς μή, 1 Cor. 7. 29–31). The believer is lord of all things (1 Cor. 3. 21–3). He enjoys that power (ἐξουσία) of which the Gnostic boasts, but with the proviso: "All things are lawful for me, but I will not be brought under the power of any" (1 Cor. 6. 12; cf. 10. 23f.). The believer may "rejoice with them that do rejoice, and weep with them that weep" (Rom. 12. 15), but he is no longer in bondage to anything in the world (1 Cor. 7. 17–24). Everything in the world has become indifferent and unimportant. "For though I was free from all men, I brought myself under bondage to all" (1 Cor. 9. 19–23). "I know how to be abased, and I know also how to abound in everything, and in all things I have learned the secret both to be filled and to be hungry, both to abound and to be in want" (Phil. 4. 12). The world has been crucified to him, and he to the world (Gal. 6. 14). Moreover, the power of his new life is manifested even in weakness, suffering, and death (2 Cor. 4. 7–11; 12. 9f.). Just when he realizes that he is nothing in himself, he can have and be all things through God (2 Cor. 12. 9f.; 6. 8–10).

Now, this is eschatological existence; it means being a "new creature" (2 Cor. 5. 17). The eschatology of Jewish apocalyptic and of Gnosticism has been emancipated from its accompanying mythology, in so far as the age of salvation has already dawned for the believer and the life of the future has become a present reality. The fourth gospel carries this process to a logical conclusion by completely eliminating every trace of apocalyptic eschatology. The last judgement is no longer an imminent cosmic event, for it is already taking place in the coming of Jesus and in his summons to believe (John 3. 19; 9. 39; 12. 31). The believer has life here and now, and has passed already from death into life (5. 24, etc.). Outwardly everything remains as before, but inwardly his relation to the world has been radically changed. The world has no further claim on him, for faith is the victory which overcometh the world (1 John 5. 4).

The eschatology of Gnosticism is similarly transcended. It is not that the believer is given a new nature (φύσις) or that his pre-existent nature is emancipated, or that his soul is assured of a journey to heaven. The new life in faith is not an assured possession or endowment, which could lead only to libertinism. Nor is it a possession to be guarded with care and vigilance, which could lead only to asceticism. Life in faith is not a possession at all. It cannot be exclusively expressed in indicative terms; it needs an imperative to complete it. In other words, the decision of faith is never final; it needs constant renewal in every fresh situation. Our freedom does not excuse us from the demand under which we all stand as men, for it is freedom for obedience (Rom. 6. 11ff.). To believe means not to have apprehended but to have been apprehended. It means always to be travelling along the road between the "already" and the "not yet", always to be pursuing a goal.

For Gnosticism redemption is a cosmic process in which the redeemed are privileged to participate here and now. Although essentially transcendent, faith must be reduced to an immanent possession. Its outward signs are freedom (ἐλευθερία), power (ἐξουσία), pneumatic phenomena, and above all ecstasy. In the last resort the New Testament knows no phenomena in which transcendent realities become immanent possessions. True, St Paul is familiar with ecstasy (2 Cor. 5. 13; 12. 1ff.). But he refuses to accept it as a proof of the possession of the Spirit. The New Testament never speaks of the training of the soul in mystical experience or of ecstasy as the culmination of the Christian life. Not psychic phenomena but faith is the hallmark of that life.

Certainly St Paul shares the popular belief of his day that the Spirit manifests itself in miracles, and he attributes abnormal psychic phenomena to its agency. But the enthusiasm of the Corinthians for such things brought home to him their questionable character. So he insists that the gifts of the Spirit must be judged according to their value for "edification", and in so doing he transcends the popular view of the Spirit as an agency that operates like any other natural force. True, he regards the Spirit as a mysterious entity dwelling in man and guaranteeing his resurrection (Rom. 8. 11). He can even speak of the Spirit as if it were a kind of supernatural material (1 Cor. 15. 44ff.).

Yet in the last resort he clearly means by "Spirit" the possibility of a new life which is opened up by faith. The Spirit does not work like a supernatural force, nor is it the permanent possession of the believer. It is the possibility of a new life which must be appropriated by a deliberate resolve. Hence St Paul's paradoxical injunction: "If we live by the Spirit, by the Spirit also let us walk." (Gal. 5. 25). "Being led by the Spirit" (Rom. 8. 14) is not an automatic process of nature, but the fulfilment of an imperative: "live after the Spirit, not after the flesh". Imperative and indicative are inseparable. The possession of the Spirit never renders decision superfluous. "I say, Walk by the Spirit and ye shall not fulfil the lust of the flesh" (Gal. 5. 16). Thus the concept "Spirit" has been emancipated from mythology.

The Pauline catalogue of the fruits of the Spirit ("love, joy, peace, long-suffering, kindness, goodness, faithfulness, temperance", Gal. 5. 22) shows how faith, by detaching man from the world, makes him capable of fellowship in community. Now that he is delivered from anxiety and from the frustration which comes from clinging to the tangible realities of the visible world, man is free to enjoy fellowship with others. Hence faith is described as "working through love" (Gal. 5. 6). And this means being a new creature (cf. Gal. 5. 6 with 6. 15).

B The Event of Redemption

1. Christian Self-Understanding without Christ?

We have now suggested an existentialist unmythological interpretation of the Christian understanding of Being. But is this interpretation true to the New Testament? We seem to have overlooked one important point, which is that in the New Testament faith is always *faith in Christ*. Faith, in the strict sense of the word, was only there at a certain moment in history. It had to be *revealed*; it *came* (Gal. 3. 23, 25). This might of course be taken as part of the story of man's spiritual evolution. But the New Testament means more than that. It claims that faith only became possible at a definite point in history in consequence of an *event*—viz., the event of Christ. Faith in the sense of obedient self-commitment and inward detachment from the world is only possible when it is faith in Jesus Christ.

Here indeed is the crux of the matter—have we here a remnant of mythology which still requires restatement? In fact it comes to this: can we have a Christian understanding of Being without Christ?

The reader will recall our criticism of the History of Religions school for eliminating the decisive event of Christ. Is our re-interpretation of Christianity in existentialist terms open to precisely the same objection?

It might well appear as though the event of Christ were a relic of mythology which still awaits elimination. This is a serious problem, and if Christian faith is to recover its self-assurance it must be grappled with. For it can recover its certainty only if it is prepared to think through to the bitter end the possibility of its own impossibility or superfluity.

It might well appear possible to have a Christian understanding of Being without Christ, as though what we had in the New Testament was the first discovery and the more or less clear expression, in the guise of mythology, of an understanding of Being which is at bottom man's natural understanding of his Being, as it has been given clear expression in modern existentialist philosophy. Does this mean that what existentialism has done is simply to remove the mythological disguise and to vindicate the Christian understanding of Being as it is found in the New Testament and to carry it to more logical conclusion? Is theology simply the precursor of existentialism? Is it no more than an antiquated survival and an unnecessary incubus?

Such is the impression we might derive from a consideration of the recent developments in philosophy. Might we not say that the New Testament lays bare what philosophy calls "the historicity of Being"?

Count Yorck von Wartenburg[1] wrote to Dilthey on 15 December 1892: "Dogmatics was an attempt to formulate an ontology of the higher historic life. Christian dogmatics was inevitably the antithesis of intellectualism, because Christianity is the supreme vitality."[2] Dilthey agrees: ". . . all dogmas need to be translated so as to bring out their universal validity for all human life. They are cramped by their connection with the

[1] *Briefwechsel zwischen Wilhelm Dilthey und dem Grafen Paul Yorck von Wartenburg, 1877-97.* Halle, Niemeyer, 1923.
[2] P. 154.

situation in the past in which they arose. Once they have been freed from this limitation they become . . . the consciousness of the supra-sensual and supra-intelligible nature of historicity pure and simple. . . . Hence the principal Christian dogmas, which include such symbols as "Son of God", "satisfaction", "sacrifice", and the like, are, in so far as they are limited to the facts of the Christian story, untenable. But once they are re-interpreted as statements of universal validity they express the highest living form of all history. They thus lose their rigid and exclusive reference to the person of Jesus, which deliberately excludes all other references."[1]

Yorck gives by way of illustration a re-interpretation of the doctrines of original sin and the atonement. He finds them intelligible in the light of what he calls the "virtual connection" which runs like a thread right through history. "Jesus is the historical demonstration of a universal truth. The child profits from the self-sacrifice of its mother. This involves a conveyance of virtue and power from one person to another, without which history is impossible. [Note the corollary—*all* history, not only Christian history, involves transference of power.] This is why rationalism is blind to the concept of history. And sin—not specific acts of wrong-doing, but man's sinfulness in general—is, as the religious man knows from his own experience, quite unpredictable. Is it less 'monstrous and repulsive' [as Dilthey had stigmatized the doctrine of original sin] that sickness and misery are inherited from generation to generation? These Christian symbols are drawn from the very depths of nature, for religion itself—I mean Christianity—is supernatural, not unnatural."[2]

The development of philosophy since Dilthey's day has, it would seem, amply justified these contentions. Karl Jaspers has found no difficulty in transposing Kierkegaard's interpretation of Christian Being to the sphere of philosophy. Above all, Heidegger's existentialist analysis of the ontological structure of being would seem to be no more than a secularized, philosophical version of the New Testament view of human life. For him the chief characteristic of man's Being in history is anxiety. Man exists in a permanent tension between the past and the future. At every moment he is confronted with an alternative. Either

[1] P. 158.   [2] P. 155.

he must immerse himself in the concrete world of nature, and thus inevitably lose his individuality, or he must abandon all security and commit himself unreservedly to the future, and thus alone achieve his authentic Being. Is not that exactly the New Testament understanding of human life? Some critics have objected that I am borrowing Heidegger's categories and forcing them upon the New Testament. I am afraid this only shows that they are blinding their eyes to the real problem. I mean, one should rather be startled that philosophy is saying the same thing as the New Testament and saying it quite independently.

The whole question has been posed afresh in the recent book by Wilhelm Kamlah.[1] It is true that Kamlah expressly attacks the eschatological character of the Christian understanding of Being, but that is because he misinterprets the detachment from the world which is consequent upon faith. He understands it undialectically as a simple negation of the world, and so fails to do justice to the element of "as if not" which is so characteristic of the Pauline Epistles. But the understanding of Being which Kamlah develops philosophically is manifestly a secularized version of that which we find in Christianity. For the Christian concept of faith he substitutes "self-commitment", by which he means "surrender to the universal reality", or to God as the source of all Being. Self-commitment is the antithesis of autonomy. It brings with it a revelation of the meaning of universal reality. Further, it is emancipation, bringing inward freedom through detachment from all sensual objects of desire. Kamlah himself is aware how close this is to the Christian conception of faith. He says: "The theologians have often observed the paradoxical character of this ability to trust, at least so far as the inception of faith is concerned. It has often been asked how the individual can come to believe at all if faith is the gift of God and is not to be won through human effort, and how faith can be demanded if it is outside the limit of human capacity. The question has often been left unanswered because the theologians have failed to see that this is a problem which is not peculiar to Christianity, but which belongs to the fundamental structure of our natural Being."[2]

Christian faith, properly understood, would then (on Kamlah's view), be identical with natural self-commitment. "Since it

[1] *Christentum und Selbstbehauptung*, Frankfort, 1940.   [2] P. 321.

offers the true understanding of Being, philosophy emancipates natural self-commitment and enables it to become what it was meant to be.''[1] Thus it has no need of any revelation.

Christian love, through which faith operates, is open to a similar interpretation. It is equivalent to committing ourselves to our familiar surroundings. Indeed, Kamlah thinks he can correct the New Testament at this point. As he sees it, the Christian conception of love interrupts what he calls the smooth flow of history. It infringes the priority of the immediate environment in which we have been placed by history. It dissipates love by universalizing it instead of directing it to our true neighbours, those who are nigh to us. Kamlah would have us see as our neighbours those who are tied to us by the inexorable bonds of history. In this way he would emancipate the true naturalness of man.[2]

But is it really true that in the last resort the New Testament means by faith the natural disposition of man? Clearly "natural" in this context means not "empirical" but "proper to man's authentic Being". This Being has first to be set free. But according to Kamlah this does not require revelation. All that is necessary is philosophical reflection. Is faith in this sense the natural disposition of man?

Yes and no. Yes, because faith is not a mysterious supernatural quality, but the disposition of genuine humanity. Similarly, love is not the effect of mysterious supernatural power, but the "natural" disposition of man. The New Testament goes part of the way with Kamlah when it calls man-in-faith a "new creation". Its implication is that by faith man enters upon the life for which he was originally created.

The question is not whether the nature of man can be *discovered* apart from the New Testament. As a matter of fact it has not been discovered without the aid of the New Testament, for modern philosophy is indebted both to it and to Luther and to Kierkegaard. But this merely indicates the place of existentialism in the intellectual history of man, and as far as its content is concerned it owes little to its historical origin. On the contrary, the very fact that it is possible to produce a secularized version of the New Testament conception of faith

---

[1] P. 326.   [2] P. 337.

proves that there is nothing mysterious or supernatural about the Christian life.

No; the question is whether the "nature" of man is realizable. Is it enough simply to show man what he ought to be? Can he achieve his authentic Being by a mere act of reflection? It is clear that philosophy, no less than theology, has always taken it for granted that man has to a greater or lesser degree erred and gone astray, or at least that he is always in danger of so doing. Even the idealists try to show us what we *really* are—namely, that we are really spirit, and that it is therefore wrong to lose ourselves in the world of things. Become what you are! For Heidegger man has lost his individuality, and therefore he invites him to recover his true selfhood. Kamlah again realizes that what he calls "genuine historical existence" may lie hidden and buried beneath the rubble of unreality, and that this is especially the case to-day when we are suffering from the after-effects of the Enlightenment. Kamlah also is aware that self-commitment is not the natural disposition of modern man, but a demand continually imposed upon him from without. There can be no emancipation without obedience.[1]

At the same time, however, these philosophers are convinced that all we need is to be told about the "nature" of man in order to realize it. "Since it is the true understanding of Being, philosophy emancipates that self-commitment which is proper to man and enables it to attain to its full stature"[2]—evidently, that means: it emancipates man for true self-commitment. Philosophy seeks to "liberate"[3] the true naturalness of man.

Is this self-confidence of the philosophers justified? Whatever the answer may be, it is at least clear that this is the point where they part company with the New Testament. For the latter affirms the total incapacity of man to release himself from his fallen state. That deliverance can come only by an act of God. The New Testament does not give us a doctrine of "nature", a doctrine of the authentic nature of man; it proclaims the event of redemption which was wrought in Christ.

That is why the New Testament says that without this saving act of God our plight is desperate, an assertion which existentialism repudiates. What lies behind this difference?

The philosophers and the New Testament agree that man can

[1] P. 403.   [2] P. 326.   [3] P. 337.

be only what he already is. For instance, the idealists believed
that the life of the spirit was possible only because they regarded
man as essentially spirit. Become what you *are*! Similarly
Heidegger can summon us to the resolve to exist as selves in
face of death because he opens our eyes to our situation as one
of "thrownness"[1] into Nothing. Man has to undertake to be
what he already is. Similarly it is reasonable for Kamlah to invite
us to emancipate ourselves by an act of self-commitment, because
he sees that our empirical life is already a life of self-commitment
—we are already members of society, we already receive its
benefits and contribute to its maintenance.

The New Testament also sees that man can be only what he
already is. St Paul exhorts Christians to be holy because they
have already been made holy (1 Cor. 6. 11, cp. 5. 7), and to
walk in the Spirit because they are already in the spirit (Gal.
5. 25), and to mortify sin because they are already dead unto sin
(Rom. 6. 11ff.); or in Johannine language, because they are not
"of the world" (τοῦ κόσμου, John 17. 16) they can overcome
the world, and because they are born of God they do not sin
(1 John 3. 9). Eschatological existence is an attainable ideal
because "the fulness of time has come" and God has sent his
Son "that he might deliver us out of this present evil world"
(Gal. 4. 4; 1. 4).

Thus the New Testament and the philosophers agree that the
authentic life is possible only because in some sense it is already
a present possession. But there is one difference—the New
Testament speaks thus only to Christian believers, only to those
who have opened their hearts to the redemptive action of God.
It never speaks thus to natural man, for he does not possess life,
and *his* plight is one of despair.

Why does the New Testament take this line? Because it
knows that man can become only what he already is, and it sees
that natural man, man apart from Christ, is not as he ought to
be—he is not alive, but dead.

The point at issue is how we understand the fall. Even the
philosophers are agreed about the fact of it. But they think that
all man needs is to be shown his plight, and that then he will be
able to escape from it. In other words, the corruption resulting

1 *Geworfenheit*: see "*Existence and Being*" Vision Press, 1949, p. 49f. (Translator).

from the fall does not extend to the core of the human personality. The New Testament, on the other hand, regards the fall as total.

How then, if the fall be total, can man be aware of his plight? He certainly is aware of it, as the philosophers themselves testify. How can man be aware that his fall is total and that it extends to the very core of his personality? As a matter of fact, it is the other way round: it is only because man is a fallen being, only because he knows he is not what he really ought to be and what he would like to be, that he can be aware of his plight. That awareness of his authentic nature is essential to human life, and without it man would not be man. But his authentic nature is not an endowment of creation or a possession at his own disposal. The philosophers would agree thus far, for they also know that man's authentic nature has to be apprehended by a deliberate resolve. But they think that all man needs is to be told about his authentic nature. This nature is what he never realizes, but what at every moment he is capable of realizing— you can because you ought. But the philosophers are confusing a theoretical possibility with an actual one. For, as the New Testament sees it, man has lost that actual possibility, and even his awareness of his authentic manhood is perverted, as is shown by his deluded belief that it is a possession he can command at will.

Why then has the fall destroyed this actual possibility? The answer is that in his present plight every impulse of man is the impulse of a fallen being. St Paul demonstrates this in the case of the Jews. In their search for righteousness they missed the very object of their quest. They looked for justification from their own works; they wanted to have a ground for glorying before God. Here is a perfect illustration of the plight of man, of his bondage to the flesh, which the Jews were trying so frantically to escape. This bondage leads to self-glorying and self-assertion, to a desperate attempt to control our own destiny. If the authentic life of man is one of self-commitment, then that life is missed not only by the blatantly self-assertive but also by those who try to achieve self-commitment by their own efforts. They fail to see that self-commitment can be received only as a gift from God.

The glorying of the Jew over his faithfulness to the law and the glorying of the Gnostic in his wisdom are both illustrations of the dominant attitude of man, of his independence and autonomy which lead in the end to frustration. We find the same thing in idealism with its *deus in nobis*:

> Lay hold on divinity; make it your own:
> Down it will climb from its heavenly throne.

In Heidegger's case the perversity of such an attitude is less obvious because he does not characterize resolve as self-commitment. But it is clear that the shouldering of the accident of his destiny in the facing of death is really the same radical self-assertion on man's part. Kamlah is relatively nearer to the Christian position when he asserts that the commandment of self-commitment is capable of fulfilment because God grants an understanding of himself[1] or because "Reality" makes self-commitment possible to man by disclosing its own meaning to him,[2] or because self-commitment receives an indication of its own intelligibility from "Reality" itself.[3] But to assert the intelligibility of Reality is to my mind a counsel of despair. Is it not a desperate act of self-assertion when Kamlah says: "It is not possible to doubt altogether in the intelligibility of Reality"?[4] This surely goes to prove that the only reasonable attitude for man to adopt apart from Christ is one of despair, to despair of the possibility of his ever achieving authentic Being.

This at any rate is what the New Testament asserts. Of course it cannot prove its case any more than the philosophers can prove the intelligibility of Reality. It is a matter for decision. The New Testament addresses man as one who is through and through a self-assertive rebel who knows from bitter experience that the life he actually lives is not his authentic life, and that he is totally incapable of achieving that life by his own efforts. In short, he is a totally fallen being.

This means, in the language of the New Testament, that man is a sinner. The self-assertion of which we have spoken is identical with sin. Sin is self-assertion, self-glorying, for "No flesh should glory before God. . . . He that glorieth, let him glory in the Lord" (1 Cor. 1. 29, 31; 2 Cor. 10. 17). Is that no more than an unnecessary mythologizing of an ontological proposition? Can man as he is perceive that self-assertion involves

---

[1] Pp. 341, 353.   [2] P. 298.   [3] P. 330.   [4] P. 358.

guilt, and that he is personally responsible to God for it? Is sin a mythological concept or not? The answer will depend on what we make of St Paul's words to the Corinthians: "What hast thou that thou didst not receive? but if thou didst receive it, why dost thou glory, as if thou hadst not received it?" (1 Cor. 4. 7). Does this apply to all men alike, or only to Christians? This much at any rate is clear: self-assertion is guilt only if it can be understood as ingratitude. If the radical self-assertion which makes it impossible for man to achieve the authentic life of self-commitment is identical with sin, it must obviously be possible for man to understand his existence altogether as a gift of God. But it is just this radical self-assertion which makes such an understanding impossible. For self-assertion deludes man into thinking that his existence is a prize within his own grasp. How blind man is to his plight is illustrated by that pessimism which regards life as a burden thrust on man against his will, or by the way men talk about the "right to live" or by the way they expect their fair share of good fortune. Man's radical self-assertion then blinds him to the fact of sin, and this is the clearest proof that he is a fallen being. Hence it is no good telling man that he is a sinner. He will only dismiss it as mythology. But it does not follow that he is right.

To talk of sin ceases to be mere mythology when the love of God meets man as a power which embraces and sustains him even in his fallen, self-assertive state. Such a love treats man as if he were other than he is. By so doing, love frees man from himself as he is.

For as a result of his self-assertion man is a totally fallen being. He is capable of knowing that his authentic life consists in self-commitment, but is incapable of realizing it because however hard he tries he still remains what he is, self-assertive man. So in practice authentic life becomes possible only when man is delivered from himself. It is the claim of the New Testament that this is exactly what has happened. This is precisely the meaning of that which was wrought in Christ. At the very point where man can do nothing, God steps in and acts—indeed he has acted already—on man's behalf.

St Paul is endeavouring to express this when he speaks of the expiation of sin, or of "righteousness" created as a gift of God rather than as a human achievement. Through Christ, God has

reconciled the world to himself, not reckoning to it its tres-
passes (2 Cor. 5. 19). God made Christ to be sin for us, that we
through him might stand before God as righteous (2 Cor. 5. 21).
For everyone who believes, his past life is dead and done with.
He is a new creature, and as such he faces each new moment.
In short, he has become a free man.

It is quite clear from this that forgiveness of sins is not a juridical concept. It does not mean the remission of punishment.[1]
If that were so, man's plight would be as bad as ever. Rather,
forgiveness conveys freedom from sin, which hitherto had held
man in bondage. But this freedom is not a static quality: it is
freedom *to obey*. The indicative implies an imperative. Love is
the fulfilment of the law, and therefore the forgiveness of God
delivers man from himself and makes him free to devote his life
to the service of others (Rom. 13. 8–10; Gal. 5. 14).

Thus eschatological existence has become possible. God has
acted, and the world—"this world"—has come to an end.
Man himself has been made new. "If any man is in Christ, he is a new
creature: the old things are passed away; behold, they are become
new" (2 Cor. 5. 17). So much for St Paul. St John makes the
same point in his own particular language. The knowledge of
the "truth" as it is revealed in Jesus makes men free (8. 32),
free from the bondage of sin (8. 34). Jesus calls the dead to life
(5. 25) and gives sight to the blind (9. 39). The believer in
Christ is "born again" (3. 3ff.); he is given a fresh start in life.
He is no longer a worldling, for he has overcome the world
through faith (1 John 5. 4).

The event of Jesus Christ is therefore the revelation of the
love of God. It makes a man free from himself and free to be
himself, free to live a life of self-commitment in faith and love.
But faith in this sense of the word is possible only where it
takes the form of faith in the love of God. Yet such faith is still
a subtle form of self-assertion so long as the love of God is merely
a piece of wishful thinking. It is only an abstract idea so long as
God has not revealed his love. That is why faith for the Christian
means faith in Christ, for it is faith in the love of God revealed
in Christ. Only those who are loved are capable of loving.

---

[1] It is worth noting that St Paul never uses the term ἄφεσις τῶν ἁμαρτι ν,
though it reappears in the deutero-Pauline literature; see e.g. Col. 1. 14;
Eph. 1. 7.

Only those who have received confidence as a gift can show confidence in others. Only those who know what self-commitment is by experience can adopt that attitude themselves. We are free to give ourselves to God because he has given up himself for us. "Herein is love, not that we loved God, but that he loved us, and sent his Son to be the propitiation for our sins" (1 John 4. 10). "We love, because he first loved us." (1 John 4. 19).

The classic statement of this self-commitment of God, which is the ground of our own self-commitment, is to be found in Rom. 8. 32: "God spared not his Son, but delivered him up for us; how shall he not also with him freely give us all things?" Compare the Johannine text: "God so loved the world, that he gave his only-begotten Son, that whosoever believeth in him should not perish, but have eternal life" (John 3. 16). There are also similar texts which speak of Jesus' giving up himself for us: ". . . who gave himself for our sins, that he might deliver us out of this present evil world" (Gal. 1. 4); "I have been crucified with Christ; yet I live; and yet no longer I, but Christ liveth in me: and the life which I live in the flesh I live in faith, the faith which is in the Son of God, who loved me and gave himself up for me" (Gal. 2. 19f.).

Here then is the crucial distinction between the New Testament and existentialism, between the Christian faith and the natural understanding of Being. The New Testament speaks and faith knows of an act of God through which man becomes capable of self-commitment, capable of faith and love, of his authentic life.

Have we carried our demythologizing far enough? Are we still left with a myth, or at least an event which bears a mythical character? It is possible, as we have seen, to restate in non-mythological terms the New Testament teaching on human existence apart from faith and in faith. But what of the point of transition between the old life and the new, authentic life? Can it be understood otherwise than as an act of God? Is faith genuine only when it is faith in the love of God revealed in Christ?

2. The Event of Jesus Christ

Anyone who asserts that to speak of an act of God at all is mythological language is bound to regard the idea of an act of

God in Christ as a myth. But let us ignore this question for a moment. Even Kamlah thinks it philosophically justifiable to use "the mythological language of an act of God" (p. 353). The issue for the moment is whether that particular event in which the New Testament sees the act of God and the revelation of his love—that is, the event of Jesus Christ—is essentially a mythical event.

(a) The Demythologizing of the Event of Jesus Christ

Now, it is beyond question that the New Testament presents the event of Jesus Christ in mythical terms. The problem is whether that is the only possible presentation. Or does the New Testament itself demand a restatement of the event of Jesus Christ in non-mythological terms? Now, it is clear from the outset that the event of Christ is of a wholly different order from the cult-myths of Greek or Hellenistic religion. Jesus Christ is certainly presented as the Son of God, a pre-existent divine being, and therefore to that extent a mythical figure. But he is also a concrete figure of history—Jesus of Nazareth. His life is more than a mythical event; it is a human life which ended in the tragedy of crucifixion. We have here a unique combination of history and myth. The New Testament claims that this Jesus of history, whose father and mother were well known to his contemporaries (John 6. 42) is at the same time the pre-existent Son of God, and side by side with the historical event of the crucifixion it sets the definitely non-historical event of the resurrection. This combination of myth and history presents a number of difficulties, as can be seen from certain inconsistencies in the New Testament material. The doctrine of Christ's pre-existence as given by St Paul and St John is difficult to reconcile with the legend of the Virgin birth in St Matthew and St Luke. On the one hand we hear that "he emptied himself, taking the form of a servant, being made in the likeness of men: and being found in fashion as a man . . ." (Phil. 2. 7), and on the other hand we have the gospel portraits of a Jesus who manifests his divinity in his miracles, omniscience, and mysterious elusiveness, and the similar description of him in Acts as "Jesus of Nazareth, a man approved of God unto you by mighty works and wonders and signs" (Acts 2. 22). On the one hand we have the resurrection as the exaltation of Jesus from the cross or grave, and on the other the legends of the empty tomb and the ascension.

We are compelled to ask whether all this mythological language is not simply an attempt to express the meaning of the historical figure of Jesus and the events of his life; in other words, significance of these as a figure and event of salvation. If that be so, we can dispense with the objective form in which they are cast.

It is easy enough to deal with the doctrine of Christ's pre-existence and the legend of the Virgin birth in this way. They are clearly attempts to explain the meaning of the Person of Jesus for faith. The facts which historical criticism can verify cannot exhaust, indeed they cannot adequately indicate, all that Jesus means to me. How he actually originated matters little, indeed we can appreciate his significance only when we cease to worry about such questions. Our interest in the events of his life, and above all in the cross, is more than an academic concern with the history of the past. We can see meaning in them only when we ask what God is trying to say to each one of us through them. Again, the figure of Jesus cannot be understood simply from his inner-worldly context. In mythological language, this means that he stems from eternity, his origin is not a human and natural one.

We shall not, however, pursue the examination of the particular incidents of his life any further. In the end the crux of the matter lies in the cross and resurrection.

(b) The Cross

Is the cross, understood as the event of redemption, exclusively mythical in character, or can it retain its value for salvation without forfeiting its character as history?

It certainly has a mythical character as far as its objective setting is concerned. The Jesus who was crucified was the pre-existent, incarnate Son of God, and as such he was without sin. He is the victim whose blood atones for our sins. He bears vicariously the sin of the world, and by enduring the punishment for sin on our behalf he delivers us from death. This mythological interpretation is a mixture of sacrificial and juridical analogies, which have ceased to be tenable for us to-day. And in any case they fail to do justice to what the New Testament is trying to say. For the most they can convey is that the cross effects the forgiveness of all the past and future sins of man, in the sense that the punishment they deserved has been remitted. But the New Testament means more than this. The cross releases men not only from the guilt, but also from the power of sin. That is why, when the author of Colossians says "He [God] . . . having forgiven us all our trespasses, having blotted out the bond written in ordinances that was against us, which was contrary to us; and he hath taken it out of the way, nailing it to the cross" he hastens to add: "having put off from himself the principalities and powers, he made a show of them openly, triumphing over them in it" (Col. 2. 13–15).

The historical event of the cross acquires cosmic dimensions. And by speaking of the Cross as a cosmic happening its significance as a historical happening is made clear in accordance with the remarkable way of thinking in which historical events and connections are presented in cosmic terms, and so its full significance is brought into sharper relief. For if we see in the cross the judgement of the world and the defeat of the rulers of this world (1 Cor. 2. 6ff.), the cross becomes the judgement of ourselves as fallen creatures enslaved to the powers of the "world".

By giving up Jesus to be crucified, God has set up the cross for us. To believe in the cross of Christ does not mean to concern ourselves with a mythical process wrought outside of us and our world, with an objective event turned by God to our advantage, but rather to make the cross of Christ our own, to undergo crucifixion with him. The cross in its redemptive aspect is not an isolated incident which befell a mythical personage, but an event whose meaning has "cosmic" importance. Its decisive, revolutionary significance is brought out by the eschatological framework in which it is set. In other words, the cross is not just an event of the past which can be contemplated, but is the eschatological event in and beyond time, in so far as it (understood in its significance, that is, for faith) is an ever-present reality.

The cross becomes a present reality first of all in the sacraments. In baptism men and women are baptized into Christ's death (Rom. 6. 3) and crucified with him (Rom. 6. 6). At every celebration of the Lord's Supper the death of Christ is proclaimed (1 Cor. 11. 26). The communicants thereby partake of his crucified body and his blood outpoured (1 Cor. 10. 16). Again, the cross

of Christ is an ever-present reality in the everyday life of the
Christians. "They that are of Christ Jesus have crucified the
flesh with the passions and the lusts thereof" (Gal. 5. 24).
That is why St Paul can speak of "the cross of our Lord Jesus
Christ, through which the world hath been crucified unto me,
and I unto the world" (Gal. 6. 14). That is why he seeks to know
"the fellowship of his sufferings", as one who is "conformed to
his death" (Phil. 3. 10).

The crucifying of the affections and lusts includes the overcoming of our natural dread of suffering and the perfection of
our detachment from the world. Hence the willing acceptance
of sufferings in which death is already at work in man means:
"always bearing about in our body the dying of Jesus" and
"always being delivered unto death for Jesus' sake" (2 Cor.
4. 10f.).

Thus the cross and passion are ever-present realities. How
little they are confined to the events of the first Good Friday is
amply illustrated by the words which a disciple of St Paul puts
into his master's mouth: "Now I rejoice in my sufferings for
your sake, and fill up on my part that which is lacking of the
afflictions of Christ in my flesh for his body's sake, which is the
Church" (Col. 1. 24).

In its redemptive aspect the cross of Christ is no mere
mythical event, but a historic (geschichtlich) fact originating in
the historical (historisch) event which is the crucifixion of Jesus.
The abiding significance of the cross is that it is the judgement
of the world, the judgement and the deliverance of man. So far
as this is so, Christ is crucified "for us", not in the sense of any
theory of sacrifice or satisfaction. This interpretation of the cross
as a permanent fact rather than a mythological event does far
more justice to the redemptive significance of the event of the
past than any of the traditional interpretations. In the last resort
mythological language is only a medium for conveying the significance of the historical (historisch) event. The historical (historisch) event of the cross has, in the significance peculiar to it,
created a new historic (geschichtlich) situation. The preaching of
the cross as the event of redemption challenges all who hear it
to appropriate this significance for themselves, to be willing
to be crucified with Christ.

But, it will be asked, is this significance to be discerned in
the actual event of past history? Can it, so to speak, be read off

from that event? Or does the cross bear this significance because it is the cross of *Christ*? In other words, must we first be convinced of the significance of Christ and believe in him in order to discern the real meaning of the cross? If we are to perceive the real meaning of the cross, must we understand it as the cross of Jesus as a figure of past history? Must we go back to the Jesus of history?

As far as the first preachers of the gospel are concerned this will certainly be the case. For them the cross was the cross of him with whom they had lived in personal intercourse. The cross was an experience of their own lives. It presented them with a question and it disclosed to them its meaning. But for us this personal connection cannot be reproduced. For us the cross cannot disclose its own meaning: it is an event of the past. We can never recover it as an event in our own lives. All we know of it is derived from historical report. But the New Testament does not proclaim Jesus Christ in this way. The meaning of the cross is not disclosed from the life of Jesus as a figure of past history, a life which needs to be reproduced by historical research. On the contrary, Jesus is not proclaimed merely as the crucified; he is also risen from the dead. The cross and the resurrection form an inseparable unity.

(c) *The Resurrection*

But what of the resurrection? Is it not a mythical event pure and simple? Obviously it is not an event of past history with a self-evident meaning. Can the resurrection narratives and every other mention of the resurrection in the New Testament be understood simply as an attempt to convey the meaning of the cross? Does the New Testament, in asserting that Jesus is risen from the dead, mean that his death is not just an ordinary human death, but the judgement and salvation of the world, depriving death of its power? Does it not express this truth in the affirmation that the Crucified was not holden of death, but rose from the dead?

Yes indeed: the cross and the resurrection form a single, indivisible cosmic event. "He was delivered up for our trespasses, and was raised for our justification" (Rom. 4. 25). The cross is not an isolated event, as though it were the end of Jesus, which needed the resurrection subsequently to reverse it.

When he suffered death, Jesus was already the Son of God, and his death by itself was the victory over the power of death. St John brings this out most clearly by describing the passion of Jesus as the "hour" in which he is glorified, and by the double meaning he gives to the phrase "lifted up", applying it both to the cross and to Christ's exaltation into glory.

Cross and resurrection form a single, indivisible cosmic event which brings judgement to the world and opens up for men the possibility of authentic life. But if that be so, the resurrection cannot be a miraculous proof capable of demonstration and sufficient to convince the sceptic that the cross really has the cosmic and eschatological significance ascribed to it.

Yet it cannot be denied that the resurrection of Jesus is often used in the New Testament as a miraculous proof. Take for instance Acts 17. 31. Here we are actually told that God substantiated the claims of Christ by raising him from the dead. Then again the resurrection narratives: both the legend of the empty tomb and the appearances insist on the physical reality of the risen body of the Lord (see especially Luke 24. 39–43). But these are most certainly later embellishments of the primitive tradition. St Paul knows nothing about them. There is however one passage where St Paul tries to prove the miracle of the resurrection by adducing a list of eye-witnesses (1 Cor. 15. 3–8). But this is a dangerous procedure, as Karl Barth has involuntarily shown. Barth seeks to explain away the real meaning of 1 Cor. 15 by contending that the list of eye-witnesses was put in not to prove the fact of the resurrection, but to prove that the preaching of the apostle was, like the preaching of the first Christians, the preaching of Jesus as the risen Lord. The eye-witnesses therefore guarantee St Paul's preaching, not the fact of the resurrection. An historical fact which involves a resurrection from the dead is utterly inconceivable!

Yes indeed: the resurrection of Jesus cannot be a miraculous proof by which the sceptic might be compelled to believe in Christ. The difficulty is not simply the incredibility of a mythical event like the resuscitation of a dead person—for that is what the resurrection means, as is shown by the fact that the risen Lord is apprehended by the physical senses. Nor is it merely the impossibility of establishing the objective historicity of the resurrection no matter how many witnesses are cited, as though once it

was established it might be believed beyond all question and
faith might have its unimpeachable guarantee. No; the real
difficulty is that the resurrection is itself an article of faith, and
you cannot establish one article of faith by invoking another.
You cannot prove the redemptive efficacy of the cross by invoking
the resurrection. For the resurrection is an article of faith
because it is far more than the resuscitation of a corpse—it is
the eschatological event. And so it cannot be a miraculous
proof. For, quite apart from its credibility, the bare miracle
tells us nothing about the eschatological fact of the destruction
of death. Moreover, such a miracle is not otherwise unknown
to mythology.

It is however abundantly clear that the New Testament is
interested in the resurrection of Christ simply and solely because
it is the eschatological event *par excellence*. By it Christ abolished
death and brought life and immortality to light (2 Tim. 1. 10).
This explains why St Paul borrows Gnostic language to clarify
the meaning of the resurrection. As in the death of Jesus all have
died (2 Cor. 5. 14f.), so through his resurrection all have been
raised from the dead, though naturally this event is spread over
a long period of time (1 Cor. 15. 21f.). But St Paul does not only
say: "In Christ shall all be made alive"; he can also speak of
rising again with Christ in the present tense, just as he speaks of
our dying with him. Through the sacrament of baptism Christians
participate not only in the death of Christ but also in his resurrection. It is not simply that we *shall* walk with him in newness of
life and be united with him in his resurrection (Rom. 6. 4f.);
we are doing so already here and now. "Even so reckon ye
yourselves to be dead indeed unto sin, but alive unto God in
Jesus Christ" (Rom. 6. 11).

Once again, in everyday life the Christians participate not only
in the death of Christ but also in his resurrection. In this resurrec-
tion-life they enjoy a freedom, albeit a struggling freedom, from
sin (Rom. 6. 11ff.). They are able to "cast off the works of
darkness", so that the approaching day when the darkness shall
vanish is already experienced here and now. "Let us walk
honestly as in the day" (Rom. 13. 12f.): "we are not of the night,
nor of the darkness. . . . Let us, since we are of the day, be
sober . . ." (1 Thess. 5. 5–8). St Paul seeks to share not only the
sufferings of Christ but also "the power of his resurrection"

(Phil. 3. 10). So he bears about in his body the dying of Jesus, "that the life also of Jesus may be manifested in our body" (2 Cor. 4. 10f.). Similarly, when the Corinthians demand a proof of his apostolic authority, he solemnly warns them: "Christ is not weak, but is powerful in you: for he was crucified in weakness, yet he liveth in the power of God. For we also are weak in him, but we shall live with him through the power of God toward you" (2 Cor. 13. 3f.).

In this way the resurrection is not a mythological event adduced in order to prove the saving efficacy of the cross, but an article of faith just as much as the meaning of the cross itself. Indeed, *faith in the resurrection is really the same thing as faith in the saving efficacy of the cross*, faith in the cross as the cross of Christ. Hence you cannot first believe in Christ and then in the strength of that faith believe in the cross. To believe in Christ means to believe in the cross as the cross of Christ. The saving efficacy of the cross is not derived from the fact that it is the cross of Christ: it is the cross of Christ because it has this saving efficacy. Without that efficacy it is the tragic end of a great man.

We are back again at the old question. How do we come to believe in the cross as the cross of Christ and as the eschatological event *par excellence*? How do we come to believe in the saving efficacy of the cross?

There is only one answer. This is the way in which the cross is proclaimed. It is always proclaimed together with the resurrection. Christ meets us in the preaching as one crucified and risen. He meets us in the word of preaching and nowhere else. The faith of Easter is just this—faith in the word of preaching.

It would be wrong at this point to raise again the problem of how this preaching arose historically, as though that could vindicate its truth. That would be to tie our faith in the word of God to the results of historical research. The word of preaching confronts us as the word of God. It is not for us to question its credentials. It is we who are questioned, we who are asked whether we will believe the word or reject it. But in answering this question, in accepting the word of preaching as the word of God and the death and resurrection of Christ as the eschatological event, we are given an opportunity of understanding ourselves. Faith and unbelief are never blind, arbitrary decisions. They offer us the alternative between accepting or rejecting

that which alone can illuminate our understanding of ourselves.

The real Easter faith is faith in the word of preaching which
brings illumination. If the event of Easter Day is in any sense an
historical event additional to the event of the cross, it is nothing
else than the rise of faith in the risen Lord, since it was this
faith which led to the apostolic preaching. The resurrection
itself is not an event of past history. All that historical criticism
can establish is the fact that the first disciples came to believe
in the resurrection. The historian can perhaps to some extent
account for that faith from the personal intimacy which the
disciples had enjoyed with Jesus during his earthly life, and so
reduce the resurrection appearances to a series of subjective
visions. But the historical problem is not of interest to Christian
belief in the resurrection. For the historical event of the rise of
the Easter faith means for us what it meant for the first disciples—
namely, the self-attestation of the risen Lord, the act of God in
which the redemptive event of the cross is completed.[1]
completed.[1]

We cannot buttress our own faith in the resurrection by that
of the first disciples and so eliminate the element of risk which
faith in the resurrection always involves. For the first disciples'
faith in the resurrection is itself part and parcel of the eschatological event which is the article of faith.

In other words, the apostolic preaching which originated in
the event of Easter Day is itself a part of the eschatological event
of redemption. The death of Christ, which is both the judgement
and the salvation of the world, inaugurates the "ministry of
reconciliation" or "word of reconciliation" (2 Cor. 5. 18f.).
This word supplements the cross and makes its saving efficacy
intelligible by demanding faith and confronting men with the
question whether they are willing to understand themselves as
men who are crucified and risen with Christ. Through the word
of preaching the cross and the resurrection are made present:
the eschatological "now" is here, and the promise of Isa. 49. 8

[1] This and the following paragraphs are also intended as an answer to the
doubts and suspicions which Paul Althaus has raised against me in *Die Wahrheit
des kirchlichen Osterglaubens*, 1941, p. 90ff. Cp. also my discussion of Emanuel
Hirsch's "Die Auferstehungsgeschichten und der christliche Glaube", 1940,
in *Theol. Lit.-Ztg.*, 1940, pp. 242–6.

is fulfilled: "Behold, now is the acceptable time; behold, now is the day of salvation" (2 Cor. 6. 2). That is why the apostolic preaching brings judgement. For some the apostle is "a savour from death unto death" and for others a "savour from life unto life" (2 Cor. 2. 16). St Paul is the agent through whom the resurrection life becomes effective in the faithful (2 Cor. 4. 12). The promise of Jesus in the Fourth Gospel is eminently applicable to the preaching in which he is proclaimed: "Verily I say unto you, He that heareth my words and believeth on him that sent me, hath eternal life, and cometh not unto judgement, but hath passed out of death into life. . . . The hour cometh and now is, when the dead shall hear the voice of the Son of God; and they that hear shall live" (John 5. 24f.). In the word of preaching and there alone we meet the risen Lord. "So belief cometh of hearing, and hearing by the word of Christ" (Rom. 10. 17).

Like the word itself and the apostle who proclaims it, so the Church where the preaching of the word is continued and where the believers or "saints" (i.e., those who have been transferred to eschatological existence) are gathered is part of the eschatological event. The word "Church" (ἐκκλησία) is an eschatological term, while its designation as the Body of Christ emphasizes its cosmic significance. For the Church is not just a phenomenon of secular history, it is phenomenon of significant history, in the sense that it realizes itself in history.

Conclusion

We have now outlined a programme for the demythologizing of the New Testament. Are there still any surviving traces of mythology? There certainly are for those who regard all language about an act of God or of a decisive, eschatological event as mythological. But this is not mythology in the traditional sense, not the kind of mythology which has become antiquated with the decay of the mythical world view. For the redemption of which we have spoken is not a miraculous supernatural event, but an historical event wrought out in time and space. We are convinced that this restatement does better justice to the real meaning of the New Testament and to the paradox of the kerygma. For the kerygma maintains that the eschatological emissary of God is a concrete figure of a particular historical past, that his eschatological activity was wrought out in a human fate, and that therefore it is an event whose eschatological character does not admit of a secular proof. Here we have the paradox of Phil. 2. 7: "He emptied himself"; of 2 Cor. 8. 9: ". . . though he was rich, yet for your sakes he became poor"; of Rom. 8. 3: "God, sending his Son in the likeness of sinful flesh"; of 1 Tim. 3. 16: "He was manifested in the flesh"; and above all of the classic formula of John 1. 14: "The Word became flesh."

The agent of God's presence and activity, the mediator of his reconciliation of the world unto himself, is a real figure of history. Similarly the word of God is not some mysterious oracle, but a sober, factual account of a human life, of Jesus of Nazareth, possessing saving efficacy for man. Of course the kerygma may be regarded as part of the story of man's spiritual evolution and used as a basis for a tenable *Weltanschauung*. Yet this proclamation claims to be the eschatological word of God.

The apostles who proclaim the word may be regarded merely as figures of past history, and the Church as a sociological and historical phenomenon, part of the history of man's spiritual evolution. Yet both are eschatological phenomena and eschatological events.

All these assertions are an offence (σκάνδαλον), which will not be removed by philosophical discussion, but only by faith and obedience. All these are phenomena subject to historical, sociological and psychological observation, yet for faith they are all of them eschatological phenomena. It is precisely its immunity from proof which secures the Christian proclamation against the charge of being mythological. The transcendence of God is not as in myth reduced to immanence. Instead, we have the paradox of a transcendent God present and active in history: "The Word became flesh".

JULIUS SCHNIEWIND

A REPLY TO BULTMANN

Theses on the Emancipation of
the Kerygma from Mythology

I

1. Introduction

SINCE its first appearance, Bultmann's essay has evoked a
storm of indignant repudiation. He has been accused of
eliminating all the facts of salvation. He has left us without
a message for our Christmas, Good Friday, and Easter sermons.
He has raised doubts about the very kerygma itself.

It would be better to approach the subject in a more re-
strained tone. To begin with, Bultmann has clearly and explicitly
repudiated any intention of dissolving the kerygma. The whole
tenor of his essay is enough to show that. And he expressly
dissociates himself from the liberalism of the older school such
as Harnack's "God and the soul" as well as from the more
mystical approach of Troeltsch and the History of Religions
school (see p. 14). Unlike the liberals, Bultmann is not in the
least interested in the evolution of religion. What he is interested
in is the once-for-allness of the deed, the revelation of God in
Christ.

Secondly, Bultmann's desire to emancipate the gospel message from mythology is something which he shares with every
preacher who is worth his salt. Every time we preach a sermon
we have to translate the language of the New Testament into the
thought and language of the present day. Thielicke[1] is equally
concerned with this question, though his terms "permanent
and transitory", "shell and content", "divine and human",

[1] *Pfarrerblatt*, 1942, No. 30; cp. also his more exhaustive treatment in the
essay in this volume (pp. 138 ff.).

are not altogether satisfactory. For Thielicke does not seek to
differentiate any more than Bultmann does between an "eternal"
and purely transitory element in the Bible. That would be only
a return to liberalism, which both Thielicke and Bultmann want
to avoid.

Here are a few incidents which will show what the problem
is really about. The present writer remembers listening about
ten years ago to a thoughtful sermon on the opening chapters
of Genesis. An educated lady in the congregation happened to
take offence at the way the preacher spoke of Adam. "How can
he", she asked, "talk about Adam as if he were an historical
person? And what has the sin committed by the first man thousands or even millions of years ago to do with me?" The trouble
was that the preacher was right in principle but uncertain in
his exposition. When we speak of Adam we are speaking of the
collective fall and guilt of man, of his *abalienatio a deo*, which is
the presupposition of every actual sin. The Reformers realized
this. There is another incident which the present writer re-
calls from his student days at Marburg in 1906. On Ascension
Day he went to the service on the Christenberg. Great crowds
were flocking thither, attracted by the display of traditional
costumes in the procession; most of them were people who
had little sympathy with the Christian religion. Would the
preacher, one wondered, be able to proclaim the message
of "Christ the King" in a way which the crowds would
understand? Alas, we were given a naïve picture of a literal
ascension, such as a non-Christian would dismiss as mere myth.
Even Luther poured scorn on such literalism: "Oh, that heaven
of the charlatans, with its golden stool and Christ sitting at the
Father's side vested in a choir cope and a golden crown, as the
painters love to portray him."[1] A third incident. As an army
chaplain in the first World War the writer remembers preaching
to the men of his Bible class an Easter sermon which met with
similar criticism. "You don't really believe that Christ's bones
came up out of the earth, do you, padre?" As a matter of fact,
he had not said anything of the kind, but evidently the word
"resurrection" conjured up in the minds of the men the
stained glass windows in their parish churches back at home,

[1] *W.A.*, XXIII, p. 131. For the reference I am indebted to Herr D. Knolle
of Hamburg.

where, in flagrant contradiction to St Paul (1 Cor. 15. 36: "Thou fool"), the resurrection of the dead is depicted in ordinary human and terrestrial categories. Again and again I came across competent theologians who were shocked by the sermons they heard from army chaplains. Most of them were well meant and carefully prepared, but they showed little indication that the preachers had been face to face with death in the company of men to whom the Bible was an utterly foreign world. These young padres did not know what a sermon really was, although they might have learned from the New Testament itself. There we learn that a sermon is an attempt to speak the Word of God to the concrete situation of the hearers so that it may readily be understood.

We are already at the heart of the problem. What e.g. is the real meaning of the parallel which Romans 5 draws between Adam and Christ? What was the ascension? Is the resurrection of the dead capable of description? Does preaching simply mean repeating word for word what the Bible says? Or are we allowed to paraphrase, translate, and change the terminology? Such a procedure might well be within the limits of what the Reformers practised and what the New Testament itself intends and demands. On the other hand, it may be argued that what the New Testament says is pure myth, at least so far as the form in which it is expressed is concerned. In that case the translation of its language and its thought-forms into our own will not be enough. More drastic treatment will be required. And supposing not only the form but also the substance is affected, what then? Let us see.

II

A. By "mythological" we mean the expression of unobservable realities in terms of observable phenomena. It is doubtful whether the human mind can ever dispense with myth. Every attempt to escape from mythology leads either to nihilism or to the question whether the invisible has in fact become visible, and if so, where? The Christian answer is, in W. Herrmann's phrase, "God is Jesus" (Col. 1. 15; John 14. 9). Bultmann would agree in principle.

Bultmann (p. 10 footnote 2) defines "mythological" thus: "Mythology is the mode of representation in which the un-worldly, the divine, appears as worldly, human, and the other-worldly as this-worldly."

This definition requires simplification. It would be better to
avoid such terms as "unworldly", "the divine", and "the
other-worldly". "Unworldly", for instance, is an ambiguous
expression (see the discussion of "acosmism" in Thesis VII,
p. 92). The "divine" is the *theion* of Hellenistic pantheism.
"Other-worldly" is the usual word for the invisible world,
but difficult to reconcile with New Testament eschatology,
which speaks of a future, a goal, and a judgement. As an alternative
we would suggest: "By 'mythological' we mean the presentation
of unobservable realities in terms of observable phenonomena."
The most striking feature of the myths about the pagan gods is
the way they speak of persons and events in an invisible world
as if they were like those with which we are familiar on earth.
Jewish apocalyptic and Gnostic speculation alike describe heaven
and its denizens, cosmic catastrophes and the end of the world,
with all the paraphernalia and scenery of the earthly stage.
Critics have often noted the sobriety and restraint of the New
Testament as compared with Judaism in its picture of heaven
and the end of the world. How restrainedly do the gospels
describe the resurrection of Jesus compared e.g. with the
Gospel of Peter. "No man hath seen God at any time." "He
dwelleth in light unapproachable" (1 Tim. 6. 16), and by
analogy the same applies to the unseen world. The visible is
temporal, the invisible eternal (2 Cor. 4. 18).

But is the human mind really capable of dispensing with myth?
After all, we can speak of the invisible only in terms of the
visible. When for instance Plato reaches the summit of his
thought, he simply says: μῦθος ἔφυ. And who would be so
rash as to try and demythologize Plato?[1] Spengler was not the
first to observe that all our scientific concepts are really myths;
Karl Heim has been saying the same thing ever since 1905.
Modern science appears to be increasingly concerned with its
presuppositions and assumptions. What remains when we have
rigorously eliminated every trace of mythology?[2]

[1] I owe this to a suggestion of H. J. Iwand.

[2] This critique of the conceptions used in natural science in Heim and
Spengler is derived from the Empirio-criticism of Mach. The results of recent
atomic research have invalidated this critique in the particular form in which
it was made. At the same time, however, atomic research has shown us that

Again, a large part of what Bultmann quotes from Yorck and Kamlah is really mythological. "These symbols are drawn from the very depths of nature, for religion . . . is supernatural, not unnatural."[1] What does "nature" mean in this connection? *Phusis, phuein,* and *nasci* are all terrestrial expressions. And what about "supernatural"? Martin Kähler used to insist that we should drop the term "supernatural" altogether. And what are the "depths" of nature? Is it just a naïve application of our ordinary idea of space? And what do "authentic" and "symbol" mean? Some sort of comparison, no doubt, is involved, but what is the *tertium comparationis*? Take again Bultmann's quotation from Kamlah.[2] "The attitude of historicity is surrender to the totality of that which is, or to God as the source of Being." What does he mean by "totality" and "source"? Here is a definite case where our ideas of activity in time and space are transferred to the transcendental sphere. And is the philosopher justified on his own presuppositions in speaking of "God"? Is not that a mythological concept? There is no need to recall Haeckel's blasphemy about a gaseous vertebrate: suffice it to remind ourselves of the classical tradition of religious philosophy with its insistence that God cannot be defined except in negatives— *apoios,* without quality, the *ontos on,* the *theion,*[3] the X behind everything that happens, the X, as Kähler formulated it, following the older theology, behind our religiosity and our humanism. We know these things as phenomena, but of the "something or other" which lies behind them we can only speak in negatives. Everything beyond that is apparently mythology.

When we analyse all our thinking in this way, we begin to see how much of it is mythological. Every ultimate question presents us with an either-or. Either nihilism or the *als ob* ("as if"). There is only one way of escape from this dilemma, and that way is open only to Christian faith. That is to see all the ultimate questions of all men from the viewpoint of Christ.

---

all visible conceptions of natural and cosmic happenings are *per se* untenable, Cp. e.g. Ernst Zimmer, *Umsturz im Weltbild der Physik,* 1942, and Sir James Jeans. *The Mysterious Universe,* 1930.

[1] Yorck, quoted by Bultmann, p. 24.

[2] These are not Kamlah's actual words, but Bultmann's summary correctly reproduces the substance of Kamlah's argument.

[3] See Philo. *Leg. all.,* sect. 36, CW.I. 121. 1ff.

All human thinking leaves us with a question mark. Has the invisible ever been made visible, and if so, where? The inescapable necessity of thinking in picture language derived from the world of space and time leaves us with exactly the same question —has the invisible ever been made visible, and if so, where? And the only answer is the Christian answer—the invisible God has entered into our visible world. Of this act of God the New Testament bears witness: "He is the image of the invisible God" (Col. 1. 15). "Blessed are the eyes which see the things that ye see" (Luke 10. 22). "He who hath seen me hath seen the Father" (John 14. 9). Here is the only solution to the question of God, the question which underlies every thought which enters into the mind of man. It is remarkable how unanimous our teachers were in impressing upon us the importance of John 14. 9. Kähler, when he waged war on the X, the god of the pantheists and the deists, and Loofs when he quoted Luther's *Ein' feste Burg*:

Ask ye who is this same?
Christ Jesus is His Name:
The Lord Sabaoth's Son.

And W. Herrmann said something in his seminar in the summer term of 1906 which was quite unforgettable: "It is wrong to say that Jesus is God, for that implies that we already know what God is. It implies that Jesus is merely *theios*, a divine being. We really ought to say that God is Jesus. Jesus is the very presence of God, the divine Being himself." Herrmann reminded us of the original meaning of *homoousios*—of *one*, not of like, substance. Above all, this is the authentic gospel of Luther. Jesus is *deus ad nos*, God gracious to us.[1] Bultmann accepts this creed in principle.

At the end of his essay he quotes Phil 2. 7; 2 Cor. 8. 9; Rom. 8. 3; 1 Tim. 3. 16; John 1. 14. But what about his formulae: "God's eschatological emissary" and "the agent of God's presence and activity"? They leave us wondering whether he is really doing justice to the New Testament. John 14. 9 goes further than this, and so does 1 John 5. 20 ("true God and eternal life"), John 20. 28 ("My Lord and my God"), and John 1. 1 ("God was the Logos"). Incidentally Bultmann's interpretation of this last passage is entirely correct: "God and the

---

[1] cf. Schumann, *Deutsche Theologie*, 1942, p. 7.

Logos are identical." This is much better than Zahn, who says
that the Logos was "a pure spirit-being like God" (!). These
Johannine passages are not isolated instances; the kerygma of
the synoptic gospels, to say nothing of St Paul, proclaims the
coming of God. In Matt. 11. 5ff. the promise of Isa. 35. 4ff. is
applied directly to Jesus: "God . . . will come and save you."
The messenger who prepares the way for Jahweh goes before
Jesus (Mal. 2. 1ff.=Matt. 11. 10). Jesus forgives sins even as
God himself (Mark 2. 1ff.: Luke 7. 49). His acts are the acts
of God (Luke 15). In his coming God is visiting (*paqad*, the
equivalent of Luke's ἐπισκέπτεσθαι) his people.[1] "Parousia is
metita, adventus, eleusis; cp. Mal. 3. 1: Zech. 14. 5, and especially
Dan. 7. 13. Hence ὁ ἐρχόμενος, Matt. 11. 3."[2] This hope of an
advent of God himself is still a vital element in late Judaism.[3]
The relative silence of the synoptic gospels on the fulfilment of
this hope is after all in line with the principle of the Messianic
secret. Bultmann's formulation of the basic confession therefore
requires a greater degree of precision than he has given it. For
the phrase: "agent of God's presence and activity" we should
substitute: "He in whom God acts in a unique and final present."
Bultmann's formula would apply just as well to a prophet (John
the Baptist might equally be called an "eschatological emissary").
The formula we propose seeks to do justice to the *ephapax* of
the New Testament.

Now the *psychikos anthropos* finds it impossible to accept the
faith of the Christians. Modern man is by no means the first to
feel the difficulty of accepting it. The great majority of mankind
have always been ready and willing enough to accept a vague and
general belief in God which makes no specific demands upon
them, but the more definite Christian belief in Christ they
prefer to reject as myth. The cultured scorn of a Celsus and the
coarse ribaldry of the nineteenth and twentieth centuries are
at one in this. The deliberate paradoxes of the early Fathers
(ὁ ἀπαθὴς παθητὸς ἐγένετο and the like) and Luther's hymn
Gelobet seist du Jesu Christ serve to express the incomprehensibility

---

[1] Such instances could be multiplied. The problem of the authenticity of
any given passage is irrelevant for the defining of the kerygma.

[2] Wellhausen, *Matthäus*, 2nd Edition, p. 118.

[3] *Test. Patr.* passim, even in the Jewish version. For the subject in general
see Volz, Moore, and Billerbeck.

of the mystery of Christ. This is exactly what Bultmann means when he stresses the element of *skandalon* in the kerygma. This *skandalon* is so acute that modern man dismisses the basic confessions of the New Testament on the ground that they are mythical. It would be easy to substantiate this point from the literature of the History of Religions school and from the idealism and rationalism of the eighteenth and nineteenth centuries. After all, is not the Christian claim that the eternal God has come to us in an individual man with all the limitations of time and space essentially mythological in character—i.e., does it not speak of the eternal as if it were involved in time and space, and of the invisible as if it were visible?

B. The Christian confession is myth for man as such, not merely for modern man. Even such language as "act of God" decision, and sin (*aversio a deo*), inevitably looks like myth. Bultmann agrees in principle with these propositions, but does not express them as precisely as one could wish.

Bultmann is acutely aware of this problem. The offence or *skandalon* consists in "the paradox of a transcendent God present and active in history: 'The Word became flesh' . . . will not be removed by philosophical discussion, but only by faith and obedience" (p. 44). So far so good, but does not Bultmann make light of the difficulty when he says: "Anyone who asserts that to speak of an act of God at all is mythological language is bound to regard the idea of an act of God in Christ as a myth. But let us ignore this question for the moment. Even Kamlah thinks it philosophically justifiable to use 'the mythological language of an act of God' " (p. 33f.)

Can the problem be shelved like this? Never; it is inescapable. True, when driven by necessity a philosopher may speak of an act of God. But unless he is a Christian he will mean it in a pantheistic sense, the *natura naturans* behind all observable phenomena. But who dares to speak of an act of God in a strictly personal sense? That the Eternal, the Infinite, the Incomprehensible should make decisions, that he should be confronted by an Either/Or, that he should grant or withhold his presence, that he should show grace or wrath, that in other words God has a history, that there is a story of personal encounter between him and man: these are things a philosopher could never admit. What would he make, for instance, of Bultmann's statement on p. 33 that "God has given up himself for us"? After all, it is not so long since we theologians have recovered the ability and the courage to say such things!

Bultmann himself is on the point of asking this question when he comes to discuss the understanding of Being with the existentialists. These philosophers are quite right in using these categories, and the discussion is all the more to be welcomed since these same categories are borrowed from Kierkegaard and Nietzsche and applied in a sense which approximates to Christian usage.

Bultmann says: (1) Philosophy knows that man has become a prey to alien powers, but believes that he can free himself from them by his own efforts. But the fact is that he can be freed from them only by an act of God.—So far so good. But man is not simply fallen a prey *to* something: he is fallen *away from* God. He is, as Bultmann himself says (p. 30f.), in rebellion against God, and therefore under his wrath. But, apart from Christ, apart from the Bible, such a notion cannot but appear to be a contemptible myth.[1] How can anyone be cut off from him who embraces and upholds the universe? How can we use such anthropomorphic language as the "wrath" of God? How can we believe that the incomprehensible, unchanging deity concerns himself about every offence we commit?

(2) Philosophy does not see that this *Verfallenheit* about which it speaks penetrates to the very core of man's Being (p. 29). This we are told is due to the arrogance and self-assertion of the philosopher (p. 29f.). The Jew and the Gnostic are equally guilty of self-glorying. Yes, but it is only when we are face to face with God that we can see that self-glorying is sin. Greek tragedy knew the sin of *hybris*, but only in the light of a personal relation with the gods it believed in—and this is something which should put many pseudo-Christians to shame. It is only in the light of the cross that we can see how deep-seated is the corruption of human nature (Rom. 9. 30—16. 4; 1 Cor. 1. 18ff.), and the God who acts through the cross is neither Zeus nor Ananké, but the Holy One of Isa. 2 and 6.

(3) In fact, however, Bultmann raises these last questions himself (p. 31): "Is sin a mythological concept or not?"

---

[1] Kant dirtied his philosopher's gown with the doctrine of radical evil, says Goethe.

The answer, he tells us, depends on whether the proposition: "What hast thou that thou didst not receive?" is universally applicable, or only to Christians. "But", he continues, "it is man's radical self-assertion which makes this understanding impossible. . . . Man's radical self-assertion blinds him to the fact of sin, and this is the clearest proof that he is a fallen being. Hence it is no good telling him that he is a sinner. He will only dismiss it as mythology."

But this involves a further point. What is true of sin is equally true of faith in the living God, of faith in God incarnate in Christ. The whole notion of sin is myth for man as such, not only for modern man, for he regards the whole idea of God as myth and the whole idea of God incarnate in Christ as myth.

We asked whether Bultmann does justice to the radical nature of this inquiry. In any case he cannot escape it. And does he do justice to the radical nature of the answer which is given us in the New Testament? Here too we should have to say that he certainly cannot escape it. However, there are still some profound questions which remain to be discussed in sections III and IV. We begin again where we left off, at Bultmann's discussion with radical philosophy.

III

In his discussion with radical philosophy, Bultmann defines the forgiveness of sin as the freeing of man from himself—i.e., from his past—and faith as being open for the future. He shows no sign of recognizing the qualitative distinction between past and future. Moreover, his definition of forgiveness as freedom for obedience leaves us wondering whether he does justice to the theonomy of Biblical thought and to the *articulus stantis et cadentis ecclesiae*.

"Sin ceases to be mythology when the love of God meets man. Such a love treats man as if he were other than he is. By so doing love frees man from himself as he is. . . . This is precisely the meaning of that which was wrought in Christ" (p. 31).

These statements are all very impressive, but they overlook one essential point. The deliverance from self is not a vague kind of new ego, a notion familiar enough in other religions, both primitive and advanced. The freedom which is the theme of the New Testament is of a wholly different order. It is the

facultas standi extra se coram deo, freedom from the curse of the
condemnation and the bondage of the law. The latter cuts us off
from God and brings us under wrath, condemnation, curse, and
death. We might say in Bultmann's own terminology that this
deliverance must be conceived in strictly eschatological terms.
It has nothing to do with the "unbecoming" of the mystics or
with Goethe's *Stirb und Werde*. Our ego is in revolt against God
and fallen under judgement, but God declares us free from the
sentence of death which he had formerly pronounced against us.
Christ pleads on our behalf, he is our new Ego (Gal. 2. 20).
He is our deliverance from the curse and condemnation.

This freedom Bultmann rightly identifies with the forgiveness
of sin, but fails to give that formula the richness of meaning it
had for the Reformers. To them it meant access to the presence
of God. "The grace of God", says Bultmann, "means the forgiveness of sins, and brings deliverance from the bondage of the
past. . . . Man is released from the bondage of the past" (p. 19).
This is the meaning of faith—"to be made free for the future"
(ibid.). Faith is (p. 32) the "freedom of man from himself
. . . openness for the future. . . . Such faith is still a subtle form
of self-assertion so long as the love of God is merely a piece of
wishful thinking. It is only an abstract idea so long as God has
not revealed his love". This is where Christ comes into the
picture, and that means "God has given up himself for us."
Bultmann appropriates those great New Testament texts which
identify the self-giving and love of Christ with that of God
himself (1 John 4. 10; 4. 19, "He first loved us"; Rom. 8. 32;
cp. also "the love of God", "the love of God in Christ Jesus",
John 3. 16; Gal. 1. 4; 2. 19f.). But surely, in justice to the New
Testament, the whole argument ought to be reversed. It is
because and in so far as we have become the objects of God's
love that we are freed from *our* past and open for *God's* future.
Because we are loved by God, our old man, our "adamite
existence" as Schlatter called it, our old life in rebellion against
God and cut off from fellowship with him, has been delivered
over to death. "The old things are passed away" (2 Cor. 5. 17).
The "old things" in question are our past qualified as enmity
to God, not the past in a merely chronological sense, the
structure of our Being in time. It means our bondage to this
present evil age, to a period of time which is moving towards

the day of judgement. The New Testament is also aware of quite
a different past, the time before all worlds, the "pre" of
"predestination" which becomes a present reality in our
"calling". Here is a past which is qualified by God, and which
eludes all our ordinary categories of time. The same is true of
this present, evil age and of the future. The future which is
opened up for us is not the future in the ordinary chronological
sense of the word. It means that we are assured that neither
things present nor things to come, neither the past nor any
future condemnation at the bar of God's judgement, can separate
us from his love. The chronological future may hold in store for
us temptations which may assault even the very elect. Even the
apostle awaits this future, which is the day of judgement, with
fear and trembling (2 Cor. 5. 10, 11), lest he be found reprobate
(1 Cor. 9. 27). Yet God's future is stronger than all these things
to come—God's future is his age to come, his ages of ages, his
last things, his future period of time, which by virtue of the
incarnation and resurrection paradoxically juts out as it were
into this present age of ours. Christ alone is the clue to the meaning of past and future, the past wiped out, our rebellion against
God, and the future of the new age of God opened up for us.

But the forgiveness of sin has still further implications.
Bultmann is right enough when he observes that "it is not a
juridical concept (p. 32) . . . it does not mean the remission
of punishment". Yes, we are not concerned with justice in the
abstract, but with the living God as Judge. In other words, the
mythological pictures of the day of judgement are simply
signposts to the truth. God either rejects us (wrath) or accepts
us (righteousness). This takes place at the last day—that is, when
our present time series and the world in which we are enchained
have come to an end. The judgement is eschatological in the
strictest sense of the word. It occurs beyond the bounds of time
and space. It is wrought out in another world where man, both
individually and collectively, finds himself on the other side of
time and space as he knows them now. This is why St Paul's
doctrine of justification is rigorously eschatological. It looks not
to a juridical judgement in foro coeli, but to the eschatological
day of judgement. Our acquittal is Christ himself. He is the
embodiment of the righteousness of God. In him God vindicates
his own righteousness (Rom. 3. 26). He incorporates his own

in himself as a King includes his people. They are in him, they are in him the righteousness of God (2 Cor. 5. 21). Here then is the meaning of the forgiveness of sin (Rom. 3. 25; 2 Cor. 5. 19)—to stand upright in the presence of God, *facultas standi extra se coram deo*. This brings about a radical change in the life of man. He can now live unto God (Rom. 6. 10; Gal. 2. 19); he can stand in the gospel, in grace, in the Lord, in the Spirit; he can walk according to the Lord, according to the gospel, to the call of God, to the God who calls us into his kingdom; he need no longer be conformed to this aeon, for he can walk in the newness of eternal life.

But in Bultmann's hands the forgiveness of sins would seem to be endangered at its very heart. "It is", he tells us on p. 32, "not a juridical concept. It does not mean the remission of punishment. If that were so, man's plight would be as bad as ever. Rather, forgiveness conveys freedom from the sin which hitherto had held man in bondage. But this freedom is not a static quality: it is freedom to obey. The indicative implies an imperative. . . . Thus eschatological existence has become possible. God has acted, and the world—'this world'—has come to an end. Man himself has been made new (2 Cor. 5. 17)".

Once more the argument should surely be reversed. The primary consideration is God and his coming judgement. It is our encounter with that judgement which betokens our sentence of death. But our acquittal is Christ himself. In the passage quoted by Bultmann (2 Cor. 5. 17) the emphasis lies on the words "in Christ". The real meaning of eschatological existence and of the renewal of man is discernible only in the light of the revelation of God in Christ. We have no other means of discovering the meaning of those things. If we had, all God would be doing in revealing himself would be helping us to achieve eschatological existence and the renewal of our being. But the truth is, it is only our encounter with God in Christ which shows us what these things really are. Without that encounter, eschatological existence is misconstrued as the absolute timelessness of the mystics and the renewal of man as moral uplift. And there is a further difficulty. It looks as though for Bultmann the forgiveness of sins does not show its true character until it has produced freedom from sin and consequent obedience to the imperative. If that were so, the forgiveness of sin would only be a means to an end, and the end would be the ethical renewal of man. This is to place a higher premium on the imperative "thou shalt" than on the indicative "thou art". Strangely enough it was Bultmann himself who taught us that St Paul's ethics are derived from the indicative (*Z.N.W.*, 1924, 123–40). Yet now he regards "become what you are" as a principle on which both the theology of the New Testament and the philosophy of the existentialists are at one.

We are back again at the old question which the Reformers asked of the Church of Rome, and which has cropped up again and again in the discussions within the Protestant church. Is there another element of equal or even greater importance than justification or forgiveness—e.g., sanctification, obedience, or Spirit? Or does the forgiveness of sins adequately describe the whole content of salvation? In the latter case there would be no need to help out the forgiveness of sins by bringing in the new obedience—indeed it would be impossible to help it out. The reason for this is not that forgiveness is far more than the freeing of man from the burden of sin or even from the burden of his existence in time. It is because forgiveness of sin means access, permanent access to the presence of God.

Above and beyond this there is no second element.[1] All that the New Testament says about obedience and hearkening is indissolubly linked to the gospel and faith, to hearing the joyous tidings of God. How a new way of life arises therefrom has been indicated on p. 55f. This way of life is in practice always subject to the imperative, because the eschatological judgement still lies in the future, and the present age is not yet at an end. Hence the whole revelation and gift of God to man once and for all in Christ must be apprehended ever anew in each successive

---

[1] Forgiveness of sin is the central theme of the Bible, as the Reformers perceived with unerring insight. In Mark the kerygma opens with the baptism of repentance unto the remission of sins. This is followed up with the episode of the lame man. In Luke the friendship of Jesus for sinners is the keynote of the whole ministry and its characteristic scandal. In Acts 10. 43 all the promises of the Old Testament and their fulfilment in Christ are embraced in the forgiveness of sin. Similarly in the Pauline Epistles the forgiveness of sin embraces faith, grace, peace, and life, to say nothing of the "blood of Jesus" in Hebrews and Revelation. Once more it was Bultmann in his article on Paul in *R.G.G.*[2] who taught us that justification is the clue to Pauline theology, after St Paul had been regarded for a generation as a Hellenistic mystic.

task and danger which confronts us in this present age. This is
our permanent vocation as Christians. It takes the form of an
imperative, a command, a demand, and exhortation.[1] It would
require a detailed analysis of the paraenetic sections of the
Pauline Epistles to show that they all presuppose the kerygma.
The reader is referred to Rom. 6. 1–11: Col. 3. 1–4 (also 5ff.);
1 Cor. 5. 7; 6. 11.

Bultmann has been accused of substituting anthropology for
theology. Our criticisms thus far—about the definition of the
Ego, of past and future, and finally of the forgiveness of sin—
would seem to substantiate this. But this would be to overlook
the stress Bultmann lays on the fact that it is essential to the
Being of man that he should search for God, for the God of the
Christian revelation. The whole discussion about demythologizing has tended to overlook Bultmann's first essay on the subject,
Die Frage der natürlichen Offenbarung. At the same time, however,
it is doubtful if Bultmann is right in adopting the existentialist
concepts of the Ego, of time, of guilt and obedience, for his
own definition of these things. That is to make the God of
Christian revelation the answer to questions which have been
raised within the framework of atheism. This is the wrong
approach—"anthroponomous" rather than "theonomous". We
should have to show that this approach is wrong and intrinsically
impossible, and that what it is really after can be understood
only in the light of the Christian revelation.

A final suspicion remains. Do our criticisms apply only to
Bultmann's argument with the existentialists, or do they affect
his own attitude to the Christian faith? What has Bultmann to
say about the event of Christ? How does he expound the kerygma
within purely Christian terms? It is—and here Bultmann agrees
with the New Testament—the kerygma of the cross and resurrection. We shall deal with each in turn in two theses, the first of
which will be divided into two parts.

[1] P. 21; "The new life in faith cannot be expressed in purely indicative
terms: it needs an imperative to complete it. In other words, the decision of
faith is never final, and needs to be renewed in each successive situation."

IV A

Bultmann regards the pictorial language which the New Testament uses about the cross as a mythological expression of the truth that the believer has been delivered from sin. The cross means no more than our being crucified with Christ, which he further defines as the crucifixion of our passions and the conquest of our natural reluctance to endure suffering. Our criticism of Bultmann's position starts once more from the fundamental article of the Reformation. This gives the whole question a greater degree of precision. The basic theme of the New Testament, no less than that of the Reformation, seems to have gone by the board. We hear nothing of the dereliction of Christ, of his intercession for sinners, or of his exaltation as the crucified yet ever-living Lord. All this, which is the heart of the message of the cross, contains not the slightest trace of mythology. It is simply the expression of a personal relation between the believer and Christ.

The cross of Christ (p. 35) "certainly has a mythical character as far as its objective setting is concerned. The Jesus who was crucified was the pre-existent, incarnate Son of God, and as such he was without sin. He is the victim whose blood atones for our sins. He bears vicariously . . ." This, we are told, is a mythological interpretation of the cross. "It is a mixture of sacrificial and juridical analogies which have ceased to be tenable for us to-day. And in any case they do not do justice to what the New Testament is trying to say. For the most they can convey is that the punishment (our sins) deserve is remitted. But the New Testament means more than this. The cross releases men not only from the guilt but also from the power of sin."

The last few words confirm the suspicion we raised at the end of the previous thesis. It was not merely the exigencies of controversy, but his own theology, which made Bultmann bring the obedience to the imperative into the foreground in his discussion of forgiveness. To become free from the power of sin, he tells us, means much more than the forgiveness of sin. Obviously "remission of punishment" means here the same as forgiveness of sin earlier in his essay. Once more Bultmann fails to do justice to the *articulus stantis et cadentis ecclesiae*. Of course St Paul, like all the other New Testament writers, has to deal always with the concrete realities of human sentiment and behaviour. He cannot avoid ethics or escape from the prob-

lem of right and wrong conduct. He must deal with obedience
to God, the obedience which breaks our bondage to sin. But
how do men attain to this new obedience? The answer is always
the same, though it is expressed in many different ways. God
turns to us men, who are flesh, cut off from God. This act of
God may be expressed as grace, word, sanctification, love,
Spirit, peace, life, joy, or fear. It may be that St Paul drops the
terms "forgiveness" and "access to God", but their essential
meaning is always present. St Paul knows that in the very act of
writing his letters he is conferring the grace and peace of God
upon the churches. The God who thus turns to man is *numquam
otiosus*—there is no difficulty in using such Reformation language
here, for in Luther and the confessional documents the situation
is fundamentally similar to that in St Paul. God does not allow
us to remain in our plight of godlessness and wickedness. This,
however, can happen only if the self-glorying which is the
besetting sin alike of legalists and antinomians is transcended in
the *koinonia* of the crucified and risen Lord, and the full and
definitive judgement of the cross perpetually renewed.

And here we are confronted with a further difficulty. Is the
notion of the cross as judgement simply mythology? And is the
whole idea of sacrifice also mythological? Now, as a matter of
fact, there is no religion under the sun in which sacrifice plays
no part. The notion that man must surrender his dearest possession
on earth to his deity—the supreme instance is that of child
sacrifice—is so fundamental that it cannot be dismissed as
mythology. The same applies to the idea that man's life is forfeit
in the sight of God, and that he accepts another life in place of
our own—which in the last resort is the meaning of sacrifice
in the Old Testament. And the same is true of the popular use
of the word "sacrifice", as when a mother dies for her child or
a soldier on the field of battle. A life is sacrificed when it is
surrendered on behalf of others. If we reject any particular
theory of sacrifice it is because we cannot square that theory
with the character of God as we know it.[1]

Even the doctrine of satisfaction was originally quite un-

---

[1] Bultmann does not discuss the idea of atonement, but what we have said
about sacrifice applies equally to that also. Every religion and every legal
system recognizes the need for atonement. The effects of guilt are far-reaching,
and the cry for redress cannot be stifled. The only question is, how far can any

mythological. As first formulated by St Anselm, it had a certain grandeur. It expressed an awareness of the majesty of God and of the terrible reality of sin (*pondus peccati*). Its fault lay in the false antithesis—*aut poena aut satisfactio*. This, however, was due not to mythology but, paradoxically, to an inadequate conception of the majesty of God. Abstract justice was substituted for a personal Judge. There is, however, no doctrine of satisfaction in the Pauline writings. In Romans 3 and 2 Corinthians it has to be read into it. Such a doctrine cannot be derived from St Paul's *anti* or *hyper*, at any rate when these are translated "for" and "on behalf of", which is what they really mean.

Nor is this the only case where Bultmann has somewhat distorted the teaching of St Paul.[1] Is the Son of God "as such" without sin? It is one of the characteristics of the Servant of Jahweh in Isa. 53. Is the Son of God as such pre-existent? It is one of the characteristics of the Son of Man in Dan. 7.[2] As for the pre-existence of Christ, it is significant that St Paul speaks of it most emphatically at the point where he is not speaking of it directly —viz., when he is speaking about the cross, in Rom. 8. 32— God sacrifices his Son (on Bultmann's profound understanding of this passage see p. 55). And where does Paul speak of Christ's enduring punishment in our stead? Our hymns sometimes speak of Christ's bearing God's wrath and our punishment, but they do so under Anselm's rather than Paul's influence, and their meaning is really quite different. Take for instance

> . . . Der du dich für mich gegeben
> In die tiefste Seelennot,
> In das äusserste Verderben . . .

---

particular doctrine of atonement be squared with the character of God. The cry for redress must be satisfied; the question is, how? By our own human efforts, or only by the act of God in sending his Son to be the propitiation, to be sin on our behalf?

[1] Is Bultmann still under the fatal spell of Wrede's *Paulus*? Strangely enough it was Bultmann himself who demolished Wrede on the crucial point of justification.

[2] There are parallels to both these figures in the Gnostic myths, but if the latter influenced St Paul in any way, they did so in a form which was already largely derived from Judaism. In content the difference between the Servant of Isa. 53 and the Son of Man in Dan. 7, on the one hand, and the Gnostic redeemer on the other, lies in the relation of the former to Jahweh and his revelation of himself in history.

So reiss mich aus den Ängsten
Kraft deiner Angst und Pein.

There is not a word here about the balancing of an account, or
of wrath and punishment as burdens which Jesus took upon
himself. The real meaning is that he entered into our deprivation
from God, although he was himself the Son of God, the One
"in whom God acts in a unique and final present" (see above,
p. 51), "true God and eternal life" (1 John 5. 20; above, p. 50).

St Paul is making exactly the same point when he speaks of
the "likeness of sinful flesh" (Rom. 8. 3), of the "curse"
(Gal. 3. 13), and of Christ's being made "sin" (2 Cor. 5. 21).
It is also implicit in the Markan version of the Agony in the
garden, and becomes explicit in Luke and Hebrews. The same
kerygma underlies John 11. 33 (D Text); 12. 27; 13. 21. And
what is the meaning of "Let not your heart be troubled" in
14. 1 and 27?[1] The same kerygma is also discernible in Luther's
preaching of the cross, which is based exclusively on the cry
from the cross as given by St Matthew. There is not a trace of
mythology in any of these passages. They make no attempt to
portray the inner sufferings of Jesus or his dealings with his
Father.[2] Nor is there any dialogue between God the Father and
the pre-existent Son about the work of redemption such as we
find in the hymns of Luther and Paul Gerhardt. St John does
indeed say that the death of Jesus was the victory over Satan
(12. 31; 14. 30; 16. 11), but again this is quite unmythological.
We may not know, we cannot tell what pains he had to bear in
entering into our deprivation from God in death. All we can do
is to express the fact with all wealth of language at our command.
In the last resort this is the meaning of every single pericope in
the gospels and epistles.

The whole kerygma, however, is inseparably one with the
proclamation of the risen Lord as the Crucified. It is the exalted
and ever-present Lord who is the Crucified. It is he who, as the
High Priest in Hebrews, shows sympathy with our infirmities.
He is the Lamb of the Apocalypse, the One who came with

[1] And what is the secret behind John 11. 10? The analysis in Bultmann's
commentary on the Fourth Gospel ad loc. shows only the *aporia*.
[2] The New Testament kerygma (a primitive baptismal confession?) speaks
of the "obedience of Jesus". Unfortunately it is not possible to develop this
point further here.

the blood (1 John). The earliest liturgy sings of Christ as the High Priest interceding for us (Rom. 8. 34; 1 John 2. 1; Heb. 7. 25, and the hymns in Revelation). Even Calvin in his commentary on John 16. 26 is careful not to take the picture of Christ's intercession literally, any more than the New Testament does. After all, it is impossible to form any literal picture of the intercession of One who is in his own, and whose own are in him. Nor is there anything mythological in the New Testament picture of Christ's enthronement. His own are the servants he has bought by his own blood through laying down his life for them. To whom did he pay the price? How is his death the ransom price for the many? The New Testament maintains a discreet silence. If, as is highly probable, there is a background of demonology in such passages, it is significant that it never comes to the forefront, despite the abundant testimony to such beliefs in other places (see Thesis VII). Instead, the New Testament confines itself to the language of sacrifice in such contexts: he laid down his life to deliver man from the bondage of sin, death and the devil, and now our life is his own.

This brings us apparently by chance to the second article of Luther's Catechism, and to the first question of that of Heidelberg. But it is really no accident, for it is the simplest possible expression of our personal relation to Christ. I belong to him because he has dethroned the powers which held me in thrall. This is the language of personal relationship, not the concrete pictures of mythology. This is the Gospel reduced to its simplest terms as the Presence of Christ. He who is one with God belongs utterly to us, though we be cut off from God. His sacrifice, though offered once and for all (*ephapax*), is a perpetual 'now.'

We have repeatedly asserted that this part of the primitive Christian proclamation is unmythological throughout. We found again and again that, of set purpose it would seem, all pictorial elaboration is lacking and that all mysteries are left discreetly veiled. There is a complete absence of visible imagery, except that the imagery of all four gospels is taken for granted in the epistolary literature, a point to which we shall return later (Thesis VII). By ordinary observation and by scientific criticism we have succeeded in demonstrating the complete absence of mythology in the New Testament proclamation of the cross. But we are fully aware that the non-Christian is bound to dismiss it all as mythology (see Thesis IIb). What do we mean when we say that Jesus has entered into our alienation from God? What do we mean by a personal relation to the exalted Christ? Strange things to say "of one Jesus, who was dead, whom Paul affirmed to be alive" (Acts 25. 19).

It is a remarkable fact that, if we have understood him aright, Bultmann never mentions the central aspect of the New Testament preaching of the cross. He sees only two alternatives. Either: "To believe on the cross does not mean to concern ourselves with a mythical process . . . or with an objective event (p. 36) . . . not necessarily a theory of sacrifice or satisfaction (p. 37). Or (p. 36): "to believe in the cross of Christ . . . means to make the cross . . . our own, to undergo crucifixion with him . . . the cross becomes the judgement of ourselves . . . crucifying the affections and lusts . . . overcoming our natural dread of suffering . . . and the perfection of our detachment from the world . . . the judgement . . . and deliverance . . . of man."

But what does Bultmann mean when he says that the cross becomes the judgement of ourselves? What he should mean is this: God pronounces the sentence of death against us and condemns us to reprobation. So heinous is our guilt that he delivered up his Son in order to remove it (Gal. 2. 21, a very significant passage for Luther). That sentence is intelligible and tolerable only because God has changed it into an acquittal by a unique act of his own. But for that, our plight would be desperate indeed. It is only God's verdict which makes this judgement a deliverance. Once we disregard that verdict, we are tempted to imagine we can achieve that freedom by acquitting ourselves. St Paul (1 Cor. 11. 31) and the Reformers are emboldened by their trust in Christ's intercession to say: "Christ, thou art my sin and I thy righteousness." But once the connection with the unique, yet ever-present act of God in Christ is disregarded, the whole notion is in danger of being reduced to the deliverance offered by the power of the Confessional, an idea as familiar to antiquity as it is to the modern world, even in a secularized form. The "crucifixion of our passions" is then no more than a striking euphemism for self-mastery, which is the quest of all the higher religions and philosophies. Even the willing acceptance of

suffering is a universal human characteristic. The false asceticism
of the middle ages and later the passion mysticism of the Lutheran
hymns reduced the New Testament teaching of our being
crucified with Christ to sheer bathos. In the end it meant no
more than the ordinary acceptance of suffering.

IV B

Bultmann is at pains to emphasize what he calls the historical significance of
the cross. But he means, not the historical uniqueness of the revelation of God,
but historicity as the pattern of human life. He completely ignores the connection between our life and the cross of Jesus as an event of the past. This has four
consequences: (1) The witness of the New Testament to the uniqueness of
Jesus, (2) the proclamation of the gospels themselves, (3) the proclamation
of the Gospels in the light of the Epistles, and (4) the earliest Christian confession of Kyrios Jesous—are robbed of their full force.

Bultmann uses strong language about the cross as an historical
event. It is something that happens in history (p. 37f.). But the
history he speaks of is not the unique event of Golgotha. It is
what he elsewhere (p. 36) calls the eschatological event. "It
is something which occurs beyond the bounds of time, it is, at
any rate so far as its meaning—i.e., its meaning for faith—is
concerned, an ever-present reality." Bultmann is not speaking
of the intercession of the ascended Christ, but of the cross of
Christ as a present reality in the everyday life of the Christians
(p. 36). It is at this point that the significance of the cross is to
be apprehended—in the concreteness of our human life as
historical.[1] Everything Bultmann says about the cross is located
not at Calvary but in our human experience. Of a unique event
wrought out in the personal relationship between God and men
on the stage of history, of a story of the dealings of God with
man, of a unique and final revelation of God in Christ crucified
(cp. Rom. 3. 25; 2 Cor. 5. 18), there is never so much as a
word.

In fact, Bultmann is at pains to divorce what he calls the
historicity of the cross from the crucifixion of Jesus as an event
in the past: "The real meaning of the cross is that it has created
a new and permanent situation in history. The preaching of the
cross as the event of redemption forces all who hear it to ask

[1] This point will be elaborated when we come to Thesis VI.

themselves whether they will appropriate this significance for themselves, whether they are willing to be crucified with Christ.''

But that is not the meaning of the cross considered as an event of the past. Bultmann of course objects that the cross cannot be considered in this way at all. It would mean reproducing an event of the past, which he says is frankly impossible: ''The cross is for us an event in the past. We can never recover it as an event in our own lives.''

All this is highly debatable. In the first place, the New Testament always attaches supreme importance to the uniqueness and finality of Jesus. The crucified One is not an X, but Jesus of Nazareth. Even as a matter of terminology, it is remarkable when and where St Paul uses the name of Jesus absolutely—e.g., 2 Cor. 4. 10f., quoted by Bultmann himself.[1] The implication is always the same. One who bore a human name and died under a particular signature of his own is the Lord whom the Church confesses. Compare also the importance attached to the *flesh* of Jesus (*sarx*). It is in our flesh, according to St Paul, that Jesus is victorious over the powers which cut us off from God (Rom. 8. 3; cp. Col. 1. 16; Eph. 2. 14; also Rom. 1. 3).[2] The same point underlies the story of Gethsemane in the Gospels and in Hebrews. But, to put the matter beyond all doubt, we should have to examine all the passages in Hebrews, Revelation, the Acts and the epistles, where the name Jesus is used absolutely, without the addition of any title. The addition of ''Christ'' and similar titles in the MS tradition only shows how quickly the meaning of the primitive kerygma ceased to be understood.

Secondly, what is at stake is not the so-called Jesus of history, but the primitive kerygma. We are not concerned with a Jesus of history whose authentic portrait we have first to recover by literary and historical criticism, but with a proclamation whose title deeds áre the gospels as such. In Bultmann's essay the synoptic gospels are never so much as mentioned as evidence for the kerygma, and John figures only as the satellite of Paul. Yet it is John in particular who tells us the purpose for which the gospels were written. In opposition to the Gnostics, who were concerned only with the Christos, the Fourth Gospel

---

[1] (P. 37) Cp. also the use of *Kyrios Christos*.
[2] Similarly John 1. 14; 1 John 4. 2; 2 John 7.

bears witness to the earthly Jesus as the bearer of the glory of God. The same is true, *mutatis mutandis*, of the synoptic gospels. The missionary preaching in Mark and in the speeches of Acts tells of him whose death and resurrection is the meaning and purpose of his conflict on earth. The logia tradition (Q, etc.) presents the earthly teaching of Jesus as the standard to which the Church of the exalted Christ is bound. The results of modern New Testament scholarship tend to confirm Kähler's dictum that the gospels are passion narratives prefixed by a detailed introduction. But it does not follow that the introduction is superfluous, for it tells us who that Jesus was who went to the cross and was raised from the dead. The gospels as the good news are part of the primitive kerygma. Now that we have learnt to regard them as the word of the Church, there is no excuse for failing to recognize the importance attached by the Church to the kerygma of the earthly Jesus.

Thirdly, we must at all costs avoid driving a wedge between the epistles and the gospels. How closely the two halves of the New Testament are interrelated may be learnt from the connection between the Acts and Luke on the one hand and the Johannine Epistles and the Fourth Gospel on the other. Yet neither the Acts nor 1 John make this connection explicit. May it not therefore be the same with St Paul? It was Bultmann himself, in his two essays on Jesus and Paul, who established that connection at certain crucial points—viz., in their teaching about the law and in their eschatology. This connection was not just the discovery of modern critics, for it is part of the kerygma itself. The link with the Jesus who was made under the law, who on a certain night was delivered up, and on that night instituted the Eucharist, who rose again the third day and was seen of chosen witnesses—all this is essential to the Pauline kerygma. St Paul's conversion on any interpretation means that he came to see that *Jesus of Nazareth* was the Messiah.

Fourthly, all this is in line with the earliest Christian confession, *Kyrios Iesous*. In the switch from this to *Christos Iesous*, the human name, Jesus, remains unchanged. Both versions, Palestinian and Hellenistic, imply an antithesis—he who was crucified on the accursed tree is nevertheless Messiah: Jesus, a figure of flesh and blood, is nevertheless Lord. This was the element in the kerygma which Jewish controversialists continued to repudiate down to the Dialogue of Justin Martyr, and which the Gnostics are already repudiating in the New Testament with their *anathema Iesous* (1 Cor. 12. 3). The *scandalon* is always the person of Jesus, its uniqueness, its finality, and its lowly form. Bultmann has no intention of mitigating this *scandalon*, indeed he seeks to accentuate it, to throw it into even sharper relief by removing every trace of mythology which obscured it. But may it not be that, as the Christian Church has always asserted, our salvation is One who was involved in all the relativity of history? It may be true that all past history can be reproduced only by the art of the historian, but the Church has always been content to trust the kerygma or tradition (*paradosis*) of the Apostolic Church about the uniqueness and finality of the incarnate, crucified, and risen Lord. It is irrelevant to object that the primitive Church could not feel the problem as we are bound to, owing to our distance from the original events and to the development of modern historical criticism. The primitive Church includes the claim of the credibility of the witnesses as part of its kerygma, a point to which we shall return later when we come to the resurrection. And whether historical criticism really presents something quite new vis-a-vis historic being as such, will be discussed under Thesis VI.

Meanwhile, we must deal with the resurrection. Throughout our present thesis it has been apparent that the cross and resurrection form an inseparable unity. Bultmann makes the same point again and again.

V

Bultmann is right in holding that the resurrection cannot be a miraculous proof. For the resurrection is itself an object of faith, an eschatological event which is actually made present in the preaching of the gospel. The event of Easter Day, however, is for him not the resurrection itself, but the beginning of the disciples' faith in the resurrection. The question is whether this theory does justice to the uniqueness and finality of the Easter event (1 Cor. 15), and to the relation between the faith of Easter and the uniqueness and finality of Jesus himself.

The cross, Bultmann observes, is identical in meaning with the resurrection. Cross and resurrection form a single, indivisible event (p. 38). The resurrection is "an attempt to express the meaning of the cross". It shows that the death of Jesus on the cross is "not just an ordinary death, but the judgement and salvation of the world", and because it is this, it "deprives death of its power".

The resurrection is not a "miraculous proof" (p. 39). It does not guarantee the saving efficacy of the cross. Bultmann admits that even the New Testament often regards the resurrection as a miraculous proof. But the passages he quotes are open to more than one interpretation, as we shall see when we come to consider 1 Cor. 15. Yet Bultmann is right in principle, for the resurrection is itself an article of faith and an eschatological event (p. 40); it is the eschatological fact in virtue of which Christ has abolished death and brought light and immortality to light (2 Tim. 1. 10).

This truth, we are told, is made manifest in everyday Christian living, in putting off the works of darkness. Hence dying and rising again with Christ are identical (Rom. 6. 11ff.; 2 Cor. 4. 10f., etc.): "Faith in the resurrection is really the same thing as faith in the saving efficacy of the cross" (p. 41). How do men come to such a faith? Bultmann answers—and here he has the whole New Testament on his side: "Christ meets us in the preaching as One crucified and risen. He meets us in the preaching and nowhere else. The faith of Easter is just this—faith in the word of preaching."

How is this Easter faith connected with the Easter event? Bultmann has stated elsewhere[1] that "the only historical event which can be established is the faith of the earliest disciples in the resurrection". Whatever the historical and psychological explanation of that experience, the Easter faith of the earliest disciples is for us as it was for them "the proclamation of himself by the risen Lord, the act of God in which the salvation-event of the cross is completed". "We are asked", Bultmann continues in the same article, "whether God acted in and through the visionary experiences of a handful of enthusiasts: that is what they believed themselves and what the proclamation asserts." This is true, for in the Pentecost narrative (Acts 2. 13) and in the judgement of Festus (Acts 26. 24) the apostles appear as enthusiastic visionaries, and all the resurrection narratives emphasize that the disciples doubted. In 1 Cor. 15 the key

[1] *Th.L.Z.* 1940, 246.

word in the evidence for the unique unrepeatable event of the resurrection is the word *ophthe,* which is the normal verb for a vision. The testimony of the New Testament to the resurrection is all along aware of its own inherent paradox. It asks us whether in the Easter event God acted in a unique and final present, whether we choose to mock at these enthusiastic visionaries. Bultmann is quite right. The witness of the original disciples to the resurrection rests upon their own experience. There is no other supporting evidence either before or after it. This testimony lives on in the Church's preaching (p. 42) and this preaching is the source of her life. It is itself part of the eschatological event. We have repeatedly insisted that within certain limits the interpretation proposed by Bultmann does justice to the claims of the New Testament about the resurrection. We have only one question to put to Bultmann, but that question is the key to the whole subject. What about the uniqueness and finality of the Easter event?

Here we seem at first sight to be on the same ground as we were in Thesis IVA. Is being crucified with Christ no more than a subjective experience in the heart of the believer? Or does everything depend here upon the uniqueness and finality of the event of Jesus Christ? What is true of dying with him is true of rising again with him. "God's judgement of the world, which is at the same time its salvation, and which therefore deprives death of its power" (*vide supra,* p. 70), is in the first instance the judgement of God upon Christ. This judgement vindicates him who was forsaken by God and man (1 Tim. 3. 16; John 16. 10; Isa. 53. 11 LXX). It glorifies him and enthrones him as Lord. The everyday life of Christians (*vide supra,* p. 70) means to be in Christ. This is the new existence. For the risen Christ, now exalted as Lord, includes his own in himself.

But Bultmann is clearer about the uniqueness and finality of the resurrection than he is of the cross. For him the faith of the disciples in the resurrection is the decisive fact which confronts us. The preaching of the Church down the ages hands on the testimony of the original disciples to the resurrection. We are forced to make up our minds whether we will accept their testimony or reject it as illusory. Here Bultmann, as it were, involuntarily breaks through the identification of Cross and Resurrection. The Easter faith of the original disciples meant faith in the "self-manifestation of the risen Lord, the act of God in which the redemptive event of the cross is completed''. The events of Good Friday and Easter Day are two separate things, humiliation and exaltation, even though there is identity between the risen Lord and the crucified Jesus. This is the justification for the change in terminology which we have already introduced without explanation. The preaching of the Church gives us not the Easter faith but the Easter *testimony* of the original disciples. Faith, if it is genuine, never calls attention to itself (see Rom. 4. 5; Mark 9. 24). The resurrection narratives are true to this. The faith of the disciples is the "faith of unbelievers".[1] Fear and uncertainty give way to joy and gladness. But the climax of the resurrection story lies not in man's puny faith, but in the triumphant witness which springs from that faith—and with this St Paul and the Acts agree.

If this be so, why does Bultmann stigmatize St Paul's argument in 1 Cor. 15. 3–8 as "fatal" (p. 39)? There are other similar passages in both the genuinely Pauline and the disputed epistles, so it does not stand alone. It is only one form of the manifold testimony of the apostolate, which is an unrepeatable charisma. Moreover 1 Cor. 15 does not really go beyond what Bultmann himself has admitted to be important—that is, the witness of the original disciples to the resurrection. It really happened on one unique occasion: men did really see the risen Messiah after his death and burial. To see him was a privilege granted only to the apostles, and is one which we can never share. The preaching of the Church down the ages is simply the unfolding of that "word which constitutes the Church" (so Kähler described the special significance of the New Testament). This is not due to any supposed superiority of the earliest preaching over that of later times, but to the uniqueness and finality of the apostles as duly qualified witnesses.

To accept the word of the apostles and to believe in the risen Lord are one and the same thing. There is no question of any before or after, or of three distinct stages in the growth of faith, as though we were first convinced of the historicity of the resurrection, and then of the witness to its import, and lastly of its redemptive power in our own lives. The word of the testimony stands on its own feet. To take that word to heart means to believe (Rom. 10. 8–10). This testimony tells us that the Christ

[1] Bultmann on Mark 9. 24.

who rose again the third day is one and the same as he who hung on the cross and lay in the grave.[1]

The apostolic witness testifies that Jesus crucified lives and reigns, and that the crucified and risen Lord are identical. It bears witness to the uniqueness and finality of what God has done in Jesus of Nazareth. As with the cross, so with the resurrection the crucial point is the uniqueness and finality of Jesus. Bultmann brings us before the problem in both cases, but each time he removes the uniqueness and finality from its place in our preaching to-day. But with the resurrection he brings us one stage further than he does with the cross.

For he admits that for the historian (p. 42 cf. Th.L.Z.) "the personal intimacy which the disciples had enjoyed with Jesus goes some way towards explaining their faith in his resurrection." He is quite right when he says that the Christian belief in the resurrection is faith in the proclamation of himself by the risen Lord. In other words, the resurrection is not an historical event which can be proved or reconstructed to a relative degree of certainty within the framework of cause and effect. But once again we are bound to ask, as we asked on p. 68, whether the historian's art is not usurping the place of the primitive kerygma. It is true that the Christian belief in the resurrection does not derive its substance and certainty from the results of historical criticism. Yet that faith is summed up in the fact that a man "whom we cannot draw too closely into our flesh" (Luther) was exalted by God to be Lord and King. The event of Easter is riveted to the Jesus who lived and died on earth. This is too obvious to require proof: it is abundantly testified in the gospels and the speeches in Acts, and also in the epistles. The references

[1] Bultmann has nothing to say about the Empty Tomb. This, like the resurrection itself, is not a miraculous proof. It produces fear and alarm (Mark 16. 9), and can be apprehended only by faith (John 20. 8f.); to unbelief it is a subject for ridicule (Matt. 28. 13–15). Yet the Empty Tomb has already asserted its place in the kerygma in 1 Cor. 15, otherwise the presence of "was buried" and "on the third day" is inexplicable. The resurrection is conceived as a physical event; see 1 Cor. 15. 44 and compare with 6. 14 and implicitly the whole section from verse 12 to verse 20. This implies a high estimation of the body, such as had already occasioned much opposition at Corinth. Unfortunately the whole idea became debased through exigencies of the controversy with Gnosticism, and *sarx* replaced *soma*, despite 1 Cor. 15. 50. Even Bultmann hints at this perspective in his article in Th.L.Z.

on p. 67 may suffice. The crucial point about both the cross and the resurrection is the uniqueness and finality of Jesus.

This argument requires expansion along three different lines. First, we must recall what was said above on p. 68 about Bultmann's essays on Jesus and Paul. "The erstwhile personal association of the disciples with Jesus" is important only because it brought them into touch with his word—which includes his deeds. That word is an eschatological one. He proclaimed the kingdom of God. He spoke of the coming of the Son of Man. He interpreted his words and deeds as signs of the irruption of the last things.[1] All that he said and did is now fulfilled in the resurrection. This is the theme of all the resurrection narratives in the gospels and of the passages in the Acts which bear witness to the resurrection. This Jesus, who once lived in the flesh on earth, is now exalted as the Messiah-King, the Son of Man and the Judge of the world. What he was in a mystery on earth he is now in power. He is the embodiment of the eschatological event, of the irruption of the hidden age to come in this present age. He is *deus ad nos*, the grace of God to man. But once more we must insist that the connection between the earthly Jesus and the event of Easter is not one which the historian may ignore if he chooses, but the key to the understanding of the primitive kerygma.

There are two further points which serve also to pave the way for the next thesis. First, there is the category of the eschatological. This will be considered here only in so far as it is relevant to the present thesis, and will receive further treatment under Thesis VI. Does "eschatological event" mean no more than belief in an invisible world? If so, what is the difference between it and any other belief in transcendental reality or immortal life? In that case the question remains why the events of the cross and resurrection were necessary for such an eschatological attitude. Do not Bultmann's disregard of the uniqueness and finality of Jesus and his interpretation of the event of Christ in terms of "historic-personal existence" betray him into reducing the Christological events to the level of symbols or stimuli? He may pay lip-service to the Church's kerygma, but that does not get us very far. Certainly we enjoy our historical

[1] We deliberately describe the message of Jesus in these minimizing terms, so as to conform with Bultmann's own presentation.

existence as Christians only as members of the Church. May it be that the meaning of the kerygma, the service of the Church, consists simply in providing such symbols and stimuli? This very point was the subject of a lively controversy during the last century, and the result was that it brought home to us the uniqueness and finality of Jesus and the inadequacy of a vague Christology of the symbol or idea. Was it inevitable that this theology of the Erlangen, Halle, and Ritschlian schools should end as it did in historicism? Could it not be that despite everything the person of Jesus is still the only key which will unlock the secrets of the invisible world, of eschatology, and of resurrection, and that only in the words, deeds, and suffering of Jesus the door of resurrection is opened? In their famous debate, Kähler and Herrmann agreed that the exalted Lord is no phantom but the Jesus of the gospels. Can we hold fast to this kerygma of a unique and final revelation while at the same time avoiding the Scylla of historicism and the Charybdis of a symbolic Christology?

This brings us to the third point. Perhaps Bultmann is aware of the antinomy here, for although he rejects what he calls the past-historical view of the cross, he never tires of speaking of Jesus of Nazareth as an historical figure, of his person and fate, of his crucifixion as an event of the past, of the faith of Easter as an historical event (pp. 34ff. 40ff. 44). He is fully aware of the paradox of the Gospel: although, nay rather because, the cross and resurrection are phenomena of past history, they are nevertheless present realities (*Pfarrerblatt*, 3A. 8).

The points which have been only hinted at here will be dealt with fully in the next thesis.

VI A

The first of Bultmann's categories which calls for consideration is his conception of eschatological detachment from the world, and of the Being of man as characterized by history and event. In his discussion with Thielicke he repeatedly insists on the vital connection between the Christian understanding of self and the event of Christ. Yet he tends to confuse eschatology with timelessness. Moreover, he lays so much emphasis on the fact that this event of the past can be real only if it is brought into vital connection with our own lives, that he undermines the historical character of the event itself.

We come at last to consider the categories employed by Bultmann. What does he mean by "eschatology" and "history"?

Eschatological existence is defined (*Th.L.Z.* 1940, 244) as "a new existence in detachment from the world . . . the attitude implied by *hos me* in 1 Cor. 7. 29–31. . . . Everything within the world is relegated to the sphere of that which has no intrinsic significance. . . . To exist means to exist eschatologically, to be a new creature (2 Cor. 5. 17) . . . to surrender all self-contrived security." "Historic" existence is contrasted with "nature". Nature is the sphere of the demonstrable and calculable, the realm of causality. "Historic" being, on the other hand, is realized in decision (p. 11) and resolve (p. 22). Nature, we may add, is always consistent, and is therefore patient of experimental research. History, on the other hand, is characterized by the Either/Or, and therefore bears the stamp of uniqueness, contingency, and spontaneity.

We may perhaps interpret this somewhat as follows. Life in faith means life based on realities beyond our control. Such a life is realized in decision and resolve, which has to be continually renewed in response to the word or kerygma of the Church. This word is not susceptible to logical proof, but when proclaimed it becomes an event. Is this a fair interpretation of Bultmann's position? If it is, there is no need for the kerygma to contain anything specifically Christian, no need for it to be riveted firmly to the Man Jesus of Nazareth. Cross and resurrection, in so far as they have a place in the kerygma at all, figure only as symbols of detachment from the world. The suspicions we raised under the two preceding theses would seem to be abundantly justified.

Bultmann, however, has vigorously defended himself against a similar charge in his discussion with Thielicke.[1] Thielicke sees Bultmann's real error in the fact that he makes the understanding of existence, of self, the crucial question. "The event takes place in the consciousness. The historical facts reported in the New Testament are not themselves the event of redemption, but merely its prolegomenon. The event is the change in my own consciousness." The truth, however (Thielicke, *Pfarrerblatt*, p. 130), is that the cross and resurrection are *present* realities for me only "when I focus my existence upon the historical uniqueness and finality of the years A.D. 1–30. Cross and

[1] See Thielicke, *Pfarrerblatt* 1942, No. 30, and Bultmann, *ibid.* 1943, No. 1, and compare Thielicke's essay in the present volume, pp. 138ff. (Ed.).

resurrection make themselves available to me as present realities only in Kierkegaard's sense of contemporaneity. But this implies that they are events in time, and that the Logos has entered into the time scheme of the *sarx.*"

To this Bultmann replies: "Understanding of self and understanding of existence do not imply timelessness. Our judgement about an encounter in the present, our meeting with a friend, for instance, may also involve a judgement about past history— e.g., about Henry IV. Hence by analogy faith, or the Christian understanding of self, owes its distinctiveness to its inseparable relation to the act of God in Christ which encounters me in the word . . . for we know that the act of God is what it claims to be only when we realize that it happened *pro me.*" Thielicke's objection "only shows that he evacuates the event of redemption of its eschatological significance. . . . A concrete historical event is the event of salvation . . . not however in the sense of a conclusive and demonstrable event of the past, but as an event which only becomes visible in the word of preaching which is based on that event and which brings it to fruition". If therefore an event of past history is also an eschatological event (which for Bultmann is synonymous with event of redemption), the event of redemption is not what happened in the years A.D. 1–30 reproduced in memory. For "what happened in those years has, in so far as it is the act of God, no end, but is itself the end of all history, and is therefore eternally present in the word of preaching". By contrast, "what happened in the years A.D. 1–30, in the sense of mere past history can be present only in the memory, and cannot be said to have existential reality". Thus (Bultmann, *Pfarrerblatt*, ibid., footnote 8) "the cross and resurrection are phenomena not only of the past, but also of the present. The paradox of the Christian Gospel is just this—those events are present realities *although* they belong to past history."

Now, Thielicke is certainly wrong when he accuses Bultmann of placing the event of redemption exclusively in the realm of individual consciousness. Bultmann never divorces Christian experience from the historical event of redemption. Moreover, Bultmann is quite right in maintaining that the saving efficacy of an historical event can be apprehended only when that event is experienced as something which happened *pro me. Notitia, assensus,* and *fiducia* do not follow one another in strict chrono-

logical sequence. To take "notice" of Jesus at all is in itself
fiducia. For the non-believer the cross is just a brute fact which
he can explain according to his own philosophy of history and
judge according to his lights—with sympathy, hostility, or in-
difference, which is simply another form of hostility. But to the
believer the cross and resurrection are not anterior facts awaiting
subsequent evaluation and interpretation: for him faith is something given "in with and under" the testimony of the cross and
resurrection. We have thus conceded what Bultmann calls the
eschatological character of the event of redemption. He is right
here too. The event of salvation is valid for all time; it is a
permanent Now. For here is the unique and final revelation of
God.

But at this point our doubts begin to rise. Does Bultmann
really do justice to the *ephapax* of the New Testament? Thielicke
also asked the same question, and it cannot be said that Bultmann
has given any satisfactory answer. Can one really say that the
happenings of the years A.D. 1–30, in so far as they represent
the act of God, have no end? The New Testament makes the
paradoxical assertion that the acts of God at that time did come
to an end. There was an end to those things that were written
(Luke 22. 37), an end of the law (Rom. 10. 4). And the action
of the crucified and risen Lord is limited by the "not yet" of
eschatological hope (1 Cor. 15. 23ff.—"then cometh the end"
—cf. Heb. 2. 8, etc.). Here we see the awkwardness of Bultmann's terminology. If eschatological attitude means a life based
on invisible, intangible realities, that is much too wide a
definition, for it covers the whole range of religion. Eschatology
means literally the "last things". Of course Bultmann is trying
to ascertain the existential meaning behind eschatology. But to
do that we must begin quite concretely with the idea of judgement. At the last day all that is now hidden will be made manifest, and the sentence of justification will be pronounced. Now
Christianity makes the staggering claim that these "last things"
have already happened here and now in the word of the living
Christ, though in another sense they still await final consumma-
tion. To St Paul the present age is a reality, not an illusion.
That is why in Rom. 5 he wrestles so vigorously with the whole
problem of death. This is where he parts company with the
Gnostics. The Corinthians, on the other hand, suppose that they

already see face to face (2 Cor. 5. 7); they are already ruling in the kingdom of God (1 Cor. 4. 8). Death is for them only illusory (Wisd. 3. 2). This is the background of 1 Cor. 15. Similarly, the belief that the resurrection is already past (2 Tim. 2. 18) is a piece of incipient Gnosticism.

The "now" of the New Testament is not the "now" of timelessness. The distinction between the two ages differs radically from our popular distinction between time and eternity (=timelessness). It is a distinction between two different but overlapping periods of time. The difference is existential and qualitative (see above, Thesis III), a difference between this *evil* age and the age to come. Such a notion takes very seriously the reality of sin and judgement. In this age of tribulation and death, of warfare with Satan, to live in the flesh means to wait, to hope, to believe, to groan. When Christ appears at the last day this age with all its sorrows will come to an end.

All this gives the *ephapax* of the New Testament its peculiar pungency. The Logos has entered into the time scheme of the *sarx*, as Thielicke has justly observed. We may perhaps put it still more strongly. It is not simply that at one unique point in the history of the world the eternal God comes to us in the form of Being-in-time; it is that Christ enters our evil age, our alienation from God. Even after his exaltation he is still the crucified, as certainly as this age continues until the parousia. The Corinthians stumbled at the notion of a crucified Messiah just as much as they did at the reality of death, and just as much as they cried *anathema Iesous* (see above, p. 69).

The *pro me* is parallel to the *ephapax*. The basic insights of Bultmann here are right enough, though Thielicke's criticisms are understandable, especially in view of Bultmann's unsatisfactory reply. True, *pro me* does not mean *ex me* or *in me*: redemption is not just a conjuring trick performed with the consciousness. But it does mean a relation to the *extra me* of Christ, and this must never be forgotten, for it is exactly the meaning of the uniqueness and finality of Christ. The unique event in Christ is in some mysterious way both past history and permanent reality. It is part of the history of man, part of the causal series, a memory of the past and a subject for historical research. This of course Bultmann does not deny. The event of redemption, he maintains, is "grounded upon that event of the past, and in it that event is continued down the ages. . . . Cross and resurrection are present phenomena *as* historical phenomena." But does not that event of the past possess eschatological and redemptive significance in its own right? Bultmann does not give us an answer. He is content to assert that it is so, and to assert that there lies its peculiar paradox. But has he not minimized that paradox when he says that what happened in the years A.D. 1–30, when reproduced in memory, cannot be the event of redemption, that those events can be present only in memory and not in existence? Is the antithesis between memory and existence a genuine one? Memory is an essential element in human existence in history. There can be neither decision nor encounter nor personality without memory. The New Testament is aware of this, for memory plays a vital part in connection with the event of Christ.[1] It would be wholly erroneous to reject these as secondary features or later accretions to the original kerygma. The tradition is identical with the Gospel and the Word (see 1. Cor. 15. 1–3, etc.). Moreover, it is not necessary for an intellectual assent to the tradition to precede the act of faith. For trust in the reliability of the tradition and of its bearer is in itself *fiducia* and an element in fiducial belief in the *pro me*.[2]

VI B

There is the further question of Bultmann's flight from history. It may be considered under four heads: (1) The concept of time and the meaning of "present". (2) The relation of *Historie* to *Ge chichte*. (3) The gravity of the *scandalon*. (4) The impossibility of giving a logical proof of the Christian faith (no minimization of the *scandalon*).

If Bultmann fails to do justice either to the *ephapax* or to the *pro me*, the reason is to be sought in his category of *Historie*

[1] See e.g. 1 Cor. 15. 1ff.; 11. 23ff.; Luke 1. 1ff.; Acts 1. 21f.; 10. 39ff.; 1 John 1. 1ff.; John 15. 27; Acts 5. 32; John 19. 35; 21. 24; and compare also the importance of the tradition (paradosis) about Jesus, and the eyewitness character of the oldest tradition about the passion to which Dibelius has called our attention.

[2] Documentary evidence and more precise proof of this would take us too far. Just one point: the *pro me* (*hyper hemon*) is paradosis (1 Cor.).

(chronological, past history). Past history is for him something
dead and done with, something which does not vitally affect us,
something which exists only in the memory, which is dependent
on tradition and all its hazards, and which is therefore subject
to criticism and essentially relative. The antithesis to *Historie* is
the present, that which affects us vitally, the eschatological, the
eternally present, the eternal "now" (see the article on "*nun*"
in the *Theologisches Wörterbuch*, IV. 1103, by G. Stählin).
This conception is open to criticism on four grounds.

1. The concept of the "present" is a doubtful one. The idea
of pure present is a speculation of mysticism. The present is
never an object of possession: it is the mathematical point
between the past and the future. It is doubtful whether we can
speak of "now" in any legitimate sense at all. To say that timelessness is the axiomatic hinterground of time is pure speculation,
so is the identification of this timelessness with the present or
with eternity. All that the human mind can perceive is the
relativity of our concept of time as such.

Nor is it permissible to identify "present" and "eschatological". The discussion begun above on p. 75 must now be
continued.

Eschatology deals with the *telos*, with the meaning and the
goal of the time process, not with the eternal present. The
reason for this is that the world is hastening towards judgement.
"Quando Altissimus faciens faciebat saeculum, primum prae-
paravit iudicium et quae sunt iudicii," says 4 Ezra (7. 70),
rightly. It is wholly erroneous to suppose that the New Testament in general and the Johannine writings in particular trans-
mute eschatology into something which happens in the present.
The stock passages quoted in favour of this (John 3. 18; 5. 24;
12. 47, etc.) derive their meaning from the fact that the judgement of God is actually coming upon the world and its ruler in
the future. But—and here is the amazing paradox—this cosmic
judgement does actually happen when men are confronted with
Jesus and his word. The so-called "transmuted eschatology" of
the Fourth Gospel has to be viewed in connection with the
rigorous cosmic eschatology which is one of the features of its
rugged dualism. The grandeur of these Johannine utterances will
be appreciated aright only if it is recognized that heaven and
earth, the time process and the world as we know it, are passing

away. In this respect the Fourth Gospel is at one with the synoptic gospels and the Pauline epistles. Eschatology, in its strictest sense, is paradoxically already present in the words and works of Jesus, in his cross and resurrection.

Finally, there is a tension between the present and the "historic" (geschichtlich). Bultmann's definition of the "historic" in terms of decision and encounter actually demands a linear conception of time. Every decision means a dividing, a choosing: B follows A. Each event is connected with other events before and after. The moment it has happened it necessitates further decisions. Despite the incalculable and personal (as opposed to mechanical) character of decision, both decision and event imply a time-process rather than an immediate and unconditional present.

2. The relation between *Historie* and *Geschichte*.

In German theology we are familiar with the remarkable distinction between *Historie* and *Geschichte*. The distinction would appear to go back to Martin Kähler (1892), though this is not absolutely certain. Von Dobschütz pertinently asked whether the distinction were possible in other languages. Be that as it may, it is undoubtedly a real distinction. *Geschichte* means the mutual encounter of persons, *Historie* the causal nexus in the affairs of men. The latter is the subject matter of historical science, which seeks to divest itself of all presuppositions and prejudices and to establish objective facts. *Geschichte*, on the other hand, cannot achieve such impartiality, for the encounter which it implies vitally affects our personal existence: it demands resolve and decision, yes or no, love or hate.[1]

We can see from this how closely related and yet how distinct are *Geschichte* and *Historie*. But the further contrast between past and present is irrelevant and misleading. We have already seen how "historic" Being is involved in the time process and therefore in the transition from past to future. On the other hand, *Historie* is not concerned exclusively with the past. Bultmann himself maintains in his illustration about Henry IV that events of the distant past may have a vital connection with our historic Being here and now. Life in time of war teaches us how all our present life is conditioned by a chain of historical causes. But

[1] The antithesis to "objective" in this context is not "subjective" but "personal", and it would be better to speak of "neutral" than of "objective."

the same holds good of all historic existence, of every encounter between persons. In every such encounter we simultaneously become aware of, get to know, and recognize the reality of what we encounter, and this includes our cognizance of the Other whom we encounter as a person. Towards him I try to be as objective as I can. What I desire is to see him as he is, even if he is my enemy. I want to avoid all illusion, to eliminate all false assumptions and prejudices. Indeed, all the virtues of the historian are needed in every "historic" encounter between persons. It often becomes explicit too: the Other whom I encounter may belong to a different social class or to another nation. If so, I must learn all the peculiarities of his life, his family background and so on. In so doing I am behaving very much as an historian would, except that the historian is concerned specifically with causation, including philology, psychology and the most rigorous logical deduction. How close the connection is between historic encounter and the science of history may be learnt from the work of the biographer. If he was personally associated with his subject he must be particularly careful to see him as he really was and let him be his real self. In fact, he needs all the accuracy and meticulousness of the historian.

If this be so, it is impossible to run away from *Historie* to *Geschichte*. We cannot reject *Historie* because it is not vitally present for us and accept *Geschichte* because it is. It is impossible to escape from the relativity of past history. That relativity is not simply due to the limitations which affect history like any other science, nor yet to our dependence on the art of the historian and his capabilities for the reproduction of the past; it is the necessary consequence of man's creatureliness. We are all inescapably enmeshed in the toils of causality. Our personal relationship with our fellow men involves us also in the relativity of each successive moment. Every personal encounter is open to ambiguity and misconstruction, yet this very relativity provides the material for the uniquenesses, the events and decisions of *Geschichte*. This inseparability of the historic-contingent and the historical-relative reappears in historical research on the level of scientific thought. The mainspring of historical research is historic encounter, and the uniqueness of events, whether singly or collectively. On the other hand, all historical research worth the name leads simply in the pursuit of its pre-

cision work to the question of decision,[1] to the historic encounter.

3. It is only when these considerations are applied to the
event of redemption that the full paradoxical character of that
event becomes apparent. Bultmann shows that he is aware of
this (p. 44), but surely his final remarks require more precise
formulation. He says (ibid.): "The agent of God's presence
and activity, the mediator of God's reconciliation of the world
unto himself, is a real figure of history. The word of God is not
a mysterious oracle, but a sober, factual account of a human life,
and this word, it is claimed, possesses saving efficacy for man."
Now, this sober, factual account of a human life includes the
gospels themselves (which are never so much as mentioned by
Bultmann) and the testimony provided by the personal association
of the first preachers with the Jesus of history (p. 38), as well as
the list of eyewitnesses adduced to establish the miracle of the
resurrection as an historical event (p. 39). For the Jesus of
history is crucial in this context, the Jesus who is deeply com-
promised in the relativity of history, where "*martyria*" always
means eyewitness. In other words, the *martyria of* God is subject
to the relativity of all human *martyria* and is therefore exposed
to the doubt and scorn of men. These *martyres* may prove to be
pseudo-martyres or even *mainomenoi*. Accordingly we must
make one addition to Bultmann's array of paradoxes. ("The
apostles who proclaim the word may be regarded merely as
figures of past history, and the Church as a sociological phenomenon, whose history forms part of the history of religion.
Yet both are eschatological phenomena and eschatological
events.") To these as their consequence and ground we must
add. "Jesus of Nazareth, a man subject to all the relativity
of history, and yet the agent of a unique, ever-present act of
God." It is just here that the *skandalon* lies—one who is a
legitimate subject for historical research, with all its uncer-
tainties and inferences, is nevertheless the unique and ultimate
revelation of God. The careful historian, we would maintain,
is bound to come up against the traces of this revelation, and
where they are obscured it is a sign that there is something
wrong with his historical methods. We might, for instance,
take Bultmann's own *Jesus* as an example, and show how, despite

[1] I deliberately avoid such formulations as "the question of truth" or "the
question of valuation".

the avowed intention of the author, the uniqueness and finality of the here and now of Jesus means the uniqueness and finality of the advent of God. Such are the real implications of the kingdom of God and the forgiveness of sins, which according to Bultmann are central to the message of Jesus.[1] Historical research may well lead to historic encounter. But the historian can never prove that this is the unique and ultimate encounter with God, even though he cannot ignore the possibility that it is so.

This still leaves us with Bultmann's treatment of the *skandalon*. Does he maintain its full force undiminished? One cannot avoid the impression that he places the event of redemption in some transcendental sphere far beyond the relativities of history. It cannot be too strongly asserted that the *skandalon* lies "in, with and under" a series of events embedded in history with all its relativity.

4. It is Bultmann's deliberate intention to maintain the *skandalon* unimpaired, and in fact this is the real purpose of demythologization. The *skandalon* is just this: Jesus, his witnesses and the Church are outwardly "phenomena which are subject to historical, sociological and psychological observation, yet for faith they are all of them eschatological phenomena". Myth, on the other hand, seeks to make things demonstrable: "From the mythological standpoint, the event of redemption must be made as evident and demonstrable as anything else in the visible world" (*Pfarrerblatt*, 1943, p. 4). It is, however, by no means certain that this is the essential character of myth. In Gnosticism, for instance, the Redeemer is always a hidden, unknown, mysterious figure. In Jewish apocalyptic there is always a secret tradition which is accessible only to the predestinated. All such esoteric traditions pride themselves on their lack of demonstrability. All the same, Bultmann is quite right in insisting that this lack of demonstrability is *part* of the *skandalon*

---

[1] This is the real meaning of the Messiahship of Jesus. Is the Bultmann of 1926 the same as the Bultmann of 1941? Would he have expressed the conclusion of his *Jesus* differently to-day? It would be interesting to show how the more conservative interpretations of Jesus, such as those of Edward Meyer, R. Otto, and H. Lietzmann, tend to do less than justice to the mystery of the presence of God in Christ. Why is this so? It is otherwise with Hoskyns and Dibelius. But if the purpose of the last two scholars is to be carried to its conclusion, we shall have to take Bultmann's interpretation of the Sermon on the Mount very seriously.

of the kerygma. This is well brought out by the demand for a sign in the synoptic gospels, by the question "What makest thou thyself?" in the Fourth Gospel, and later by the scorn of Celsus and Porphyry.

Now there are two problems here. First, is this aspect of Jesus a *skandalon* to mythical thought only, or to all purely human thought down to the present day? Secondly, is not this aspect of Jesus—viz., the lack of demonstrable proof—the reason why the opponents of Christianity reject it as mythology? The closed world view of modern science, both in physics and in psychology, leaves no room for a unique historical event with an eschatological—i.e. final and absolute—significance. ("Idealism shrinks from attributing the absolute to an individual person, and accidental facts of history cannot bear the whole weight of eternal truth.") Bultmann says somewhere,[1] commenting on the *mythoi* of the Pastoral Epistles, that every religion rejects the claims of its opposite numbers as myths, and claims absolute truth for itself. So instead of saying (p. 44) "The transcendence of God is not as in myth reduced to immanence. Instead we have the paradox of a transcendent God present and active in history (John 1. 14)", Bultmann ought to have said: "The proclamation of the Word made flesh means the presence of the transcendent God in history. But to those who reject Christianity this appears to reduce the transcendent God to immanence." We may even ask whether this lack of demonstration and proof does belong to the cross itself—whether *skandalon* is in fact the cross itself, not the form in which it is proclaimed. Most people are ready to accept something which cannot be proved so long as it does not make any concrete demands on them. They will even accept myths, as the expression of eternal truths that cannot be uttered (e.g., the myths of Plato and the Stoics), and so long as they magnify the Emperor's divinity (Vergil, Horace, and the Giessen Papyrus). But to claim that a man who was forsaken of God and reviled of men[2] is salvation defies all tangible proof. It cannot be

---

[1] Where? (Bultmann adds a footnote that he thinks he said so verbally). Is he right in view of the situation presupposed in the (antignostic) Pastoral Epistles?

[2] See the Jewish and Hellenistic evidence cited by Lietzmann at 1 Cor. 1.18ff.

proved by signs or wisdom, not even the wisdom which un-
fathoms the secrets of mythology.

To sum up then: Bultmann's demythologizing will not
automatically bring out the *skandalon* as clearly and acutely as it
ought to be. There is still a chance that the gospel message, just
because it cannot be proved, may be misunderstood, and once
more this misunderstanding is a manifestation of the *skandalon*.
At the same time we agree with Bultmann that the kerygma must
always be interpreted in contemporary language, and that means
in terms of contemporary thought. Questions which came up
as early as Thesis I and later in the course of our work must now
be pursued to a conclusion and clarified in the light of similar
problems.

VII

Bultmann's challenge still stands. The world view and language of the Bible
must be translated into our own. Examples: the last things as event, the intercession of Christ for us, the belief in spirits and demons, the various conceptions of the Spirit. These Biblical ideas must not be caricatured beyond recognition, but neither must they be taken over as they stand. The right imagery is
to be won from the narratives of the gospels.

The reader is now full aware of the nature of Bultmann's
challenge. Belief in the Word made flesh does not oblige us to
accept everything the New Testament says whether it be
intelligible or not. The kerygma does not require that; in fact,
everything it says about understanding, apprehension, truth, and
teaching implies the contrary. It is of the essence of the Word of
Christ that it seeks expression in the contemporary world; in
fact, this is implied by the whole principle of the incarnation.
"The last twenty years have witnessed a movement away from
criticism, and a return to a naïve acceptance of the kerygma.
The danger both for theological scholarship and for the Church
is that this uncritical resuscitation of the New Testament mythology may make the Gospel message unintelligible to the
modern world" (p. 12). There is a good deal of truth in this,
but in the course of this essay we have seen reason to doubt
whether the trouble really lies in the mythology at all. May it
not be that "critical" and uncritical" means the "*krinein*"
which the kerygma itself demands. If so, this is always the service

performed by systematic theology. At the same time, the last twenty years have taught us that there is not and cannot be an "historical" theology which provides the data for systematics. The question is simply whether any given systematics does justice to the data.

Let us first consider eschatology and the heavenly intercession.

It has been argued that detachment from the world and time-lessness are not adequate categories for the understanding of eschatology. The eschatology of the early Church is not just a vague belief in the transcendent or in immortality. It is orientated towards a future day of judgement, which is held to be the goal towards which the whole time-process is moving. The New Testament knows nothing of an ascent of the soul, whether of the individual or of mankind as a whole, into some invisible world. Each individual is involved with the rest of mankind in the stream of human history, in the time-process, and in this present age. For the New Testament this age is evil, and mankind and all its history stands under a common sentence of inevitable judgement. This judgement, however, is not wrought out immanently in and through the time-process (*"Weltgeschichte ist Weltgericht"*), but by the manifestation of the "hidden things of the heart" in the presence of the hidden God. The goal of history and of the time-process in which we are involved arrives when we meet the living God, who transcends all our categories of time and space. The day of judgement comes when the veil is lifted which conceals the Invisible from our eyes. The recent dogmatic theology of Stange, Althaus, and Holmström, has followed up the suggestions of Luther and worked out an eschatology on genuine New Testament lines. Such an eschatology begins with resurrection rather than with transcendence, with the day of judgement rather than with immortality. The changes made by Althaus in the successive editions of his Dogmatics indicate the progress which has been made in this subject, as also do the questions which Holmström has addressed (without being able to answer them himself) to the New Testament and systematic theologians. In any case we have here a genuine antinomy. Just as the time-process is a reality and not an illusion, just as historicity (*Geschichtlichkeit*),[1] guilt, and judgement are

---

[1] We still do not know how far the idea of historicity, when rightly under-stood, is part of our common involvement in history. Let it suffice to recall

inseparably woven together, so too we are bound to believe
that the time-process will come to an end one day. It is of course
absurd to think of an end of time in time, but it is impossible to
dispense with such a notion. And so we are faced here with a
genuine antinomy.

Hence the New Testament is right and Bultmann wrong:
eschatology *is* ultimate history. There is a *synteleia*, a completion
of this aeon. The hostility of the world to God reaches a climax,
and the Church is gathered together. And there really is another
aeon, a new time-process and a new spatial order (a new heaven
and a new earth), in which there will be "no more death, neither
mourning, nor crying, nor any more pain". But this future hope
is already realized in part. That is why the New Testament speaks
of "now" (*nyn*). The eschatological wrath of God is at work
already here and now. The kingdom of God has already dawned
in Christ. At death each individual encounters the world to
come. In Phil. 1. 21 and 2 Cor. 5. 1ff. this present realization is
placed quite naturally by the side of the expectation of future
judgement (Phil. 1. 6; 10f.: 2 Cor. 5. 10). Here we have a
profound critique of our popular ideas about time, as Luther
saw when he said that in the sight of God the whole history of
man from Adam down to the present moment happened "as it
were but yesterday".[1] But the early Christians made no attempt
to work out a philosophy of time. It was simply a naïve conviction
resulting from their overwhelming experience of the reality of
Christ.[2] The early Christians did not believe in an eternal timelessness or that time as we know it is an illusion. They believed
that the two ages overlapped one another in some mysterious
way. This too was the outcome of their experience of Christ,
and again it is reproduced in Luther.

If all this be true, we must tread very warily in attempting to
recover the existential meaning behind the eschatology of the
New Testament. Its naïveté may arise not so much from an

---

such New Testament words as Adam (*anthropos*), *sarx*, and *kosmos*, on the one
hand, and *ekklesia* and *koinonia* on the other. Bultmann, I think, would agree
with this.

[1] WA 10 III, 194; WA III, 525, 5f. 21ff.; Althaus 4151.

[2] A vivid eschatological expectation may have a similar effect, as may be
seen e.g. in 4 Ezra—I know that several books have recently appeared on the influence of Luther on Kant.

obsolete view of the world as from an experience of Christ. Consider for example the important part played by music in the pictures of the End—e.g., the last trump, the harp, and the songs of the redeemed. There may actually be something eschatological about music. I do not mean that music represents timeless reality. I mean that a new language is an essential element in the new life in fellowship, the life which is defined in such eschatological words as peace, righteousness, and redemption.

All this of course cuts right across the world view which is usually held to be derived from modern science. But that need not trouble us unduly, for there is just as sharp a cleavage between modern science and personal existential Being. We have been trying to see the eschatology of the early Church as a serious attempt to apprehend the meaning of historic Being.[1] Yet the paradox and *skandalon* remain. The unchanging God enters the time-process, its relativity, and even its alienation from God. At the same time it must be remembered that modern science is perhaps not so confident as it was at the turn of the century that time and space are infinite.

We turn now to Christology. We saw above (pp. 60–66) that the dereliction of Jesus as presented in the New Testament and the doctrine of Christ's heavenly intercession do not contain a trace of mythology, though they will certainly appear entirely mythological in the eyes of the non-Christian. Nevertheless, it is always the task of the dogmatic theologian and the preacher to translate the language of the New Testament into that of the contemporary world. The idea of sacrifice, for instance, is completely foreign to the modern mind. We have to explain what we mean by Christ's "pleading" for us. The "blood" of Christ means the surrender of his life. "In Christ" means that Christ includes his own in himself. Then there is the perplexing language about the Body of Christ and the doctrine of his Kingship. Are these in the same category? If one remembers that St Paul uses both ideas to combat the attacks of Gnosticism, the uniqueness and finality of Christ are only thrown into still

[1] The light which existentialism has thrown on the meaning of history (*Geschichte*), personality, and existence is due entirely to Christian influence. Of course these phenomena are constituents of all human Being, but it was Christianity which first discovered them.

sharper relief.[1] The same considerations apply to the later phases of Judaism.[2] Only now are we beginning to realize the true nature of the *skandalon*. The stumbling-block is never, as Bultmann rightly maintains, the unintelligibility of any given concept: it lies in the revelation itself. Are we doing sufficient justice to the *skandalon* when we speak of Christ's dereliction or of our personal relationship with him? Here the whole material of the gospels must be presumed. From the days of the primitive kerygma which lies behind the speeches in Acts, behind the oral tradition which was eventually crystallized in Mark and Q, the primary source of the theology of the cross is the words and deeds of Jesus of Nazareth. The Jesus who was crucified was the same Jesus who overcame the power of Satan and the evil spirits, who was the friend of publicans and sinners, who was condemned to death by the "righteous", who preached the Sermon on the Mount, who disputed with the Pharisees and denounced them, who was always an enigma to his disciples and in the end was rejected by them, who was reviled by Jews and Gentiles. His life was a continuous temptation and conflict with Satan. Every pericope of the gospels is thus a preaching of the cross. This is what makes the doctrines of Christ's dereliction and heavenly intercession not vague abstractions, but the quintessence of the Logos of Jesus, as it was expressed in the Gospel-preaching of the Church, since the days of the oral preaching which lies behind our gospels.

The question whether there is an intrinsic incompatability of Christology with the world view of modern science must be taken very seriously. The life work of Karl Heim has been largely devoted to this subject. It seems absurd to assert the unique and ultimate presence of God in one Man in face of an infinite universe. Yet the incidence of the *skandalon* has shifted somewhat since the days of the Enlightenment and Idealism (Lessing and Strauss). To-day it is much more like what it was in New Testament times. For the *skandalon* then was not so much the historical uniqueness and finality of Christ, but the alternative "Christ or Caesar". Either Caesar in all his glory is Lord and Saviour, God or the Son of God, or else Jesus of Nazareth is. But if Jesus, then his glory lies in the cross and resurrection.

[1] Cp. e.g. H. Schlier, *Theol. Wörterbuch* s.v. *kephale*.
[2] O. Schmitz, *Die Opferanschauung des Spätjudentums*, 1910.

The difficulties in Christology are similar to those occasioned by demonology and the idea of the Spirit. Here are two instances which provide useful tests for Bultmann's proposed restatement of the kerygma.

Can the belief in evil spirits be dismissed so casually as Bultmann does? The real issue is the trans-subjective reality of evil. The "Adam" theory is true as far as it goes, but it does not bring out this trans-subjective reality sufficiently. It indicates the solidarity of man in his alienation from God, but the opposition of the whole universe to the will of God is so deliberate and so well organized that it is more than the product of the human will. Hence the New Testament is obliged to bring in the figure of Satan, though it does so with remarkable reserve. This has often been noticed in connection with St Paul, though at the same time it must be remembered that he tends (Rom. 5–8) to personify sin (*hamartia*), and this concept plays rather a similar role to the personal devil elsewhere in the New Testament. The reason for this reserve lies in the complete absence of dualism (Mani-cheeism). Nor is there any mythological elaboration of the story of the fall of Satan and his angels. Yet Satan himself is a very real figure, and he is the measure of that insight into our human plight which is afforded by the conflict of Christ with the powers of evil. The trans-subjective reality of the evil one is inseparable from that of evil itself. Evil is a cosmic reality, not a notion of man imposed upon the universe. Death, mourning, crying, and pain (Rev. 21. 4) ought not to be. They are "powers" which have enslaved man and cut him off from communion with God. When they are doing their worst with us there is no comfort in being told that they are figments of our imagination, and that they must be accepted as part of the world we live in. Such suggestions can console us only if we are prepared to believe that the external world is less real than the inner world—which leads to "acos-mism", a theory which assumed a variety of forms in the later phases of antiquity. Acosmism is utterly irreconcilable with the Biblical faith in a Creator. Hence the New Testament never tries to answer the problem of suffering after the manner of Gnostic-ism or Stoico-cynicism, though it does face up to questions which those philosophies ask. For the New Testament invariably regards daemonic possession in the light of Christ's victory over it.[1] The synoptic gospels (Mark, Matt. 12. 28=Luke 12. 20), St Paul (Rom. 8), the Fourth Gospel (John 16. 11, etc.), and the Revelation (chap. 1), are unanimous on this point. Hence we should be wary of dismissing the revival of such New Testament convictions as superstition. We speak of superstition where phenomena susceptible of a naturalistic explanation are attributed to invisible powers. But belief in such powers *per se* is no more affected by scientific knowledge than belief in God himself. Belief in God enables the physician to see disease in a totally new light, and gives him quite a fresh attitude to his patients— and this is particularly so when he works with all the precision of scientific method. Similarly, belief in God fosters insight into the nature of *apoleia*, the combating of which is the physician's special charisma.[2] But once again we would do well to emulate the reserve of the New Testament. Much patient investigation was needed before the underlying meaning of the New Testament daemonology was discovered. That meaning is not immediately apparent, for it is not due to cosmological speculation or to Manicheeism: it neither provides man with an excuse nor does it make him the victim of irrational fears and anxieties. Nevertheless it recurs in one way or another in all that the New Testament has to say about Christology or salvation. Our contemporary preaching and dogmatics would appear to be recovering an understanding of the New Testament here. And this recovery is all the more profound since our view of man and the world is less optimistic than it was.

The doctrine of the Spirit is closely akin to the belief in evil spirits. Both are encountered by man as another ego. In St Paul the double ego occurs both with sin (Rom. 7. 17, 20) and with Christ (Gal. 2. 20). Modern man, however, as Bultmann assures us, regards himself as a unity, whether he be a naturalist or an idealist (p. 6f, cf. 19ff). But the problem of the Ego is

---

[1] The Gnostics evolved an elaborate demonology, but since they regarded the powers of evil as ultimately unreal, they were not afraid to dabble in the "deep things of Satan".

[2] Bultmann also tries to play off "electric light and wireless, modern medical and clinical methods . . . press, radio, cinema", etc., against the Christian faith in God (p. 5 footnote 1). But belief in God is more than a convenient way of accounting for the First Cause; it reckons with the intervention of God in all these phenomena of the visible world.

not only psychiatric, but psychological and metaphysical. Indian philosophy has known this from its beginning, and it has been a vital issue in Western philosophy since the time of Fichte. Contemporary theology has been largely concerned with the nature of authentic Being, which it defines as eschatological existence as contrasted with death, to which our life in this present age is a prey. This existence can be attained only by rebirth: "Ye must be born again from above." This rebirth, as we have learnt from the History of Religions, is the universal longing of man, and the New Testament satisfies that longing by pointing to him who is exalted on the cross and to heaven (John 3). Through him men are reborn in the Spirit.

Bultmann maintains that St Paul shared the popular notion of the Spirit as "an agency which works like any other natural force . . . as if it were a kind of supernatural material" (p. 21). But St Paul, he tells us, transcended this popular view: "The 'Spirit' (p. 22) does not work like a natural force. . . . Rather, it is the possibility of a new life, which has to be appropriated by a deliberate resolve (Gal. 5. 25). . . . Being led by the Spirit (Rom. 8. 14) is not an automatic process of nature, but the fulfilment of an imperative: 'live after the Spirit, and not after the flesh'." Bultmann is here following Gunkel, whose work, though half a century old, is in its approach to the problem by no means out of date. Gunkel's thesis, briefly, is this. The Old Testament, later Judaism and popular Christianity equate the "Spirit" with a supernatural power to whose agency they attribute such phenomena as are not patent of a natural explanation. St Paul gave this popular conception a new ethical note by tracing the Christian life as a whole to the operation of the Spirit.[1] But Gunkel's approach to these questions is really alien both to the Old Testament and to the New. Kähler's bold definition that the Spirit means God present gives a better explanation of the historical phenomena. Wherever the Old Testament speaks of the Spirit, whether it be in connection with warfare and art, or with the renewal of the human heart, it always implies an immediate presence of the God of revelation. This, and not the supernatural *per se*, is the essence of the Biblical

[1] We may note in passing that (1) We know far more to-day than Gunkel did about the place of the Spirit in Hellenistic Gnosticism. (2) Bultmann's fundamental approach to the problem is far more profound than Gunkel's.

doctrine of the Spirit. The common distinction between the personal and the natural is to be applied with caution, for the activity of God embraces what we call the sphere of nature. Even ecstasy and miracle may be signs of the new age. What St Paul is combating at Corinth is a false spiritualism which regards the pneuma as a sort of divine fluid whose injection imparts divinity to man. This belief is the source of that self-glorying which depreciates love and undermines the Church of God. We may say, if we like, that St Paul transcends the naturalism of the Corinthians. But we must remember that St Paul uses quite different language, and that he has his own special reasons for doing so. St Paul is not concerned with the difference between nature and decision, but between a right decision and a wrong one. The Corinthians, carried away by their enthusiasm, had drifted into a decision against God. Bultmann observes, rightly enough, that the Spirit can never become a permanent possession of the believer (p. 22). But the real antithesis lies elsewhere. The Spirit is the gift of God, and the man who has it becomes God-controlled instead of self-controlled. "Your body is a temple of the Holy Ghost which is in you, which ye have from God, and ye are not your own" (1 Cor. 6. 19). Bultmann prefers to say that the Spirit "is the possibility of a new life which has to be appropriated by a deliberate resolve". We must remember, however, that Gal. 5. 25 is the conclusion of the whole section 5. 16ff., and that it takes for granted the trans-subjective antithesis of flesh and Spirit. As Bousset comments on 5. 17: "The will of man is impotent in the grim conflict with these supernatural powers." The same is true of Rom. 8. 14 (Bultmann, p. 22): to be led by the Spirit means to be called sons of God. This is the point at which, according to St Paul, the deeds of the body are mortified. Bultmann is right in saying that the possession of the Spirit never renders decision superfluous, but the decision is God's rather than man's. God has delivered man from the flesh—that is, from his own human existence—and given him his Spirit. But until the last day there is always the possibility of apostasy and perdition. This brings us back again to the old question of Bultmann's categories—the relation between the indicative and the imperative, between forgiveness and ethics.

But here we must break off. Bultmann's problem has been

transposed to a different key. Demythologizing raises the much wider problem of our theology as a whole. Dare we apply the categories of personal life ("the living God") to our relation with him? That is the root of the matter. Have we made too little of the question of mythology? At all events, our essay will have made clear that when we come to ask what the New Testament really means we cease to be worried by mythology. It tends to take second place. The thought and language of the New Testament often strike us as alien to our way of thinking; it is often incurably paradoxical. But after all what else could we expect when we remember the limitations of the human mind? The paradox and *skandalon* of the revelation of God in Christ are the only key to its understanding.

Are we still left with a hard core of mythology? Bultmann asked the same question at the end of his own essay (p. 43). However that may be, we should have to test our conclusions at every point and see whether we have been caricaturing the New Testament, and all we could do was to offer a few illustrations taken at random. The History of Religions did us a great service by opening our eyes to the strangeness of the New Testament world, and that was far better than the credulity which was blind to the gulf between modern thought and the New Testament. But did the History of Religions altogether escape caricature? We asked similar questions in connection with the doctrine of satisfaction, eschatology, demonology, and the Spirit. But it is even doubtful whether the Bible believes in a three-storied universe. Even the Old Testament wavers at times: ". . . the heaven and heaven of heavens cannot contain thee" (1 Kings 8. 27); "Do not I fill heaven and earth" (Jer. 23. 24). And the New Testament has completely abandoned the three-storied universe. See e.g. Heb. 4. 14: "Who hath passed through the heavens", and Heb. 7. 26: "made higher than the heavens". These and the "*en Christo*" are illustrations of the way in which the concept of space breaks down in the light of the revelation of God in Christ. And the concept of time breaks down for the same reason (*supra*, p. 88). Of course that does not mean that the whole world view of antiquity is suddenly shown to be false, but it does mean that the reality of God's revelation proves the inadequacy of the pattern of thought. We found the same naive critique of our popular notions of time and space in Luther and Calvin (*supra*, p. 88). A similar case could be made out for Apocalyptic and Gnosticism.[1]

At the same time the problem of mythology *per se* is left open. It cannot be mitigated by rejecting those elements alien to our way of thinking on the ground that they are simply picture language, and by replacing them with a different picture language of our own. The idea of the Son of Man coming on the clouds of heaven is not just picture language, any more than the doctrine of Christ's pre-existence. At the same time we may justly speak of the pictorial character of the New Testament imagery, for after all the invisible can only be expressed in terms of the visible. In each case the meaning is obvious. The Son of Man, for instance, means the Judge of the world, and the decisive question is not about this image as such, but whether Jesus really is the Judge of the world. If under the influence of Rudolf Otto modern scholars are once more ready to agree that Jesus regarded himself as the Son of man, this would drive him into a mythological twilight: the interpretation of all he said did not make clear that it is the Judge of the world who is speaking. Similarly the pre-existence of Christ means that in the words and deeds of Jesus God himself is uniquely and finally present. Thus Odeberg, in his book *The Fourth Gospel*,[2] in commenting on John 8. 58, "before Abraham was, I am", aptly coins the term "over-existence". But once more this claim can be made intelligible only if it can be shown that the whole gospel material is a *theologein Christon*: "Brethren, we ought so to think of Jesus Christ as of God, as of the Judge of quick and dead" (2 Clem.1.1)

Here we must take up and pursue to the end a line of thought which we suggested in Thesis II. The starting-point for a right understanding of eschatology is the words and deeds of Jesus.[3] Eschatology is neither a mythological picture of the end of the world nor a mythological expression of the idea of timelessness, but the message of the age to come. In the words and deeds of Jesus of Nazareth that age has become a present reality. What eschatological existence and authentic Being really are can only be interpreted aright in the light of Jesus of Nazareth. Only in him, in his cross, is the wretchedness of man made fully apparent. Only in him, in his victory, are Satan and the evil spirits really

[1] Even the concept of the *pleroma* transcends the popular conception of space; cf. e.g. Eph. 4. 10: "He that descended is the same also that ascended far above all the heavens that he might fill all things."

[2] Uppsala, 1929.   [3] *Vide supra*, pp. 8off.

intelligible and not just an obscure piece of mythology.[1] The signature of Jesus is the cross, and the cross is *totalis derelictio*, his complete desertion by God.[2] The Gospels themselves are meant to be read as a preaching of the cross. He, the embodiment of the unique and final presence of God among men, plumbs to its depths the distress of our human life.[3] This is the only proper theme for our Good Friday sermons, and it is the burden of every pericope in the Gospels. This is the only way to preach Christ and him crucified without making him an unintelligible piece of mythology or a mere symbol of an abstract truth. The signature of Jesus is the unique and final presence of God.[4] He who hath seen him hath seen the Father. In him the invisible God has become visible. The primitive Church knows that the glory of God is made visible in the word of preaching. This was the way in which St Paul and Luther preached Christ crucified. And the rugged paradoxes of patristic dogma—"very God and very man"—make explicit what the whole New Testament says indirectly. The New Testament speaks indirectly like this because what it says will only be understood aright on the other side of the day of judgement. Jesus' signature is the resurrection and the life. In him as the risen Lord the whole meaning of his words and deeds is fulfilled. He, the ever-present, is the same who called sinners and rejected the righteous. He is the fulfilment of his own eschatological word. He is in person present with his own as Lord. He is in person for ever the Crucified who makes intercession for his own. He is (Matt. 28. 18, 20) the Ruler of heaven and earth, and who is with his own until the end of the age. But this too (N.B.—heaven and earth; invisible and visible) is only rightly proclaimed when he who utters these words is for ever the same who (Matt. 28. 20) taught on earth and issued his commands, whose words remain though heaven and earth pass away (Mark 13. 31). Proclaimed otherwise, the proclamation

---

[1] Above. p. 92.   [2] Above, pp. 60ff.

[3] Bultmann, *Johannes*, p. 327, on 12. 28: "In John—and here he part company with the Gnostic myths—the Father is glorified through the Son, by his taking upon himself the very depths of earthly existence." In the text we have preferred to speak of "*human* existence". Bultmann's "*earthly* existence" is somewhat dangerous, for it could be taken in a Gnostic sense. Perhaps it would be better to speak with the New Testament of Jesus' taking the *curse* upon himself, adding what was said on p. 60ff. The idea of the curse is not mythological; it is the curse of the law. Gal. 3. 13 is the link between the Pauline doctrine of the law and the tree (xylon) of the apostolic kerygma.

of the risen Lord becomes a piece of mythology or a symbol of and abstract truth.

The proclamation will never escape the charge of myth. This possibility is part of its *skandalon*. But where it is rightly understood it is seen at once to be the answer to the question posed by myth. When late Jewish eschatology asked about the future judgement and the world to come, its question was a legitimate one. The answer is the crucified and risen Lord, an answer which at the same time means the judgement of the Jewish hope, which sought to evade the judgement by pictorial elaboration and by rites of consecration. The same holds good, *mutatis mutandis*, of the Gnostic myths. All the questions they ask about light, life, the way to heaven, the agent of redemption, are answered in the person of Jesus. But at the same time he is in. all that he says and does and suffers, the judgement upon the Gnostic hope, which sought mastery over the invisible.

Does this dialectical judgement apply equally to modern man? Bultmann has been accused in different ways of ignoring the fact that modern man is tending to return to mythology. Myth, it is held, is an indispensable element in all religion. Have we here a possible point of contact between Christianity and modern man? To suppose that we have is to overlook the fact that wherever the New Testament speaks of the invisible in terms of the visible, its assertions can be understood only in the light of its central message—i.e. the cross and resurrection. Apart from these, for instance, the eschatology and the daemonology of the New Testament will always be misconstrued. They will lose their *skandalon* because they are not understood in the light of the *skandalon* of the cross. On the other hand, there is little substance in Bultmann's contention that modern science and mythology are intrinsically incompatible. Modern man is no longer scientific man. Either science has become the handmaid of technical progress—that is what it means to most people, even the educated; medicine, law, and history are then merely departments of technology. Or, alternatively, with the indefatigable pursuit of the separate sciences, science is becoming philosophy again. And this means that, whether it is aware of it or not, science cannot ignore the problems of God, of the invisible, and of existence, as these were treated in Theses II and III. But that only makes the task of the Christian preacher to-day more serious. He must not in deference to modern man make light of those elements in the kerygma which modern man is likely to regard as myth, for the simple reason that every attempt to preach Christ God is bound to seem myth to him. Now that modern man is prepared to take the question of God seriously, there is no need for the preacher to begin by trying to give an existential explanation of the Christian disposition and to disregard everything that might look like myth. The moral of Bultmann's argument with Kamlah is that the theologian must take the offensive, and that the point of attack is the question of sin (p. 30f). Maybe the attack should have been still more radical. All the more so since Kamlah's attitude is defined in the light of the Biblical faith in God, and despite all his disagreement with that faith he is full of respect for it. If Kamlah is really right in affirming that there is no ontological statement which is not at the same time an affirmation about God,[1] ought he not to put the question of *hybris* much more seriously than he has done?[2] And does not Kamlah's God bear the marks of a *deus absconditus*? He is the X behind our self-commitment to the community or fatherland, and yet such a God permits the extinction of the individual at death. Although he is the affirmation of all that is, yet the terror of the infinite and mysterious, and the grim realities of evil, guilt, and death are camouflaged by the formula *me on*, but never really overcome. Even the Attic tragedians knew better than this. So did Nietzsche the atheist, whom Bultmann never mentions. What is Kamlah's glib self-commitment to the "All-One" compared with the profundity of the Attic tragedians and Nietzsche? So the real point at issue between Christianity and modern man is not mythology but the Krisis: it is man's rebellion against God.

There is one last possibility to be considered. Is modern man perchance Nihilist Man? This perhaps is a truer diagnosis than any other. Yet in practice nihilism is an impossible philosophy of life, for it is itself the unanswered problem of God. It is really a striking confirmation and indeed an accurate description of what the Bible calls the wrath of God.[3] Will the modern man believe us when we tell him that the Christian revelation gives us a better understanding of his own predicament than he has

[1] *Christentum und Selbstbehauptung*, p. 328ff., etc.
[2] *Saepe*—e.g. the excellent criticism of modern man on pp. 399ff., and the admission on p. 407f.
[3] I owe this to a suggestion of H. Iwand.

himself? To convince him lies not in our own power. But in any case the real difficulty lies not in myth but in the profoundest of all problems, the ultimate problem, the problem of God.

If this be so, then the central theme of this essay as worked out in theses I–VII is by no means irrelevant. Each particular inquiry has forced us back upon the ultimate question, and in every case it is we Christians who ask that question. The terms of the discussion among Christians do not differ in principle from those of the discussion with non-Christians. Its starting-point will always be a deep awareness that we only know in part. For our observations about the scandal of the gospel and the impossibility of proving it arise from this partial character of our knowledge. Our exposition of the cross and resurrection is the knowledge of the love of Christ which passeth all understanding. We have been concerned with the task of the Christian preacher in the modern world as that task is conditioned by the problem of myth. But from start to finish we have found ourselves forced back upon another problem. Can we accept the kerygma of the New Testament as good news for our generation? This much at least is true: that kerygma alone possesses the intrinsic power of awakening the conviction of its truth in the hearts of men.

(*Concluded on 27 October* 1943.)

RUDOLF BULTMANN

A REPLY TO THE THESES OF J. SCHNIEWIND

On Thesis I

I NEED only say how pleased I am that you have so clearly recognized my aims, and that you agree in principle that the mythology of the New Testament constitutes a very real problem.

On Thesis II A

I agree that my definition of "myth" is open to misunderstanding, but at the same time I am convinced that it is more satisfactory than the alternative you suggest (p. 48). For one thing, "observable" may prove too narrow a term and "unobservable" too broad, since all spiritual attitudes are unobservable. In mythology—e.g. in the legends about the gods—we constantly meet such unobservable phenomena as will, wrath, fear, etc. Hence the term "observable" is just as misleading as "unworldly". The degree of elaboration in any given piece of mythology is irrelevant for its classification as mythology, whereas to define myth in terms of "observable" and "unobservable" tends to suggest the contrary. The New Testament pictures of heaven or of the resurrection of Jesus are, despite their reserve, just as mythological in principle as the corresponding pictures in Jewish literature or in the Gospel of Peter (p. 48). It may be true that the result of modern atomic research is to convert natural phenomena into processes which are no longer accessible to observation (p. 48 note 2), but those phenomena do not thereby cease to be "worldly" in character.

You ask whether we can ever really dispense with myth (p. 48). That is in my view an ambiguous question. Much of our ordinary language is based on mythology in any case, and there are certain concepts which are fundamentally mythological, and with which we shall never be able to dispense—e.g. the idea of transcendence. In such cases, however, the original mythological meaning has been lost, and they have become mere metaphors or ciphers. As for mythology in its original sense, I maintain not only that we can dispense with it, but that it is essential to do so. You ask who would be so rash as to try and demythologize Plato. G. Krüger in his *Einsicht und Leidenschaft* shows that even Plato himself indulges in demythologizing.

When you say that natural science thinks in mythological terms, you are using the word "myth" in an improper sense. After all, it is in the nature of things that the sciences should evolve a system of concepts derived from the visible world of time and space, for that is the world with which it has to deal. If any particular series of concepts subsequently proves inadequate, that does not make them "mythological" in the proper sense of the word. If science attributes natural phenomena to non-natural causes, it may degenerate into mythology, but then it will have ceased to be science. But things have not reached that pass when it employs such concepts as "totality" and "source" (p. 49). And when such terms are used in philosophy, they do not necessarily retain their original reference to the realm of time and space. I see no need whatever to say that the philosophers can speak of ultimate questions only in mythological terms, however hypothetical their speculations must inevitably be. They may tell us that in dealing with such phenomena as "religiosity" or "humanism" (p. 49) it is irrelevant and out of order to inquire about the "something" that lies behind them, and thereby protest against the conclusion that the only answer to all ultimate questions is the Nihil. If, on the other hand, they choose to postulate the existence of God in order to account for these phenomena, as Kant and Hegel did, and as Krüger has recently done, I would contend that it is really God they are talking about, not, however, in the mythological sense, but in the Greek sense of the Arché.

On p. 49f. you appear to have been misled by Karl Heim. To point to revelation as the only solution to the dilemma is to labour from the outset under a false assumption about the answer of revelation to the question of faith, and to substitute a *Weltanschauung* for faith. The question which faith asks is quite different from that asked by philosophy or by the natural sciences. And conversely, the revelation of God in Christ gives no answer whatever to the questions asked by philosophy and the natural sciences. You say: "All our thinking leaves us with the question mark: has the invisible ever been made visible, and if so, where (p. 50)?" That would seem to be the wrong question, at any rate if by "invisible" you mean what faith means by it. For the only invisible reality which science can seek is the Arché.

You doubt (p. 50) whether I am doing justice to the faith of the New Testament when I call Jesus "the agent of God's presence and activity" (sc. towards us). Whether you are right or not will only appear from the subsequent argument. At any rate, it should be clear that I have done justice to the *ephapax* of the New Testament (p. 51), from the fact that this characteristic is postulated precisely of the unique, historical Jesus. The addition of "in a unique and final present" seems to me to lead to misunderstanding. But this will become clear when we deal with the thesis on eschatology.

On Thesis II B

I deny that the Christian faith is for man intrinsically mythological. At any rate, it is not so for modern man in the sense in which I speak of the myth of the New Testament. You tell us that even when Christianity has been emancipated from myth modern man continues to reject it because it speaks of an act of God and of sin. But that is another matter altogether. Christianity is then rejected not because it is myth, but because it is *skandalon*.

I left the question as to whether it was mythological to speak of an act of God unanswered on p. 34, only to answer it later on p. 43f. Of course a philosopher cannot in his official capacity speak of an act of God (p. 52), for he never speaks of concrete events such as transactions between persons. All he can do is to show what is meant by personal event in general. But this is just the point at which he can help the theologian to find a non-mythological language in which to speak of God.

Similarly the philosopher can help the theologian to give a sound definition of *aversio a deo*. Of course he cannot identify his "*Verfallenheit*" with the theologian's *aversio a deo*: only faith can do that. For it is only by faith that God is encountered as Person. Yet the only way to rescue *aversio a deo* from mythology is to show that it corresponds to a real experience in human life—that in fact it is equivalent to the "*Verfallenheit*" of which the existentialists speak. This is where I part company with Thielicke.[1] When we preach that life before faith is sin, we must show what life before faith is like, otherwise it is just a piece of mythology.

This is one of the crucial points in my restatement of the kerygma. Hence I am bound to say that to speak of faith in the living God and in his presence in Christ (p. 52f.) is pure myth unless these things are given an existential*ist*[2] interpretation. This explains why I deny that Christianity is intrinsically mythological. It would be true to say that natural man finds it to be pure *skandalon* precisely when it is made intellectually intelligible to him. The Christian preacher can demand faith only when he has demonstrated sin and grace to be real possibilities of human life, and their denial and repudiation to be unbelief and guilt. It is the great merit of the existentialist interpretation that it makes this clear. Or perhaps it would be more modest to claim that such is my conviction, unless someone can show me a better interpretation.

On Thesis III

If we are to arrive at a satisfactory definition of forgiveness and freedom, the need for an existentialist interpretation again becomes vital. True, freedom, in the New Testament sense of the word, means *facultas standi extra se coram deo*, freedom from condemnation, freedom from the bondage of the law, etc. (p. 55). But all this requires interpretation; these things must be shown to be real experiences in human life. The same applies to the judgement of God and to Christ as our freedom from the curse and condemnation. Otherwise all this is simply unintelligible mythology. I am seeking to elucidate this freedom by interpreting it as the freedom of man from himself and his past for himself and his future. And it is quite legitimate to look for parallels in the other religions or in mysticism or in Goethe's *Stirb und Werde* in order to show that man as man can know that

[1] *Deutsches Pfarrerblatt*, 1943, p. 3 footnote 4.
[2] N.B., Not "Existential".

the trouble with man is himself, and that in order to achieve authentic Being he must be delivered from self. Apart from such an interpretation the New Testament message of freedom remains utterly unintelligible. At the same time, by defining freedom as freedom from my own particular past for my own particular future, I have made my difference from Goethe and the mystics self-evident. For they speak not of freedom from the past for the future, but of escape from history into non-history.

This notion of freedom from the past does not in my opinion lack a qualitative reference, for it is concerned with my own particular past, with what I have made of my self under the illusion that self-hood is something to be achieved by my own efforts. Here we have your primal sin of rebellion against God. Similarly, the future I speak of is my own particular future in which true self-hood is received as a gift. The future is thus always *extra me*, and my past, my "old" self, is always present as a state of being forgiven. Deliverance is not therefore a vague kind of new ego (p. 55). That is why I may rightly claim that faith means to open ourselves to the future.

I do not see why the terms of the argument should be reversed (p. 55). If faith (and, after all, I did say so) is possible only as faith in the love of God, then "it is because and in so far as we have become the objects of God's love that we are free from *our* past and open to *God's* future" (p. 55). But there is no need to stress the contrast between our past and God's future. After all, God's future is our future too, and unless it is shown to be so it remains a myth. I agree with your remarks on p. 55. That is just what I am trying to put into effect by my restatement of the kerygma.

I would interpret eschatology and the day of judgement along similar lines. It is not enough merely to abandon the elaborate mythological symbolism (p. 56), nor to define eschatology as that which lies "beyond the bounds of time and space" (ibid.). The only true interpretation of eschatology is one which makes it a real experience of human life. You say: "Our acquittal is Christ himself. He is the embodiment of the righteousness of God." But surely that requires interpretation. And such a metaphorical statement as "He incorporates his own in himself as a king includes his people" (ibid.) serves only to darken counsel.

Again, I asserted that eschatological existence has become a possibility because human life has been refashioned by the act of God. You say I should reverse this, but again I cannot see why. I do not deny that God and his impending judgement ("impending" in the sense that it confronts us already here and now) is the primary consideration. Nor do I deny that we can know the true nature of eschatological existence only through God's revelation of himself in Christ. Our previous knowledge of it was but ignorance or error, but it was not purely negative, otherwise the revelation could not convey any real knowledge. That revelation would not be a life-shattering event, but merely the imparting of information on the subject. It would be better to call it "suppressed knowledge" such as blossoms forth in a perverted form in mysticism and idealism.

Yes, indeed. Forgiveness shows itself in freedom from sin, and that in turn in obedience to the imperative (p. 57f.). Of course, I do not mean that ethical renewal is the real end and forgiveness merely the means, for that would exalt the imperative above the indicative. There can never be a second moment parallel with or additional to justification. The whole gift of God is comprised in the forgiveness of sins. But I am quite sure that we will not understand this aright unless we insist that forgiveness is freedom from sin, not only from past guilt, but also from sinful behaviour in the future. It is "access to God", certainly, but what do we mean by that? What does it mean in actual experience? Human life continues to be "historic" even when it is eschatological—for that I take it is what you mean by "the eschatological judgement still lies in the future" (p. 58)— and it issues forth in a new life (ibid.). It is therefore controlled by the imperative. Through the gift of God "Thou shalt" becomes "I will". We are "led by the Spirit". The peculiar quality of the indicative is manifested in its inseparable unity with the imperative, and *vice versa*. It was Karl Barth, I believe, who first charged me (p. 59) with substituting anthropology for theology. This is an easy misunderstanding of the existentialist position. Anthropology is here being used rather as Feuerbach used it, and existence is identified with subjectivity. Using "anthropology" differently, I would heartily agree: I *am* trying to substitute anthropology for theology, for I am interpreting theological affirmations as assertions about human life. What I mean is that the God of the Christian revelation is the answer to the vital questions, the existential questions. But he is not the answer to the theoretical questions raised by the existentialist philosophers. That is why, in my opinion, you cannot write off existentialism as atheistic for not taking God into account. Such an objection is wholly irrelevant. After all, why should you take God into account? Are the existentialists raising the wrong questions? Is it impossible to analyse the meaning of existence in the abstract? I do not think so. They would be wrong if they tried to discover what gives meaning to my own particular existence. This question they rightly leave for the individual to answer for himself, and they do so just because they are concerned with the meaning of existence in the abstract.

Thesis IV A

First let me repeat that I do not mean that to be free from sin is something more than the forgiveness of sins (p. 60). That would be a one-sided interpretation, as if it were no more than the blotting out of past sins. It may be that I have laid too much stress on the future reference of forgiveness, but I did not forget to insist that there can only be freedom for the future where there has been deliverance from my own particular past. All I need do is to elucidate what I said on p. 35f. I agree with what you say on p. 61f.

I still maintain that the underlying assumptions of sacrifice as practised in the primitive cults and in the religions of classical antiquity (including the Old Testament) are incurably mythological. There may of course be nothing mythological in the belief that man must be ready to sacrifice to the deity what is dearest to him (p. 61). But such a belief becomes mythological the moment it ceases to be controlled by a true conception of God. Take for instance the case of a child being sacrificed in order to insure the success of an enterprise or to avert misfortune. Such a practice implies a crude mythological conception of God. It cannot be denied that a similar belief underlies the practice of sacrifice in the Old Testament—the belief that God will accept the life of a substitute when the offerer's own life is forfeit. The modern use of sacrifice in connection with the mother or the soldier is entirely different. In these cases the offerer is himself the victim. He is not seeking to insure his own safety by offering a substitute, or to gain anything for himself.

The idea of atonement is juridical, and when applied to God mythological; so is the doctrine of satisfaction, which is at least echoed in the teaching of St Paul (p. 62). I cannot see how Isa. 53 and Dan. 7 make St Paul's assertions about the sinlessness and pre-existence of Jesus any less mythological (p. 62). And to say that "Jesus entered into our deprivation from God" is in my view undeniably mythological, unless indeed you are prepared to interpret it. It makes no difference that the New Testament avoids all pictorial elaboration (p. 63). The fact itself is still mythological, and still requires interpretation. And if that is the meaning of every pericope of the gospels and epistles, it is even more imperative to interpret it.

You say that no attempt is made to elaborate the picture of Christ's enthronement and heavenly intercession (p. 64). But that again does not make them any less mythological. It is true that the variations in the formulae and the vagueness of the terminology is a warning that when we have stigmatized them as mythological we have not pronounced the last word on the subject: all the more need then for an interpretation in non-mythological terms. But you have not gone far enough to give us that. Above all, I cannot discover the hermeneutical principle behind your interpretation.

I must now confess—and here perhaps the gulf between us is most obvious—that the language of personal relationship with Christ is just as mythological as the other imagery you favour; that is, unless it is strictly conceived on the lines of John 14. 9 or of Herrmann's "God is in Christ". You ask: "What do we mean when we say that Jesus has entered into our deprivation from God? What do we mean by a personal relation with the exalted Christ?" (p. 64). Your questions only go to show how mythological in form is the New Testament theology of the cross. It is highly significant that these questions come not from one committed to agnosticism, but from a Christian exegete. Surely you are confounding the stumbling-block of the mythological language with the real *skandalon* of the cross, and the exegetical problem with that of faith. It seems that you are afraid to abandon mythology lest you should surrender the real *skandalon* with the preliminary stumbling-block.

You say (p. 65) "That sentence is intelligible and tolerable only because God has changed it into an acquittal by a unique act of his own." I agree with this. But when you say: "So heinous is our guilt that God delivered up his Son in order to remove it", I can regard that only as mythological. "Everything hinges upon God's judgement." Granted, though exactly how that judgement was wrought out in Christ is just what we have to explain. The explanation I proposed was this: when we appropriate the judgement of God we have to take up the cross for ourselves and affirm the divine judgement in self-judgement. I think that here I have St Paul and Luther on my side, and hope you agree too.

On Thesis IV B

To ignore the connection between faith on the one hand and the cross of Christ as a past event on the other (p. 66) would certainly mean surrendering the confession and the kerygma. But that was not at all my meaning. What I am concerned with is the "historic" significance of the unique event of past history, in virtue of which it possesses eschatological significance although it is a unique event of past history. That is how the New Testament interprets that event, and it is the task of the theologian to decide whether this is just mythology, or whether it is capable of an existentialist interpretation.

Now, it seems to me that the only way to explain this event is by means of a paradox. The unique event of past history is an ever-present reality. I do not mean that it is timeless like an abstract idea, for that would make the cross a bare symbol. I am seeking rather to give full weight to the New Testament conception of the cross as an ever-present reality, first in the kerygma and the sacraments (both of which are forms of personal encounter) and secondly in the daily life of the Christians. For faith the unique event of the past is an ever-present reality (as indeed you add on p. 66 in reference to p. 37f.). You speak of "a unique event wrought out in the personal relation between God and man on the stage of history" (p. 66). I have no objection to such language, especially in liturgy. But it still requires interpretation if it is not to remain mythological, and that is what I am trying to do. After all, we have to remember that we are using history in a different sense from what it bears in a phrase like "the history of Anglo-German relations".

Nor, again, do I object to your speaking of a unique and final revelation of God in history (p. 67), so long as the context puts the meaning beyond all doubt. It would, for instance, be quite legitimate to use such language in refuting a pantheistic conception of revelation. At the same time such language is dangerous, for it is liable to obscure the eschatological character of the Christian faith in revelation, and to make that revelation a *revelatum*, something which took place in the past and now an object of detached observation, and the kerygma a bare report about something now dead and done with. And that is to forget that "now is the day of salvation".

It cannot be denied that as a past fact the cross cannot be an event in our own lives (p. 67). It is only through the proclamation that the cross can become a personal encounter and so an ever-present reality. But this is not to deny the uniqueness of Christ (p. 67). On the contrary, it gives full weight to "the word made flesh", in which alone the proclamation has its origin and its credentials. So far from denying that uniqueness I am therefore confirming it. Behind your whole argument on p. 67f. there lies the difficult problem of our relation to Jesus, though I would rather not embark upon that at this point.

Certainly we must avoid driving a wedge between the two halves of the New Testament, the gospels and the epistles (p. 68). But the relation between those two halves still requires explanation, and to my mind it is by no means easy to explain it. I agree with your remarks on p. 68f.; it is indeed part of the *skandalon* that, "as the Christian Church has always asserted, our salvation is One who is involved in all the relativity of history". But did I not say the same, only in a different way? It was what I meant, anyhow.

On Thesis V

With regard to the resurrection (p. 69), let me begin by assuring you that I have no intention whatever of denying the uniqueness of the first Easter Day, in spite of my insistence on the "historic" significance of our being crucified and risen with

Christ. But I would not call dying and rising again with Christ a subjective experience, for it can occur only through an encounter with the proclamation and the present act of God in it.

On p. 71 you say: "God's judgement of the world, which is at the same time its salvation, and which therefore deprives death of its power, is in the first instance the judgement of God upon Christ. This judgement vindicates him who is forsaken by God and man. It glorifies him and enthrones him as Lord." I should accept such a statement only with reservations, for it seems to me wrong to isolate the person of Jesus in this way. When St Paul speaks of Jesus as the last Adam or the Second Man (1 Cor. 15. 45, 47; cf. Rom. 5. 12ff.; 1 Cor. 15. 20ff. and the exposition of the Church as the Body of Christ), he uses these concepts of Gnostic cosmology because he refuses to isolate the person of Jesus. His destiny was bound up with that of the whole human race, though of course its universal significance can be realized only through encounter with the kerygma and the response of faith. This seems to me to be identical in effect with the *extra nos* of the Reformers. And this is exactly what gives the event of Christ its eschatological significance. It anticipates that future event in which the time process is destined to culminate, while to speak of it as happening "first" is to speak in terms of the empirical time-process, not in terms of the eschatological event. Similarly, the events of Good Friday and Easter Day (p. 72) are two separate events only from the standpoint of man in time; in their eschatological character they are a single indivisible event.

I gladly accept your criticism on p. 72, that what encounters us in the Church's kerygma is not the Easter faith, but the Easter testimony of the original disciples. It is the purpose of the resurrection narratives to record that witness in its full authoritative force. But I cannot accept 1 Cor. 15. 3–8 as kerygma. I call that line of argument fatal because it tries to adduce a proof for the kerygma. Nor am I convinced that the legend of the Empty Tomb was part of the kerygma, or that St Paul himself knew anything about it. But I am glad to note your agreement with me on the other points (p. 72f.), and I do not deny that the resurrection kerygma is firmly rooted to the earthly figure of the crucified Jesus.

I did not mean that the eschatological event is no more than the conviction of the reality of an invisible world (p. 74). It would be better to say that it means translation into an unworldly existence, or, in New Testament language, being in Christ. It is certainly wrong to interpret Christ "merely in terms of our existence as persons in history" (ibid.), if that existence is understood in a purely idealistic sense. That would be to reduce the great Christological events to bare symbols or stimuli to religious devotion. But, granted a true conception of historicity, granted that our "historic" self transcends our subjectivity, so that we are always *extra nos* as well as in ourselves, in good as well as in evil, then the above quotation is perfectly correct, and the word "merely" serves only to protect the Christological event from a mythological interpretation. For the fact is that we can apprehend invisible reality only in the light of a fact encountered in a concrete encounter in life (p. 75). We cannot prove theoretically that this fact is Christ; we can only know it in faith.

On Thesis VI A

That which happened in the years 1–30 has, as the act of God, no end (p. 77). Nor have faith, hope, and love, which are grounded in that act and have it for their object. That there is an end of those things that were written, that Christ is the end of the law, does after all mean that God has set an end to all purely historical happening (cf. *Th.L.Z.*, 1939, 255, on H. D.-Wendland, *Geschichtsanschauung und Geschichtsbewusstsein im N.T.*).

I do not believe that "a life based on invisible, intangible realities" is too wide a definition of eschatology (p. 78). If this covers religion as a whole, that only goes to show that the definition is correct. For the chief aim of every genuine religion is to escape from the world, and in that sense every genuine cult is an eschatological phenomenon. That is particularly true of the Old Testament, for which cf. my *Glauben und Verstehen*, p. 162f. If in the Old Testament, in Judaism, and in the New Testament, the unworldly takes the form of a future hope, of *eschata*— "last things" in the traditional sense—that is only one among other possible conceptions of man's relation to the unworldly, though no doubt it enshrines a genuine insight into human existence, namely that from a human perspective the *eschaton* can only be future. (In mythological thought a future event in time is substituted for futurity in the abstract.) Now, the New Testament advances the paradoxical claim that to faith the future has become a present reality. This point could be illustrated from the New Testament doctrine of righteousness.

It is equally true that eschatology in the New Testament sense of the word is controlled by the idea of the day of judgement (p. 78). Hence my insistence that faith, in the sense of openness for the future, is also an acceptance of the judgement of God which has happened and still happens in the cross. On the other hand, I maintain that the "last day" is a mythological concept, which must be replaced by the language of death, as is actually done on p. 78. To ignore with the Gnostics the certainty of death is to forget that our existence is and remains essentially "historic" and that the future, though apprehended, is never an assured possession so long as our earthly "historic" existence endures and so long as faith is still *in via* (Phil. 3. 12–14). I am surprised how readily people conclude that my interpretation of the New Testament eschatology implies a timeless "now". To say that two ages or cosmic periods overlap is to my mind totally inadequate. If the point of the contrast between the two ages is that the present age is evil (ibid.) and that in the age to come there will be no more temptation or death, the age to come cannot be conceived as a further period in history or as overlapping the old age like two epochs in history. It would be better to say that in the new age the indispensable conditions of the time process come to an end. The overlapping is possible and the age to come a present reality only in virtue of certain events and responses to those events within the old age. Faith interprets these as the irruption of the new age. I refer of course to the event of Christ, the kerygma, the response of faith, and the church or community of believers. What happens in these phenomena *now*—that is, at particular points along the time process—has ceased to be an event in time. Therefore in the last analysis each particular Now is to the eyes of faith that one Now which isthe fullness of time.

We may perhaps say that the Now of the New Testament is both timeless and temporal. Here we have the exact equivalent of the paradox in the assertion that "the Word was made flesh". This is not the timeless Now of the mystics, stoics, or idealists. It is not as if all events in time were but parables of eternity. Rather, the Now of the New Testament implies that the supra-temporal reality becomes an event for each particular individual only by virtue of an encounter in time; it has itself the character of encounter. This realization of the supra-temporal as event, this entrance of the supra-mundane into the world, the "Word made flesh"—this is the mystery of the New Testament eschatology. I think this does full justice to the *ephapax* (p. 79). And I also think that my emphasis on our relation to Christ as one of encounter gives full weight to the idea of *extra nos*.

I cannot regard the reproduction of the events of the years 1–30 in memory as the equivalent of the eschatological encounter. Of course, memory plays an important part in human life, but it has existential significance only when I make my own particular past present through recollection. In so far as the history from which I come is operative in my past, the recollection of that history also belongs thereto. But the memory with which the historian is concerned, in so far as it reproduces facts of the past in their purely worldly actuality, is of wholly different order, and memory in that sense can imperil and even destroy "historic" existence, as Nietzsche showed in *Vom Nutzen und Nachteil der Historie für das Leben*. Of course, there is also the historian's personal encounter with the past. But this takes place not by his reproducing the events of the past in memory, but by his encountering in those events of the past (as his own history) human existence and its interpretation. With the recollection of the kerygma it is otherwise. This does not present us with facts of the past in their bare actuality, nor does it lead to encounter with human existence and its interpretation, but, as a sacramental event, it re-presents the events of the past in such a way that it renews them, and thus becomes a personal encounter for me.

Nevertheless, like the sacraments (which would otherwise become bare symbols), the kerygma necessarily assumes the form of tradition, for it is more than a summary of general truths, and is itself part of the eschatological event. The Now of the kerygma (2 Cor. 6. 2) is not purely fortuitous, but identical with the advent of Jesus and his passion. On the other hand, I

do not think that trust in the reliability of the tradition should
be identified with fiducial faith (p. 80). Of course, the reliability
of the kerygmatic tradition must not be questioned, for otherwise the eschatological event to which the kerygma testifies
would be implicated in the relativity of all historical knowledge.
But for the moment I will leave aside the difficulties which this
raises.

On Thesis VI B

1. We possess the present through encounter, and encounter
imposes the necessity of decision. I do not identify the present
tout court with the eschaton, for that would be an over-simpli-
fication, but I do assert with the New Testament that we are
confronted with the eschaton in the Now of encounter, in a
Now which is neither an eternal nor a timeless present nor a
nearer or remoter future. Here indeed is the paradox of the
faith of the New Testament, and here is the answer to the question of *eis ti* and of the *telos* (p. 81). Eschatology tells us the
meaning and goal of the time process, but that answer does not
consist in a philosophy of history, like pantheism, where the
meaning and goal of history are to be seen in each successive
moment, or like the belief in progress, where the goal is realized
in a future Utopia, or myth, which offers an elaborate picture of
the end of the world. Indeed, eschatology is not at all concerned
with the meaning and goal of secular history, for secular history
belongs to the old aeon, and therefore can have neither meaning
nor goal. It is concerned rather with the meaning and goal of
the history of the individual and of the eschatological community. Moreover, the meaning is fulfilled and the goal attained
in the *fullness of time*—that is, wherever the word of the proclamation establishes an encounter (Rev. 12. 10–13; John 12.
31; 4. 23; 5. 25; 2 Cor. 6. 2, etc.). Certainly, the world is
hastening towards judgement, but that judgement cannot be
called the meaning and goal of history, for *now* is the judgement
of this world (John 12. 31). You also say: "Eschatology in its
strictest sense is paradoxically already present in the words and
works of Jesus, in his cross and resurrection" (p. 82). But what
is the relation between the present and the future eschatological
event? For my part, the only interpretation I can give to the
Pauline and *a fortiori* the synoptic eschatology is a critical one.

Decision, in existentialist thought, is always a phenomenon
in time (p. 82). I trust I have sufficiently allayed your suspicions

on that score by my emphasis on the Now as encounter.

2. *Geschichte* and *Historie*, as you rightly observe, are closely connected and yet distinguishable (p. 82f.). I can also agree with what you say on p. 83. All the same, I do not think that it really gets to the root of the problem.

It would certainly be wrong to run away from *Historie* and take refuge in *Geschichte*. If I desire an encounter with the Jesus of history, it is true that I must rely on certain historical documents. Yet the study of those documents can bring us to an encounter with the historical phenomenon "Jesus" only on the basis of one phenomenon of past history. Yet we can hope, by means of this study, to recognise the historical phenomenon "Jesus" only on the basis of one's own historic (*geschichtlich*) encounter. That was the aim and method of my *Jesus and the Word*.

The Jesus of history is not kerygma, any more than my book was. For in the kerygma Jesus encounters us as the Christ—that is, as the eschatological phenomenon *par excellence*. Neither St Paul nor St John mediate an historic encounter with the historic Jesus. Even if the synoptic gospels appear to do so, that is only when they are read in the light of the historical problems which have arisen since their day, not when they are read in their original sense. To understand Jesus as the eschatological phenomenon (that is, as the Saviour through whom God delivers the world by passing judgement on it and granting the future as a gift to those who believe on him), all that is necessary is to proclaim that he has come, and that is what St John does so clearly.

So far, then, from running away from *Historie* and taking refuge in *Geschichte*, I am deliberately renouncing any form of encounter with a phenomenon of past history, including an encounter with the Christ after the flesh, in order to encounter the Christ proclaimed in the kerygma, which confronts me in my historic situation. That, in my view, is the only way to preserve the paradox or *skandalon* of Christian eschatology, which asserts that the eschaton has actually entered history.

3. The *skandalon* may perhaps be brought out by demonstrating the fact of the Lord's humanity from the story of his life as portrayed in the Gospels, though it must always be remembered that the disciples' apprehension of him was conditioned by the limitations of their age (p. 84). Though I am prepared to agree with your argument on p. 84, I still deny that historical research can ever encounter any traces of the epiphany of God in Christ

(ibid.); all it can do is to confront us with the Jesus of history. Only the Church's proclamation can bring us face to face with Kyrios Christos.

4. The impossibility of proving the kerygma need not surprise us, for the Saviour, as he appears in history, identifies himself completely with men (Phil. 2. 7). This Scriptural incognito is something very different from the veil in which the Gnostics enshrouded him, for the Gnostic Jesus did not identify himself with men. Of course, this impossibility of proving the truth of the kerygma is an offence to human thought as such (p. 86). I did not wish to deny that. What I do maintain, however, is that myth makes the mistake of getting rid of the offence as it does the incognito. The modern opponent of Christianity (p. 86) cannot charge it with being mythical because it cannot be proved, at least if he is using myth in the sense in which we have been using it, and not in the sense of "fable" as in the Pastorals and 2 Pet. 1. 16. Of course, our opponents are bound to dismiss this claim that a unique event in past history is the eschatological event as an absurdity. But that is another matter. The way in which the transcendence of God is reduced to immanence here is quite different.

I think the line you adopt on p. 86f. is dangerous. For an eternal idea is just as discernible in the mythical presentation of the cross as it is in pagan mythology—e.g. the idea of sacrifice or heroism. There is nothing to prevent the cross from being interpreted as the symbol of a sentimental or pessimistic *Weltanschauung*. The real offence in the fact that we cannot prove the kerygma lies rather in the "formal" sphere, in the historical fact of the eschatological Redeemer. To the formal naturally corresponds the "material", the cross, which makes the fact clear in all its paradox.

On Thesis VII

(a) *Eschatology*.—I do not see why it is necessary to think of a temporal end of time (p. 89). Indeed, it is impossible to do so. All we can think of is the end in time of everything that characterizes the world of time, the end of time as we know it. That in my opinion is all that need concern us. Hence I cannot see what right you have to insist on the permanent truth of the New

Testament mythology, or how exactly the Now is relevant at this point. The idea of the remarkable overlapping of two periods of time does after all require interpretation (p. 89). Your interpretation strikes me as a curious blend of mythology and existentialism. I agree, of course, that the naïveté may arise less from the obsolete world view than from the peculiar character of Christian experience (p. 90), but that is just what my existentialist interpretation is intended to show. How music has something eschatological about it I really fail to see.

(b) *Christology.*—I will not allow that the New Testament language about Christ's dereliction and his heavenly intercession contains no mythology (p. 90). Nor is it true to say that the "blood" of Christ is just a striking metaphor for the surrender of his life (p. 90). I would agree that it is in ordinary secular use—e.g. of the soldier's death on the field of battle—but in the case of Christ it means something entirely different. It is sacrificial blood in a cultic sense, and moreover it is the blood of the pre-existent Son of God. Of course it was the blood of his human body, but that gives his self-surrender quite a different meaning from what it has in an ordinary secular context.

Of course, "in Christ" means that Christ includes his own in himself, but everything turns upon how that is understood. Thus on p. 90 you seem to go some distance along the road of demythologizing, but not far enough, and you fail to bring out the scandal of mythology in the New Testament language about Christ's dereliction and his heavenly intercession. I agree that the real *skandalon* was the same in New Testament times as it is for us to-day. But I object to the ease with which you make the unreal *skandalon*—i.e. the mythology of the New Testament language—the real *skandalon*.

(c) *Daemonology.*—I still maintain that the belief in evil spirits is obsolete. I agree with you that it enshrines the important truth of the trans-subjective reality of evil (p. 92). This is one of the points I am trying to bring out in my restatement. But I cannot accept what you say about an organized rebellion against God (p. 92), for that is undoubtedly mythological. Who organized the rebellion? Satan is a mythological figure, however cautiously we speak of him.

You say it is impossible to separate the trans-subjective reality of the evil one from that of evil as an impersonal force. This raises a theological problem which bristles with difficulties. The same applies to wickedness and evil as "powers". But I need not dwell on this now, for I am sure I agree with what you say on p. 92. At the same time, I maintain that to revive or perpetuate the daemonology of the New Testament in the modern world is to incur the charge of obscurantism and superstition. The Church should do all in her power to root it out, for it can only stultify her proclamation. The Blumhardt legends are to my mind preposterous.

Your argument on p. 92f. is right as far as it goes, but I think it obscures the real problem. Everything turns upon how precisely we abandon natural causation in favour of supernatural explanations—i.e. whether by the "nevertheless" of faith (cf. *Glauben und Verstehen*, pp. 214ff.), or by recourse to mythology. The real *skandalon* of faith in God *vis-à-vis* modern technology (p. 93 note 2) can become clear only when we have abandoned the false view of God which that technology has exploded.

(*d*) *The Spirit.*—I am inclined to agree with your criticism about modern man's understanding of himself (p. 93f.) as a unity. I am of the opinion that, as the understanding of historicity itself implies, he is wrong in identifying his authentic ego with his subjectivity. Considerations of psychology, philosophy, and theology do not appear to shed any light on the problem or help us to define the ego. This much, however, is clear: while modern man may be wrong in identifying his ego with his subjectivity, he is undoubtedly right in regarding it in its subjective aspect as a unity, and in refusing to allow any room for alien powers to interfere in his subjective life. The mythical thought of the New Testament on the other hand, does reckon with such interferences, and if such thought enshrines a profound and genuine insight into the nature of the human ego, it requires restatement to make it plain, and that means the complete abandonment of mythology.

Your argument on p. 94 seems to me only to obscure the problem. After all, it is not to be doubted that the Old Testament, as also the popular view in the New Testament, regards the Spirit as a supernatural power, a kind of mysterious fluid, a "mana", to which it attributes all abnormal phenomena, including those of art and warfare (p. 94). But this does not mean that those phenomena are attributed to the God of revelation. For the God of revelation is the God of judgement and forgiveness, not the Cause of abnormal phenomena. To think otherwise is to surrender faith in God for an abstraction. Of course, the presence of that God is discernible in art or any other achievement of man, but only in the light of his word, only as he makes himself known as the author of judgement and grace. To put it another way, God's handiwork cannot be labelled and docketed like the work of an artist or an engineer.

Miracles and ecstasies may of course, as you say (p. 95), be the signs of the advent of the new age; the only question is, to what extent? They certainly cannot be conclusive proofs, but only encounters in a concrete situation in life. And since miracle is an essential feature of the Spirit in the New Testament, we must interpret the meaning of miracle. We must show that it is a phenomenon of the historical life, not one of nature. Nor do I think it wrong to use the distinction between the personal and the natural. It is quite true that the drifting of the Corinthian Gnostics spelt a decision against God (p. 95). They preferred a naturalistic to an "historic" understanding of self. To that extent the distinction between right and wrong decision is identical with that between nature and decision.

You say: "The Spirit is the gift of God, and the man who has it becomes God-controlled instead of self-controlled." I say: "The Spirit is the possibility of a new life which has to be appropriated by a deliberate resolve." I do not see there is any essential difference between these two statements. For (1) The content of God's gift to us requires definition, and I think "possibility of life" is adequate. (2) The resolve by which the gift is apprehended is identical with the abandonment of control of one's own life. Moreover, in this resolve, so clearly demanded by St Paul, the gift of God is already at work. The Spirit is not the prime cause behind the human will, but operates *in* that will. To be led by the Spirit means not only that we are called sons of God but that we can appropriate the sonship and discern the imperative in the indicative. The decision God pronounces over man (p. 95) takes effect in the resolve of the human will.

It is my aim also to show that the appearance or garb of mythology can to a large extent be removed from the New Testament kerygma. We agree about this, and also, in principle at least, that demythologizing throws into sharper relief the paradoxical or scandalous character of its claims, so that they become as clear for modern man as they were in apostolic times. But I would not say that the paradox or *skandalon* is due to the limitations of the human mind (p. 96). This is obviously a place where you are under the influence of Karl Heim. It is due rather to the natural self-understanding of man.

I would not deny that the reconstruction offered by the History of Religions school was frequently an exaggeration and a caricature (p. 96), or that the Old Testament as well as the New provides precedents for demythologizing.

I do not see why it is necessary to speak of the unobservable in terms of the observable. Why could we not substitute an intelligible language for an unintelligible imagery? Or, if the traditional imagery is preserved—e.g. in liturgy, where its use is perfectly legitimate—we should see that its real meaning is given adequate interpretation. Your sample interpretation on p. 97, however, does not go far enough. You interpret eschatology, for example, as the word of the age to come now realized in the words and deeds of Jesus (p. 97). But "age to come" is still a mythological expression, and to say that "Jesus is present in person to his own" does not make matters any clearer. When you say that he "is in person forever the Crucified pleading for his own", that again is a mythological statement.

You observe that modern man is returning to myth (p. 99), but that is true only if myth bears a different sense from that which it has borne in the present discussion. Modern man *par excellence* is technological man, and for that reason he is doubly enslaved to the modern scientific world view, even if in theory he disclaims all interest in and knowledge of it. If he is prepared to take seriously the question of God, he ought not to be burdened with the mythological element in Christianity. We must help him to come to grips with the real *skandalon* and make his decision accordingly. The preaching of Christ (p. 100) must not remain myth for him. If he still calls it a myth even after we have emancipated it from mythology, he is using myth in a false sense of that word.

It is interesting to note that my discussion with Kamlah did not begin until after I had endeavoured to make the Christian view of life intelligible by removing the mythology and restating it in existentialist terms. (Incidentally, Kamlah is an old Marburg pupil of mine.) This shows that we can establish communication with modern man only when the unreal *skandalon* has been set aside by demythologizing, and that in such a discussion it is for the Christian to take the initiative. We can talk to modern man about the crisis in which he stands in rebellion against God (p. 100) only after the question of mythology has been solved. The Church can re-establish communication with modern man and speak with an authentic voice only after she has resolutely abandoned mythology. In this connection it would be pertinent to ask why Kamlah is prepared to discuss matters with me and not with yourself, or with Schlatter or Büchsel. The discussion mooted on p. 101 can take place only when the preliminary question of mythology has been settled, so that it ceases to side-track or obscure the real points at issue.

I am glad that I can agree with you (p. 101) that our domestic discussions as Christians do not differ in principle from our approach to those outside the fold. And that is why I believe that the issue of demythologizing is a burning issue for our own domestic discussions.

ERNST LOHMEYER

THE RIGHT INTERPRETATION OF THE MYTHOLOGICAL[1]

I HAVE been asked to speak to you on the demythologizing of the New Testament proclamation, a subject which was thrown up a year ago in an essay by Rudolf Bultmann. The problem in itself is an old one. You may find it in the scorn with which the cultured Athenians greeted St Paul when he preached to them on the Areopagus about the resurrection of the dead. But in the form in which it has engaged the attention of Protestant theology it goes back to the seventeenth century. Ever since the principles of historical criticism have been applied to ancient documents the criticism of the Old and New Testaments has never been silent. The Enlightenment sought to emancipate the eternal ideas of reason from the cloak of historical tradition, to lay them bare in their stark purity and truth, and to do away with every bit of mythological sense—or, from their standpoint, nonsense. It was their dogma of reason that led them to demythologize. In idealism we find a more profound approach to the subject. The idealists believed that myth was the indispensable form which the spirit of Christianity had assumed: therein lay its right and its justification. But it meant the replacement of Christianity by abstract philosophy. Once more the aim is the removal of mythology, but this time it springs from a dogma which is less inappropriate. Demythologizing is now required by the actual content of the Christian revelation, however much the heritage of the Enlightenment is still evident in the working out of the detail. This particular solution has profoundly affected the course of liberal theology right down to our own times, though there has been a great deal of change and a weakening of its influence. But to-day, it may be said, the partnership between the Christian revelation and philosophical idealism has been dis-

[1] Based upon a lecture delivered at Breslau on 9th January, 1944.

124

solved, at any rate in the field of New Testament exegesis, and Bultmann himself has played a prominent part in the process. It is not therefore surprising that Bultmann has reopened the problem whose solution in earlier times had been provided by German idealism. Once the partnership between the myth of the gospel and the truth of philosophy had been dissolved and their mutual relation left uncertain, the need for a fresh elucidation was bound to occur. The effects of this heritage are clearly discernible in the answer Bultmann gives to the question of demythologizing. For just as the philosophy of idealism had a twofold concern, the purity of philosophic thought and the truth of the Christian proclamation, so these two tendencies are clearly at work in Bultmann's exposition. He is fighting for the freedom of the New Testament message from falsification, and at the same time for the clarity of scientific, and particularly theological, thought. Only the watchword has been changed. The phenomenology of the spirit, as Hegel called it, has been replaced by a phenomenology of existence after the model of Kierkegaard. But there is one difference: the mythological thought of the New Testament is abandoned like an empty and useless husk as it was in the early days of the Enlightenment. For existentialist philosophy is concerned with man, whereas myth is concerned with God and gods. The only truth behind myth is therefore, as Bultmann says, the understanding of human existence which its imagery enshrines. We must first define these two tendencies with greater precision.

I

What is meant by myth? Bultmann accepts the definition of the History of Religions school—viz., that it is the presentation of the unworldly and divine in terms of the worldly and human, of the transcendent in terms of the immanent. He takes this definition for granted without stopping to ask whether it is true or appropriate to the New Testament revelation. It tells us nothing about the particular faith which the myth enshrines, but is deliberately "formal", in order to cover every possible religion. But what do we mean by form and content in this connection, and in what way do they differ from one another?

Even if we accept this definition for the moment, there is still the question whether it is appropriate to the actual content of religion. It is based on a rigid distinction between the unworldly and the worldly, the divine and the human, and sees the essential characteristic of myth in its fusion of these two distinct elements into one. That is certainly right, but does not this fusion correspond to the true nature of every religion? How else can we believe in God or speak of the gods, unless we conceive of him or of them as working and having their being in this world among us men in the same mode as men speak and work? To conceive the divine in terms of the human—that is the problem and the solution, the consolation and the mainstay of all religion. It is its secret and ultimate basis that human conceptions, while they remain human, are nevertheless capable of apprehending the divine and so surpass all human conception. On Bultmann's definition, however, it follows that myth is the language of all religion, the form in which it is expressed, and that to demythologize a religious proclamation of whatever kind is to condemn every religion to silence and therefore to destroy it. Bultmann himself is alive to this consequence, for he says at one point: "Anyone who asserts that to speak of an act of God at all is to use mythological language is bound to regard the idea of an act of God in Christ as a myth. But let us ignore this question for the moment." But can this question be ignored once the problem of demythologizing has been raised?

At this point it would seem that Bultmann is helped by the nature of myth itself. For myth contains many elements which are irrelevant to the pure relation between God and man and between God and the world. For instance, there is the idea of heaven as a kind of vault suspended over the edges of the earth's disk, of an underworld like a turbulent cauldron in a deep, dark cavern under the lid of the earth, of the stars as spirits which control human destiny. There is abundant material of this sort in the New Testament, and so far from being the lumber of a past age, it is embedded in the heart of the gospel. For instance, what becomes of the miracles of Jesus, in which evil spirits are cast out and all manner of sickness is healed? This is just a further example of the way in which myth combines religious utterance and objective definition. It borrows material from the system of objective conceptions and historical circumstances and uses it to explain in narrative or teaching, in oracular utterance or rule, in controversy or judicial pronouncement, what it has to say of the pure relation between God and man. It is always tempting to peel off the historical shell and extract the pure and fruitful kernel, but, as with any tradition, that is to do violence to the inner and unbreakable unity in which permanent truth and historical form are combined in myth as in other things. This may be shown from an illustration which Bultmann uses himself. Bultmann holds that the mythical eschatology "is untenable for the simple reason that the parousia of Christ never took place as the New Testament expected. History did not come to an end, and—as every schoolboy knows—will continue to run its course." That is certainly right. But is all eschatology on that account "untenable"? Why is it that during the classical ages of Christianity the Last Day has always been a close and familiar friend whose arrival was hourly expected? And that not only in the sectarian fringe, but in the heroes of the Christian faith like Augustine, Luther, and Calvin, to mention only a few. That the Lord is nigh, that the believer is standing at the end of time and history—is only a way of expressing the ultimacy and the certainty of the truth and reality which the Christian confesses in faith. We shall have more to say about this in a moment.

We must pursue Bultmann's theses further. He emphasizes that myth by its very nature demands demythologizing. All myth, he says, requires not cosmological but anthropological or, better, existential interpretation. The conception of such an interpretation itself is important. It is certainly true that myth speaks of the existence of man—or rather, of man-in-faith; it speaks of the limits and the foundations of his world, of the powers which control it, which confront him with succour or demand. Certainly there is knowledge of human existence to be derived from every myth. But is that the whole story? Is that the only purpose of myth? Even if all religion (and religion always uses the language of myth) were exclusively concerned with the relation between God and man, the existentialist approach would be too narrow to comprehend its whole range. For religion knows that divine power only as the foundation or limit of this existence, not what that divine power is in itself in its absolute independence and self-sufficiency. God is more than just the foundation or condition of human existence. It is just here that the enigma of myth lies: it dares to speak of an absolute Deity in human words and with analogies from human relationships, and moreover is successful in doing so. In other words, the existentialist interpretation of myth provides the clue to only one aspect of the relation and the gulf between God and man, but it cannot do justice to the wonder of its full range and depth. Almost more important is that other relation between God and the world. Hence the cosmogonies, which are always the most perspicuous examples of myth. Of course, an existentialist interpretation does not ignore this other relation, but, as Bultmann's essay shows, the importance of the world in that interpretation is limited to providing the stage for human life. But God is the true centre of the world as well as of man. It would be more in accord with the spirit of myth to regard man as just one element in an infinite universe—even the New Testament does so in clear and classical language; it says, not "God so loved mankind", but "God so loved the world". And this limitation becomes even more acute when this world, in the sense of familiar and tangible reality, is handed over to man's control. The teaching of myth at this point is rather the reverse, that man, as tangible reality, is handed over to the control of the world. In other words, human life is just one element in the universe and, moreover, both have their source in God and rest in his hands. Myth revolves round the inexhaustible wealth of these relations between God and the world and man: it lives and springs like a ceaseless fountain from these three sources of theology, cosmology, and anthropology.

II

If things so stand with regard to myth, what does "demythologizing" then mean? We will not press the point that Bultmann defines it in a kaleidoscopic variety of ways. Its literal meaning, which it bears in large parts of his essay, is the removal of the inappropriate mythical garb with the false objectivity of its cosmic imagery—and this means the abolition of the myth. But elsewhere it has a different meaning—the *interpretation* of the myth in the existentialist sense—and this means the preservation of the myth. For every interpretation preserves the text: the text is not only its material, but the master which it endeavours to serve. From a logical point of view, however, these two conceptions are not mutually exclusive, especially if Bultmann is right in regarding the true sense of myth as the disclosure of the "self-understanding of man", and the objectivizing imagery with its implied mythical world view the inadequate means for the expression of that sense. Now, that is to make the interpretation the master and judge of the myth it is interpreting, instead of keeping it in its rightful place as a servant. What right have we to do that? Sometimes Bultmann says this is the task of the theologian, sometimes the task of preaching, of the parson in the pulpit. But are theology and preaching the same thing? Only if theology is simply the proclamation of faith and proclamation the same as theology. But that would be the end of theology as a science, and there could hardly be a keener champion of theology as a science than Bultmann. His discussion with secular existentialist philosophy would also be rendered superfluous, a point to which we shall return at a later stage. More important for the moment is the question whether it is the task of Christian proclamation to give an existentialist interpretation, and whether it lies within its competence to do so. Here we touch on a great problem which has often been neglected. All Christian preaching is based upon the New Testament as the title-deeds of its revelation and faith. The New Testament provides preaching with its subject matter and principles, its truth and reality. But the relation between preaching and the New Testament is a curious combination of subservience and freedom. On the one hand the New Testament is an historical document relating to a long-vanished past, with its own peculiar concepts and images, its problems and solutions, its doubts, needs, and troubles, its hopes, consolations and promises, all of which are quite different from our own. In respect of these the Christian proclamation is free. For its standard and its centre lie in the faith vouchsafed to it in the here and now, in the revelation which is its abiding heritage; Jesus Christ the same yesterday and to-day and for ever. On the other hand, Christian preaching is grounded upon that revelation, which it must obey as the "steward of the mysteries of God". In this sense it is bound to the letter of the documents of this revelation. This blending of freedom and subservience springs from the distinctive charac-

ter of the revelation. It is an historical religion, and at the same
time the final, eschatological, only true religion—Jesus Christ,
not only yesterday, but to-day and for ever. In other words,
this freedom and subservience are once more a reflection of the
Word made flesh. This subservience and freedom apply to each
separate book and to the document as a whole, to every chapter
and every sentence, to the earliest Christian confession and the
earliest Christian world view, to mythical miracle and historical
event. All this is at once the ground and abyss of faith, its
encouragement and stumbling-block, its mainstay and problem,
its answer and question. There have been times in the history of
Christianity when the whole of revelation has seemed to be
comprehended in myth so-called, and other times when it has
seemed to be comprehended in the historical reality of the
Master. Many ages have seen only the Christus Rex, while others
—one need think only of St Francis of Assisi—have seen only
the humble and kindly Brother who conquered the world by
love. The secret behind this constant swing of the pendulum—
whose mid-point is always the same—is that each successive
generation is faced anew with the privilege and responsibility of
apprehending and realizing the whole of God's revelation in
the whole of its contemporary life and time. This is what moulds
tradition and destroys it, affirms and denies, creates myths and
abandons them. And although Christianity may often take a
wrong turning or be led astray by the spirit of the age, it may
always be sure that the Spirit of God is leading it into all truth,
even though that assurance may often be shattered and may
have to be fought for all over again. In this never-ceasing process,
often frustrated, often getting bogged down in the mire of human
sin, but always rising again—in this process of appropriation,
even demythologizing has its proper place. But demythologizing is not confined to the destruction of myths in order to
extract the existential kernel and enjoy the fruit, whether it be
sweet or bitter to the taste. It also means to appreciate that
myth is the mode in which God reveals himself, and that the
apparently empty and worn-out husk is the symbol of the
historicity of that eschatological revelation of God in which
"the Word became flesh". And that applies not only to the
central event of salvation, to Christ himself, but also what we
call the mythical world view which provides the framework of

the picture. Even to say "Our Father which art in Heaven" is to make a confession of faith which depends on a three-storied universe of heaven, earth, and hell.

You will immediately protest that I am canonizing every syllable of the New Testament as if it were part of the unchanging wisdom of God, and that I am varnishing its errors and its obsolete thought with the splendour of abiding truth. Surely, you will say, this is shutting up the revelation of God in the sanctuary, cutting it off from all that is true in modern thought, and erecting a wall between them which gets harder to penetrate the longer it lasts. But such an objection only betokens a profound misconception of the change which the Christian revelation has undergone in the course of history. The sole reason for this change is that the Christian revelation allies itself with the thought of each successive age, and so makes faith and appropriation possible. At this point, however, we meet another difficulty. Bultmann has handed out the task of demythologizing not only to the New Testament proclamation, but also to theology, and how important that task is in his eyes may be seen from the space he gives to the discussion of a profane existential philosophy.

What then does demythologizing mean in the field of scientific theology? A theology of the New Testament has but one all-embracing task, which is to give a lucid and methodical presentation of the New Testament material with due regard to its systematic relations and the varied nature of its historical background. Hence it is not enough simply to reproduce the material word for word as past history or to ossify it as timeless, abstract doctrine. There is only one way in which to present it —that is, in a way which not only answers the question: What was it actually like? but also the further question: what "it" now is which really was then. Now, whatever else may be said of it, the New Testament material—and here Bultmann is quite right—is undoubtedly mythological. By designating it as such we have already advanced one step in defining what that material is, though that step is based on science and not demanded by faith. We have recognized its affinities with and more particularly its differences as regards the nature of its myth from the documents and contents of other religions. But the language of myth is not that of science. In the one we have imagery,

parable, and the reality of a divine-human event: in the other,
the abstract concept and the truth of historical fact. At this
point therefore demythologizing means the translation of the
New Testament material from the language of myth into that of
science. This is a possible procedure, as there is only one truth,
which is intended by both kinds of language, and it is a necessary
procedure, as the New Testament material assuredly contains
perceptible truth. For myth never recognized any limit to its
applicability, any more than modern science does. Both are
potentially capable of drawing all truth into their own sphere,
and even where something happens which does not fit into its
conceptions, it is brought into relation with those conceptions,
and even the most ordinary occurrence may become the vessel
of a mythical revelation. Take for instance that famous text
from the Fourth Gospel: "And it was night." In such instances
it would be wrong to set aside the mythological element because
of its supposed incompatibility with modern thought. Instead,
we must try to ascertain the abiding truth it enshrines and accept
its mythical expression as a symbol of the unique character of
its historicity. This is the same process which the scientific
historian applies to every historical fact—a process which must
be applied anew in each successive generation, and which testifies to the inexhaustible vitality and fruitfulness of the tradition.

Two questions may be asked at this point. The first concerns
the scientific concept. Is it really capable, as we have assumed,
of comprehending and defining religious truth in all its fullness?
We hear so much, especially in the New Testament, of the
inexhaustible riches and the unsearchable nature of the religious
or mythical revelation, and that makes us ask whether it is not
a hopeless task to try to define it in the concepts of science,
which after all are only human. This is the old problem of
"negative theology" so called, which we can only deal with
summarily here. For it would require a thorough and methodical
examination of the nature of religion and its relation to other
branches of human knowledge. In so far as all these branches
may be classified under the concept of the one truth, and in so
far as this truth is precisely the aim and task of scientific apprehension, to that extent that concept is capable of apprehending
the truth in all the data of religious experience. It apprehends
it in the way appropriate to it—that is, it investigates the

possibility and necessity of it in the strict sense, and leaves it for faith to affirm in action this possibility as the ultimate truth. Thus faith is left free to perform its own essential function, while scientific apprehension assesses its rationality. In other words, the idea of an historical or even of a mythical revelation requires to be apprehended in two ways. In so far as it is historically given, it may be classified with other knowable historical data. For it is a fundamental proposition and a fundamental fact of the New Testament that God has revealed himself fully and completely at the end of history in his Son. And in so far as it is revelation, it demands the assent of faith—which is the justification of speaking of the unsearchability of the revelation. It is the characteristic of religion that it submits itself unreservedly to thought, and in the very act of doing so transcends all thought. The second question is whether the translation of myth into the language of concept leads to the existentialist interpretation rather than any other. Rightly understood, and with the reservations of which I have already spoken, the concept of existence in this sense is not open to any objection: it simply means man standing before God in judgement and grace. Of course the New Testament has much more to say than this idea of human existence in faith. It speaks of the *kingdom* of God, it speaks of the world, of its passing away and its coming into being, though all these things are obviously related to existence in faith. But it is quite another matter to interpret this idea of existence in faith in terms of this existentialist philosophy. With that philosophy existentialist interpretation has only this much in common—though the connection is absolutely firm and inalienable: it defines the place which religion occupies in its system. In this way it furnishes the terminology for the definition of religion, as it does for any other science. Its function is thus of a methodological or logical nature, and therewith it embraces theology as for instance it does natural science. But on the actual subject matter of theology it has no more right to pontificate than it has about physics, and it makes no difference whether the philosophy be existentialism or naturalism or idealism or materialism. It may be true that existentialist philosophy arrives in the end at statements almost identical with those of Christian theology, but that is not because it is a philosophy, but because it borrows its thesis from other spheres which belong to another kingdom and another order, or

else it posits them dogmatically. Certainly the theologian, or
more precisely the apologist, has the additional task of assessing
the primary justification of its own propositions and of detecting
surreptitious importations from alien spheres. And in this task
demythologizing has also a part to play, in bringing to light
the original deposit of truth which the mythical language of
the New Testament conceals just as much as it reveals. But this
task belongs to a wider field, where the controversy between
Christian faith and a so-called new *Weltanschauung* is being
carried on. My impression—it is only a personal impression,
and I cannot stop to argue the point now—is that existentialist
philosophy is no more than a secularized form of Christian theology. It has borrowed a number of propositions from Christianity and wrested them from the context of faith on which all
theological affirmations depend for their existential reality.

III

Thus the problem of demythologizing seems to belong to
two spheres; though perhaps it would be better not to speak of
two distinct spheres, but of two interconnected approaches to
the subject. For they are both concerned with the same object,
and both are demanded by it. God requires faith—an almost tauto-
logical statement, but it includes the requirement of a believing
theology. By this I mean a theology which starts with faith, raises it
to a knowledge informed by faith, and produces a theological
system. Every word of faith and every word of revelation
which faith apprehends is not content until it has found its
proper place in a believing theology. Every halting, unspoken
prayer is at heart a theological affirmation or a theological idea.
They differ only in degree, in the extent to which they are conscious and explicit in word and thought. But in unfolding itself
like this, faith follows the categories of scientific thinking and
assesses its own validity in accordance with the rules of judgement
and conclusion. And here we are concerned not only with an
external system of concepts embracing the object of theological
affirmations but with the thing itself, with the nature of the
concept as it is appropriate to the object of faith. Thus believing
theology can begin its work by taking for granted a system of

theological concepts and affirmations with a proved scientific basis. And how could it be otherwise, seeing that every judgement of faith is a judgement in the real sense of the word with its proper place in a whole system of judgements, which follows the pattern of scientific thought? But just as believing theology needs scientific theological thinking, so in its turn scientific theological thinking needs believing theology. For the task of scientific theology is to assess the possibility and necessity of what faith asserts. And this task is a legitimate one, as certainly as the object of faith (particularly when it provides the foundations for all possible objects or, in religious language, when it creates them) still remains the object of *faith* and is the immediate and exclusive object of human activity. And this task is not only developing systematically in the present, it has done so historically throughout the past. Thus the two kinds of theology need each other, and we may best define their relation by adapting a famous dictum of Kant: "Without believing theology all scientific theology is empty, and without scientific theology all believing theology is blind." What then will demythologizing mean for these two kinds of theology? We have seen already that it is a legitimate task for the scientific interpretation of the New Testament, though not because it is myth, but because that myth is given in history. In this connection therefore the interpretation of myth does not differ essentially from that of any other expression of faith—e.g. a dialogue, a doctrine, or a prayer. Interpretation must always establish the permanent content of truth behind the mode of expression, and ascertain why historically it was uttered in that particular mode. As on the day which created it, myth must be refashioned from the possibilities furnished by its content and history, and its form and content redefined: its obsolete elements must be removed and its permanent truth restated. In this way scientific theology teaches us that myth and history are not opposites, but complementary aspects of the same truth. This may be illustrated from the call of Moses or the covenant of Mount Sinai, or from the death and resurrection of Jesus. Scientific theology teaches us the questionable character alike of myth and history—indeed, one may say of the history of redemption and of the history of the world, of revelation and of the nations. It teaches us both the connection and the difference between them, and that both always

are worthy of new questions. In all this activity, which owing to
the investigator and his subject matter is rarely brought to a conclusion, scientific theology must adhere faithfully to the text and
to what the text says. Its task is to remember and meditate upon
the text, though it must never make that the determining principle of its activity or the reality by which it stands or falls. Its requirement is, to apply a much misused word, relevance, or, more
accurately, objectivity. When the truth is established as valid
apart from the investigator himself, scientific theology has
achieved its aim. For believing theology, on the other hand, demythologizing has quite different implications. It is the hallmark of Protestant theology and Protestant faith that it never en-
trenches itself in a province of its own where it can enjoy its own
content untouched by outside movements and upheavals. Its weakness is that it has too often surrendered to the spirit of the age.
Yet that weakness is also its strength, for despite its association
with the world, it has managed to preserve the unbounded freedom
of its own faith and its location by God in the here and now. This
is a matter for wonder and gratitude. That is why Protestant theology cannot, as Catholic theology could and does, ignore the
challenge of demythologizing. It is therefore the special vocation of Protestant theology to associate itself with all the developments in science, and to reap the fruits from all the trees of
secular knowledge. It cannot therefore ignore the challenge of demythologizing and, since that problem has a legitimate place in
scientific theology, it becomes its own problem too. But believing
theology engages in demythologizing with quite a different
purpose—not to bring criticism to bear upon myth, nor yet to
eliminate myth, but to experience in the process the purity
and godliness of its own revelation and affirmations of faith.
Myth can become the solid rock on which the faith is built,
the place where believing theology can experience the wonder
of its own faith. But it can also become the rock of offence which
must be surmounted if that theology is to acquire a clearer and
purer understanding of itself. This applies, however, not only
to myth but, as we have seen, to every sentence in the New
Testament. Only under the pressure of doubt, doubt in everything and doubt in itself, can theology experience the triumphant
power of its divine vocation. To have its faith tried and tested
in the fires of doubt is of the very essence of Protestant theology.

It may freely admit both its strength and its weakness, but it knows that the act of God which is the ground of its own experience is greater than myth, and that it can experience that act more genuinely the more it penetrates behind mythology to the essential core of truth. Protestant theology knows that myth is the mode in which God has chosen to reveal himself. That revelation is a treasure which we have to bear in earthen vessels, not only because we are men of earth, but because it has pleased God to place it in this vessel. It is not for us to smash the vessel, but to make proper use of it and to learn that after all it is an earthen vessel. The more sincerely we devote ourselves to the cause of demythologizing, the more surely shall we preserve the treasure God has given us.

HELMUT THIELICKE

THE RESTATEMENT OF NEW TESTAMENT MYTHOLOGY[1]

PRELIMINARY OBSERVATIONS

The Importance of Bultmann's Challenge for the Church

Bultmann's essay on the demythologizing of the New Testament has become an event which everybody is talking about. I deliberately speak of it as an event of more than theological or academic significance: it is an *ecclesiastical* event. My reasons for so doing are as follows:

Bultmann has asked the question whether salvation history, in its formal aspect at any rate, is to be regarded as myth rather than history, and as myth not only in its outer framework but in its essential core, in the event of Jesus Christ.

Before proceeding to examine this challenge in detail, we should state at the outset that it affects the very foundations of the Church.

When the Reformers made *sola fide* the *articulus stantis et cadentis ecclesiae*, they meant by faith faith in Jesus Christ, *fides*

[1] This essay is a discussion of Bultmann's *Offenbarung und Heilsgeschehen* (1941). See also my article in the *Deutsches Pfarrerblatt*, 22 August 1942. The present essay, first produced as a theological memorandum in 1942 at the request of the *Oberkirchenrat* of the Lutheran Church of Württemberg, is reproduced here without any important changes. Since then, the discussion has been carried an important stage further by Oscar Cullmann, in his outstanding work *Christ and Time* (Eng. trans., S.C.M. Press, 1951). Despite the subsequent appearance of this book, I had to leave my own contribution in its original form. It was first read as a paper at a conference of theologians convened by Bishop Wurm at Stuttgart in 1943 and afterwards circulated in typescript by the *Oberkirchenrat*. The only other course would have been to rewrite it completely. All I have done is to remove its obvious wartime references on the suggestion of Hans v. Soden, to whom I am indebted for detailed criticisms and appreciation.

Jesu (objective genitive).[1] The Reformers were not concerned with faith as a subjective disposition as contrasted with works, but with its object, Jesus Christ. Luther was always emphasizing that what mattered about faith was not its subject, but its object, which was located *extra me*. In his exposition of Psalm 90 he even used the daring metaphor that the subject of faith was a mathematical point, so far was he from regarding faith as a subjective experience through which man's understanding of himself is illuminated, and so exclusively should faith be defined in reference to its object, the *extra se* of the historic Christ. As it became secularized, Protestantism lost sight of this, and *sola fide* became a subjective disposition of man, an emotional experience, the famous "defiant faith" of Lutheranism.

Hence it would be more accurate to speak of *sola fide Jesu Christi*. This makes the controversy with Bultmann a *status confessionis*. Only when faith is controlled by its object and riveted to Christology does it become the *articulus stantis et cadentis ecclesiae*. It is not merely faith as such, but, more important, the historical basis of faith, which belongs to the standing and falling of the Church. If that be so, then Bultmann's challenge, concerned as it is with the contamination of that historic basis with mythology, affects the very foundation of the Church.

Bultmann is not just a voice in the wilderness. He is the mouthpiece of a quite definite spirit of the age. More than that, he represents a historism which grew out of the swaddling clothes of the History of Religions, passed through dialectic theology, and reacted negatively to it. All this means that the Church is challenged here to take a confessional stand. This is more than a theological discussion. Of course, all we can do here is to offer a few preliminary considerations of a theological character to pave the way for such a confession.

Quite apart from the solution Bultmann proposes, he raises problems which concern every theologian, whenever he opens his Bible in the study, lecture room, or pulpit. A few examples will make this clear. He must, for instance, make up his mind about what is "true" in the Biblical text, and what is only

---

[1] There is something to be said for taking it as a subjective genitive, but the point need not detain us here. See the important work by H. Iwand, *Rechtfertigungslehre und Christusglaube*, Leipzig 1930, which is particularly illuminating on this subject.

"temporary"—i.e. to be interpreted in the light of the world view or the religious environment of the age. He must decide what is the kernel of the gospel, and what is merely the outward husk which has been shaped by human imagination, by traditional interpretation, by the tendency to produce credal formulae, by the subsequent historical consolidation of the truths of faith. What is "truth" and what is "mythology"? What is divine and what is human?

Bultmann does not set out with any practical concern, whether secret or avowed. He does not ask what bearing his conclusions may have on our preaching of the gospel. He approaches the problem from a purely academic standpoint and asks, How far does the essential message of the gospel confront us—(1) In the framework of a mythical world view conditioned by its environment and therefore irrelevant to the modern world? If so, how is that message (2) to be detached from its setting and presented so to say in its chemical purity?

No one will be able to deny Bultmann's radical honesty. He does not shrink from the consequences, however terrifying they may be, either in his personal responsibility towards the Scriptures, or in the positive or negative conclusions he is forced to draw for his own preaching. This is the most serious challenge theologians have had to face for many a day.

As a matter of fact, we all draw the distinction between mythology and truth, but the point at which we draw it varies with our school of thought or our individual preferences. The vagueness—nay more, the downright insincerity—of much modern preaching may be gauged from the way we tend to draw the line between truth and mythology at different points, at one point in the study and at another in the pulpit. We tend to be influenced by practical considerations. How much will the congregation stand? This leads to insincerity, and is not a healthy sign. Perhaps this pragmatism affects the personal faith of the preacher: he stands helpless in face of mythology, and lacks the courage to draw the distinction as sharply as he should. However this may be, it is a fact that up to now the problem of mythology has never been a regular part of the curriculum of theological study. It will certainly have to be in the future.

We see then from the outset that there is no escaping Bultmann's challenge. It must be boldly met in the confidence that the outside world cannot and must not possess a monopoly of the truth, and that here too the truth can make us free. We must go forward with the conviction that as our faith is steeled in the fires of doubt we shall open up a new chapter in the progress of theological knowledge.

Let us make it quite clear that we do not dispute the distinction between the husk of mythology and the kernel of revelation. That goes without saying. What we ask is, Where exactly should the line be drawn?

In the first part (A), we shall endeavour to arrive at a clear understanding of Bultmann's aim. This will enable us to see that the logical consequence of his restatement of mythology is the elimination of salvation history and the substitution of philosophy for theology.

In the second part (B) we shall use the Memorandum of the Confessing Church of Hesse as our basis, and ask whether myth is a permanent element in human thought, and therefore an indispensable vehicle for the expression of the Biblical revelation.

Both Bultmann and the Hessian memorandum (hereafter quoted as HBK) agree that the message of the Bible is not just straightforward history. Between us and the historical reality which lies behind that message there is an intermediate layer of myth. On historical grounds, both religious and secular, Bultmann believes that myth affects the actual message itself: the mythical element encounters us, so to say, "objectively", and is part of the message itself. To HBK, on the other hand, the reason for myth lies in the nature of man, in the way he inevitably approaches religion. Here myth is, so to say, "subjective": it arises from the way we look at things. Bultmann thinks he can get rid of the mythological language which conceals the truth by carefully extracting the Biblical message from its setting in a contemporary world view. To HBK such a procedure is impossible, since the mythological setting is due not to historical circumstances or to the contemporary world view but to the way man looks at things. We can no more abandon mythology than we can cease to think in terms of time and space. Thus Bultmann rejects, while HBK accepts and affirms, the mythological elements in the Bible.

These two works provide a pattern for the treatment of the problem of mythology and history in Holy Scripture. In the last analysis they form a unity in tension. Hence we shall use them as a guide for our own consideration of the problem, not for any polemical reasons, but because they lay down the best lines for its treatment.

We shall endeavour to take up an independent line on the problem of myth as a whole, without losing sight of the practical implications of our conclusions for the Church's proclamation. We are fully aware that we can do no more than throw out a few suggestions and make a few preliminary assaults on the problem, for it will probably need the work of a whole generation of theologians for a final solution. We shall endeavour not to suppress the difficulties in this preliminary assault. In fact, we shall bring to light an even more formidable array of problems than either Bultmann or HBK have raised so far.

A. The Consequence of Demythologizing: The Conversion of the Gospel into a Philosophy

I Bultmann's Task

Bultmann maintains that the essential kerygma is embedded in a double framework:

1. A world view which implies a three-storied universe of heaven, earth, and hell (p. 1).

2. Jewish apocalyptic and the Gnostic myth of redemption. Both of these are now untenable (p. 15). They provide the source for many of the teachings and narratives of the New Testament, and are indispensable for its interpretation. Neither these teachings nor these narratives may be imposed as articles of faith on those who seek the ultimate truth of which these things are but the temporary vehicles, and who are themselves conditioned by a totally different world view.

Bultmann believes that this affects not only the periphery of the New Testament, but even its central features like the miracles, the daemonology, the doctrine of the End, of death as the punishment of sin, of vicarious satisfaction through the death and resurrection of Christ (p. 4ff.). "At this point absolute clarity and ruthless honesty are essential both for the academic theologian and for the parish priest. It is a duty they owe to themselves, to the Church they serve, and to those whom they seek to win for the Church. They must make it quite clear what their hearers are expected to accept and what they are not" (p. 9).

It will be seen here how profoundly Bultmann is influenced by the History of Religions school and its historical relativism. Yet the difference between them is equally obvious. That school tended at the outset to remove the kerygma as a kind of erratic boulder, and to plant it down in the general history of religion. Thus they deprived the kerygma of its distinctiveness. Bultmann, on the other hand, tries to avoid this threat to the kerygma, not by denying the influence of its environment, nor by a naïve dogmatism which the study of the History of Religions has rendered obsolete, but by penetrating through the temporary framework of mythology to the permanent truth behind it.

We may admit that whatever the final outcome may be, such a plan is a great one, and in the way in which it has been begun represents a legitimate task for the Church. For the only real answer to the History of Religions school will come from a theologian who recognizes its discoveries and who realizes the complete change in the situation which those discoveries have brought about. It must, if I may say so, come from one who has been through it and suffered with it. It cannot come from an obscurantist who behaves as though nothing had happened and is content to repeat the shibboleths of a short-circuited dogmatism, or to take over the exegesis of Luther naïvely and uncritically, to say nothing of the allegorical interpretations of the Rabbis.[1]

Bultmann takes the History of Religions seriously, but he is not a slave to it. It is important to give him credit for that, not only for his own sake but for the sake of the cause he has at heart. In fact, he is looking for the answer to it. And from the outset—we owe this to him too—we must recognize that such an enterprise will demand sacrifices: we must face the risk of heresy, and even the likelihood that we shall have to shed our own theological blood. "Nothing venture, nothing win", that is the rule in the kingdom of God as it is in the world, for faith

[1] As is done e.g. by Hans Halbardt, and to some extent by Wilhelm Vische himself.

is precisely a venture. But in any case this venture possesses theological dignity, not because of its dangers and its magnitude, but because of the name in which it is undertaken. That is to say, whether it is undertaken in the name of a deliberately secular criterion to which the Bible is subordinated, or in the name of the Lord who will not suffer the truth to fail. For he himself is the Truth, and he will always distinguish between the faith of his servants and their theological ventures. Hence it is important to recognize that Bultmann is thinking as a servant of the Lord and of his Church.

II Earlier Restatements of the Kerygma now Outmoded

Bultmann believes that we cannot penetrate to the permanent truths of the New Testament by the reduction or subtraction of the mythological element (p. 9). Such a procedure would be merely eclectic, and would not solve the whole problem of mythology as a system.

Nor will the older liberal theology help us. For by dissolving the evangelical events into the symbol of an eternal idea it forfeited the element of event in the Christian revelation. Bultmann agrees that modern man cannot accept the mythology, but he does not want him to have to content himself with a timeless sublimation of the gospel: he is looking for another alternative, which will rescue the historicity of the gospel and so retain its character as kerygma. It would be unjust to Bultmann if we forgot his genuine pastoral concern in our zeal to repudiate his conclusions. Whether Bultmann's methods are adequate, and whether he can sustain his intention, is another matter, to which we must address ourselves forthwith.

III Mythology to be Interpreted, not Eliminated

So far then we agree with Bultmann. We cannot penetrate to the kernel of history behind the husk of mythology by critical subtraction, nor can we sublimate the gospel into a timeless truth after the manner of liberal Protestantism. The former procedure failed to do justice to the principle of myth and to its ubiquity in the Bible, while the latter deprived salvation history of its historical roots and reduced it to a *Weltanschauung*.

The only way to penetrate to the eternal truth behind the mythological husk is, according to Bultmann, not to eliminate the mythology but to interpret it (p. 12). The real purpose of myth (e.g. the creation stories) is not to give an account of what actually happened in the past, or what may happen in the future (e.g. another ice age), but to convey a particular understanding of human life.

What Bultmann is really driving at may perhaps be demonstrated from a further consideration of the doctrine of *creatio ex nihil*. This particular doctrine does not tell us how the world actually came into being, but seeks rather to convey the implications of the fact that we stand as responsible beings before God. It teaches us that God is the source of all our being. He calls us out of nothing, and stamps us with the insignia of his Fatherhood. We are not made out of some material alien to God which we can blame for our sins and failures. Further, there is no ground for refusing to recognize his absolute sovereignty. Beside him there are no other gods, and apart from him there can be no material world. To deny the doctrine of *creation ex nihil* is to limit God's sovereignty, as happens in the various theories which make God himself part of the evolutionary process.

Hence it will be seen that Bultmann is groping after a really important truth. The cosmological assumptions of myth are not literal truths: what we have to do is to discover the existential meaning behind them. This meaning is valid for all time, for though world views change, human nature remains the same. Incidentally there would appear to be nothing really new in Bultmann's enterprise. It has been going on now for several decades in the controversy between religion and science. In the course of it theologians have rediscovered the kerygma which is enshrined in the cosmology of the creation myth.

The truth then embodied in myth is not scientific, but anthropological, or better, existential (p. 10ff.). The question is, what particular understanding of man's Being does the New Testament convey?

IV Myth as an Understanding of Human Life

It is when Bultmann speaks of the understanding of human life that our suspicions are first aroused, especially when we know what a prominent part this conception plays in Bultmann's thought.[1] By "understanding of human life" he means a timeless abstract truth. When I think I understand some piece of history (e.g. the Reformation), I thereby claim that my understanding of it transcends my subjectivity and temporality, and possesses supra-temporal validity. And although I am aware that historical understanding is always subjectively conditioned, it nevertheless acquires supra-subjective, timeless status. Convinced as I am that my understanding is genuine, I am bound at the same time to claim that my subjectivity is in a special manner subordinated to its object, and is therefore adequate to it. Hence it is more than accidental that the mind is able to regard its understanding as timeless.

If the content of the New Testament message is, as Bultmann claims, an "understanding", the emphasis lies on the subjective element, the change in our self-consciousness which produces that understanding. This experience may in some way be connected with an event of revelation (p. 4), and it may be necessary first to extract the distinctive Christian self-consciousness, but that does not make it any the less subjective.

All we have to do is to substitute Schleiermacher's famous "self-consciousness" for Bultmann's term, "understanding of human life" (after all, the two terms are practically synonymous) in order to see this. We may call this self-consciousness existential, we may say it needs an external event to bring it to birth, but that does not alter its essential character as timeless truth. In any case, the emphasis rests upon its timeless character and permanent validity.

Such an outlook really leaves no room for an historical revelation in time, at least not in the sense of an intervention on the plane of reality, including reality external to man, and an intervention which changes that reality, as in miracle. Such an idea would be too mythological for Bultmann. The only event of revelation he can allow is one which brings to birth

[1] Cf. Bultmann's characteristic article on Paul in *Religion in Geschichte und Gegenwart*.

an understanding of human life such as man could never have produced for himself.

Consequently the event in the process of revelation is not an objective reality, it is simply a change in the subjective consciousness of man. When the prologue of the Fourth Gospels says "The Word became flesh" it means by "flesh" not the historical fact in the manger at Bethlehem but the acquisition of a new understanding of human life which has its origin in that point of history. This would seem to be a legitimate interpretation of Bultmann's argument. The historical narratives of the New Testament are, to put it bluntly, not events in their own right, but only the prelude to an event. The real event is the change which takes place in human self-consciousness.

V Historicity in Danger

At first sight it would appear that Bultmann has done more justice to the kerygma as event, when compared with Liberal Protestantism. But we cannot delude ourselves as to the status of this event. We get the impression—and this will be confirmed in the ensuing argument—that the event is a kind of inference deduced from the Christian or the existential understanding of human life.[1]

Thus it would appear that the new understanding of existence is rendered possible only by an act which stands in the background—i.e. Christ. But this act never comes out into the open, any more than Kant's hypothetical God. We seem to be relegated with the men of the New Testament to Plato's famous cave. All we see is the shadows of our own consciousness, and all we can do is to draw inferences about the reality which lies behind them and produces the effect. Of the kernel of history which transcends the myth, Bultmann can speak only in negative terms: "Our interest in the events of his life, and above all in the cross, is more than an academic concern with the history of

---

[1] To avoid misapprehension, let us emphasize that the event we speak of is not the historical data—e.g. the facts about the life of Jesus. These facts are not deducible from the Christian interpretation of human life. They are the subject of historical investigation. What we mean by event is these historical data elevated to cosmic dimensions by the acquisition of an understanding of human life which those data produce (p. 36). Thus the event is not the Jesus of history, but Jesus valued as the Christ.

the past. We can see meaning in them only when we ask what God is trying to say to each one of us through them. Again, the figure of Jesus cannot be understood simply from his context in human evolution or history. In mythological language this means that he stems from eternity, his origin transcends both history and nature." "Eternity" is thus only a description of the fact that entry of the Logos into *sarx* involves a particular understanding of human life[1] which cannot be discovered as immanent in the world around us. The implication is that it would be nearer the truth to say: "The Word did not become flesh."

We said earlier that for Bultmann the crucial event takes place in the human consciousness. To this we must add that the change in consciousness does not produce itself. It is not, so to say, "congenital" or socratic, or in any other way self-originating. It needs an event to bring it to birth. It must as it were be "cranked up" like the universe in deism. Such would seem to be the fundamentally negative implication in Bultmann's thought about the event which underlies the New Testament kerygma and the understanding of human life of which it is the expression.

What matters in theology, however, is not the recognition of the event, but the status accorded to it. Is the history recorded in the New Testament just a vague reality which underlies the Christian consciousness, the contours of which can no longer be recovered, or is it not rather the event *par excellence*, quite apart from our subjective consciousness? Is it not the light whose miraculous appearance is quite unaffected by whether the darkness apprehended it or not? Everything turns upon the status accorded to the event. Even Lessing in *The Education of the Human Race* would seem to recognize that revelation meant event, but he again conceived that event in a deistic manner, and so transformed the truth of revelation into an abstract philosophical truth. It became in fact an understanding of human life.[2] The status accorded by Bultmann to the event in revelation would appear to be essentially indirect and negative.

[1] Since, according to Bultmann, its basis in history is unimportant, the Logos is important not because of what it *was* in history but merely because of what it *said*. What it was involves history, whereas what it said involves no more than this particular understanding of human life. Bultmann is logical.

[2] See my *Vernunft und Offenbarung, A study of the Religious Philosophy of Lessing*, Tübingen, 1942, 2nd ed. It is surely no accident that Bultmann repeatedly echoes the ideas of Lessing.

VI Revelation Disintegrated into Philosophy

This raises the question—and it shows how radical Bultmann is that he is prepared to face it—as to what happens to this understanding of human life once it has been created. Is it detached from the event which gave it birth and left suspended in mid-air? Does it become philosophical and unhistorical? Must we not conclude with Lessing in *The Education of the Human Race* that the aim of God's revelation of himself in history was to render itself superfluous by becoming an abstract idea loosed from its historical moorings—in fact, an understanding of human life?[1] Or, to put it concretely in reference to Bultmann's problem, Is not the Christian understanding of human life detached from its basis in history, which is Christ? Does not Christianity become a philosophy of existence? Does there not come a time when the child no longer needs a teacher to guide him? Does not Christ become an outworn myth of ever-decreasing importance?

In this connection Bultmann himself calls attention to the striking fact that Jaspers, Heidegger, and quite recently Kamlah, have transposed the Christian understanding of human life into the sphere of philosophy (p. 24). Reading between the lines, it would appear that Bultmann is anxious lest he too should be driven to the same conclusion. By interpreting the New Testament as he does in terms of Heidegger (p. 25) he would seem to have no other course left open to him. He is compelled to carry the method he has chosen—namely, that of secular philosophy—to its logical conclusion.

Let us digress for a moment to notice a fact which emerges from the study of the history of theology. Wherever a non-Biblical principle derived from contemporary secular thought is applied to the interpretation of the Bible, the Bible's *facultas se ipsum interpretandi* is violated, with fatal results. This is what happened in Kant's philosophy, and again in theological idealism. It is happening with Bultmann too. By adopting Heidegger's conception of understanding he is surrendering to the sovereignty of an intellectual world view, which deprives him of any feeling

[1] See the author's *Krisis der Theologie*, and for Bultmann's unhistorical interpretation of miracle his *Das Wunder*, both in Hinrichs-Verlag, 1938 and 1939 respectively.

for the distinctiveness of the Bible. What, for instance, can he make of the phenomenon of prophecy on such an assumption, to say nothing of the resurrection? This explains why the section dealing with the resurrection is so confused and bewildering. It is significant that Kamlah, whose philosophy is at once anti-Christian, yet closely related to the Christian conception of faith (at least, Bultmann thinks so), is a renegade pupil of Bultmann, one might say a Bultmann-turned-philosopher. It just shows what might happen to Bultmann himself.[1]

VII Bultmann's Defence against the Philosophizing of his Thought.

How does Bultmann attempt to resist this philosophizing of his interpretation of the New Testament?

As we have already seen, Bultmann's conception of understanding allows the element of event in revelation to fall into the background. If this be true, he would seem to have surrendered the strategic point from which alone this infiltration of philosophy could be warded off.

This is apparent in the points of agreement and difference Bultmann sees between the Christian and the philosophical understanding of human life.

He considers that they agree that something has gone wrong with human life. Man is lost, gone astray, fallen.[2] As a matter of fact, the biblical conception of sin is quite distinctive: it is an event, not an abstract philosophical conception of man's predicament. It is an act which separates man from God, from a "Thou" external to himself. In the philosophers, however, there is only a dim awareness that man is fallen from *himself*, his destiny, his true nature, his ego. But what the philosophers regard as the authentic ego of man is, from the Christian point of view, still fallen man, unless we are to assume that the spirit and reason are unaffected by the fall.

Once more Bultmann sides with the philosophers. Sin is man's consciousness that he is lost, and therefore it is not in any real sense an event. At most it is but the shadow of an event projected on the screen of our understanding of human life. The consequence is that the Thou in relation to whom the event

---

[1] Kamlah, *Christentum und Selbstbehauptung*, Frankfort-on-Main, 1940.
[2] Bultmann quotes Heidegger and idealism as illustrations, p. 27.

of sin takes place is thrust into the background, for events are transactions between a plurality of entities. Sin is thus a phenomenon of the ego on the same level of immanence as the philosophical understanding of human life.[1]

Not that Bultmann would wish to draw such a conclusion: in fact, he would vigorously resist it. Even in his essay he lays great stress on the event. But the event and the divine "Thou" in relation to whom it occurs receive only formal recognition. Sin, for Bultmann, as we have seen, is at least the shadow of an event. But he thinks that the Christian and the philosophical understanding of human life are so close to one another in their conception of sin that he refuses to distinguish between them at this point. The difference between them lies rather in the different ways in which they offer man deliverance from their fallen state. Philosophy takes the road of Socrates. All man needs is to be told what his real nature is, and he will be able to realize it (p. 27). What he needs is information rather than redemption.

The New Testament, on the other hand, asserts that if man tries to achieve his own redemption he cannot escape from his own autonomy, and therefore cannot escape from his predicament. So the New Testament offers man a way out where philosophy sees none: "At the very point where man can do nothing, God steps in and acts—indeed, he has acted already—on his behalf" (p. 31).

For Bultmann, then, the difference between the message of the New Testament and the theories of the philosophers lies not so much in their interpretation of Being as in the way of redemption they offer from a fallen state about whose nature they are more or less agreed. In philosophy that redemption is achieved by Socratic midwifery, in the New Testament by the act of Christ (cf. p. 14). This act of Christ conveys a new understanding of man's being which it is beyond his own capacity to achieve. (Whether that understanding, once it has been granted, can stand on its own feet is, as we have seen, a different question.)

---

[1] This point was established by E. Hirsch in his younger days in a critique of idealist philosophy. His chief objection to the intellectual approach is its solipsism. It confines itself to the ego and ignores the Thou, and thus blinds itself to the idea of fellowship with Another. (*Die idealistische Philosophie und das Christentum*, Gütersloh, 1926, esp. p. 69ff.)

VIII The Futility of Philosophy as a Way of Redemption

Can we be happy about this sudden appearance of the Christ event? Does it offer a firm barrier against the philosophical understanding of human life, which, as we have seen, is inescapably socratic and immanentist? How would Bultmann answer the objection that the Christ event, regarded as an actual intervention on the plane of reality, is just as mythological as the rest of the kerygma? For this reality is, Bultmann maintains, a closed system determined by the laws of cause and effect, and any idea of an intervention *ab extra* necessarily implies a mythical world view which is no longer tenable (p. 6f). This can be seen clearly from his treatment of miracle in his *Glauben und Verstehen*. This modern assumption that the world view of modern science is absolute is, we think, the reason for Bultmann's repeated retreat from revelation as an historical event into an abstract philosophy of life. Self-consciousness is the only sphere unaffected by the closed system of cause and effect, and therefore the only sphere which religion can claim as its own, and which is uncontaminated by mythology.

We are told by the author of the HBK memorandum that Bultmann dealt with this point when it was raised by the *Brüderrat*. He tried to save the objective historical basis of the Christian understanding of human life with particular reference to the resurrection. The resurrection, he says, is not just a subjective experience. "A vision is never purely subjective. It always has an objective basis. In the vision the encounter which precedes it attains fruition, so that the vision itself becomes a further encounter. . . . Similarly, in a dream our eyes are opened upon ourselves, and our sleeping conscience awakened. It is foolish to regard dreams and visions merely as subjective experiences. They are in a real sense objective encounters. What the disciples saw was the product of imagination in the sense that they projected what they saw into the world of space and sense. But that does not make what they saw imaginary. The faith evoked by the preaching of the gospel is no more subjective than a man's love for his friend. It is directed towards an object, though an object which is not purely external to him, but which operates as a reality within him" (ibid.).

Bultmann has confirmed our thesis with his own words.

First, we see that he is desperately concerned to avoid drifting into an immanentist philosophy of consciousness, and striving at all costs to preserve the historical basis of the kerygma. Secondly, we see how impossible it is to guarantee that historicity along the lines he has chosen. Faith has ceased to be dependent on the resurrection. Instead, the resurrection has become dependent on faith, the faith which springs from an encounter with Christ, or rather, with Jesus of Nazareth as he walked upon earth. The resurrection is no more than the pictorial symbol of an encounter, not an event in its own right.

Bultmann will surely have to admit that this encounter is susceptible of other interpretations: it does not necessarily demand a symbolic resurrection to explain it. Could it not be explained as a martyrdom for an idea, or as a survival in the memory of the disciples? Or perhaps the kind of immortality Goethe allowed to his friend Wieland, when he said in his conversation with Falk: "I would not be at all surprised if I met Wieland again some thousands of years hence as a star of the first magnitude . . ., and saw with my own eyes how he infused everything around him with a pleasant light."[1] If faith in the resurrection is only the reflex of an experience of an encounter, and devoid of any objective historical basis, it is in the last resort vulnerable to all the attacks of the psychologists.

We must not, however, overlook the element of justice in Bultmann's case against a certain kind of dogmatic orthodoxy. Lessing had the same degree of justification in his controversy with Goeze, the Chief Pastor of Hamburg. Faith in the resurrection does not spring from the historical narratives of the resurrection, the empty tomb, etc. These narratives are by their very nature open to historical criticism, and even when their reliability has been established beyond all doubt, they can never provide an adequate basis for faith, for they are still relative. The resurrection is not just an event of the past; it must still be authenticated in the encounter with which Bultmann is so much concerned. The resurrection must always be the logical outcome of the earthly life of Jesus, of his power over sin, disease, and death, and of his uniqueness. The resurrection must always appear as a flash of light which illuminates a whole host of traits in the life and teaching of Jesus and gives them new

[1] Goethe to Falk, on the day of Wieland's funeral, 25 January 1813.

meaning, so that apart from the resurrection they remain an unfathomable mystery and an ultimately meaningless fragment of history.

If all this be true then, to put it pregnantly, the resurrection of Jesus must be much more than a by-product of an encounter with him or its mythological after-effect. It is just the opposite: the resurrection is the only thing which creates a real encounter with Christ. Apart from it, he is an enigma with which there can be no real encounter. To put it even more pregnantly, the encounter with which Bultmann is concerned does not cause faith in the resurrection: the resurrection is the cause of an encounter with Christ. It is only through the resurrection that we can say to him: "My Lord and my God." Just as the Old Testament can only be understood and can only become an encounter in the light of the fact of Christ, so too the life of Jesus makes sense only in the light of the resurrection, and only so can it become an encounter.

And just as it is impossible to interpret the fact of Christ as a mythological inference from Old Testament prophecy, so also the resurrection cannot be regarded as a mythological inference from an encounter with Christ. In both cases the past has been absolutely superseded by a stark fact of history, and placed in an entirely new light. And this is done without bringing human subjectivity or inventiveness into play, nay rather in such a way that human subjectivity is produced by it, inasmuch as it is won over to faith.

We see then that Bultmann has left himself defenceless. Having once surrendered the fact of the resurrection, he cannot recover it again. Faith is cabined and confined in the narrow limits of subjectivity and consciousness, and receives no external impact from history. Having begun in the Spirit, i.e. with a genuine concern with the kerygma, Bultmann threatens to end in the flesh (Gal. 3. 3), i.e. in a "sarkic" philosophy.

We are left wondering why the event of Christ is not myth like everything else. Surely "*logos sarx egeneto*" implies an intervention in the closed system of reality?

The only point Bultmann can make against philosophy is that the New Testament bears witness to a fact which (presumably) could not be produced from a Socratic understanding of Being or transposed into that understanding. Once again the shadow

of the Christian understanding of human life points indirectly
to an event beyond itself. But must not this event on Bultmann's
own premises once more assume the character of a mirage
instead of a fixed point on the landscape of history? And if this
is so—and we are sure we have succeeded in proving that it is
—if the one remaining event (i.e. the fact of Christ) disappears,
and the ground of history gives way under our feet, what can
prevent Bultmann's thought from disintegrating into philosophy?
Is not Kamlah an awful warning of what happens when someone
else understands and sees through Bultmann's thought better
than he does himself?

*IX Tasks for Exegesis: Christmas, Good Friday, Easter Day, and
Pentecost, as Events*

Before we close this part of our discussion, let us sketch a
few of the tasks which will have to be faced if Bultmann's
challenge is to be taken up seriously by the theologians. These
tasks centre on specific problems of exegesis.

If Bultmann's concern for demythologizing is a valid one,
and if the sole point at issue is where exactly the line is to be
drawn between myth and kerygma, the only way forward is to
take certain specific problems of exegesis one by one. This will
be more fruitful than a purely general discussion of the problem.
Let us ask how Bultmann deals with the fundamental Christological events of Christmas, Good Friday, Easter, and Pentecost.
How does he extricate them from mythology as he conceives it?

Take for instance his treatment of Good Friday and Easter
Day. Here we shall have no difficulty in proving the case we have
been arguing, for in them we can see how he eliminates the
historical element in a way which abundantly justifies our
suspicions. Cross and resurrection are reduced to present
phenomena (I die and rise again with Christ, p. 36f.). We might
almost add that this happens in moments of illumination, when
we understand the meaning of human existence. As events,
these things—viz., dying and rising again with Christ—certainly
have their place in the New Testament message, especially as
presented by St Paul, but only in the sense that we bring our
existence into relation with what happened once for all in the
history of A.D. 1–30. Cross and resurrection become present

realities only in Kierkegaard's sense of contemporaneity. It is this contemporaneity that makes them events in time. It is in this sense that the Logos enters into the time-scheme of the *sarx*.

Once again we ask how Bultmann can still hold fast to the idea that redemption is an event in time, if he makes salvation history evaporate into this questionable "present" of his. Once more he would seem to be unable to do so. Contemporaneity is once more a timeless, abstract truth within my self-understanding.

His discussion of the cross and resurrection looks like a tragic wrestling with this terrible consequence. The narratives of the New Testament become ghostly figures which haunt us in the twilight between "being" and "validity", between reality and the bare data of consciousness. The question how all this is to be put across to the man in the pew need not detain us here, for it is scarcely relevant for the moment, though one cannot help wondering.

It is then the task of New Testament scholarship to continue the discussion by concentrating on specific points of exegesis. At all events, let no one run away with the idea that he has finished with Bultmann. That would be entirely wrong. Bultmann's challenge is not to be dealt with so summarily, even by the simplest, most practical-minded parish priest. The fundamental problem posed by demythologizing is, What elements in the New Testament revelation are temporary and what are eternal, what are "human" and what are "divine"? Obviously it is imperative to know where exactly the line of demarcation lies at many points. We are as sure of that as we are that temporal myths and views surround the core of the gospel message.

This line of demarcation, however, is clearly not one of principle. The distinction between the human and the divine is not absolute. For after all the miracle of the incarnation asserts that God has broken down the barrier between them and has established communication with man. He has thrown a bridge over the chasm and removed the cherubim out of the way. "He was found in fashion as man", and: "He was tempted like as we are."

We conclude this first half of our discussion with a rhetorical question. It is rhetorical, because the answer is already implied in the question, and it is a question because it opens up a wide field of problems which demand further exploration.

Does not every attempt at demythologizing, seeking as it does to probe the dividing-line between the eternal and the temporary, the divine and the human, come up against a barrier which has been put there by God, and beyond which it dare not ask any more questions? This barrier is the mystery of the God-man. It is no accident that Bultmann regards this God-man as the product of a myth (p. 3f.). For him therefore the barrier is non-existent. That means that in the last resort he does not really take seriously the assertion that the Logos *sarx egeneto*. The innermost point of Bultmann's work appears to me to be a latent but irremediable "crisis" of the fact of Christ.

B. THE PERMANENT PROBLEM OF THE MYTHOLOGICAL FORM OF SPEECH AND THE ATTEMPT TO SOLVE IT

I Mythology as a Form of Thought

We have approached the problem of demythologizing so far on the assumption that there is a real distinction between the form of the New Testament narratives, a form conditioned by the contemporary mythology, and the actual content which the form enshrines.

Our case against Bultmann is not that he makes this distinction, but the method and principles he uses to carry it out. For the criterion he uses to distinguish between myth and reality is the "self-understanding" of the men of the Bible. The unintended result is that the kerygma is disintegrated into a philosophy. The historical reality of the truth is made relative, true only for a particular age.[1]

[1] If I understand it aright, the HBK memorandum criticizes Bultmann on similar grounds. Our identification with the death of Christ, it maintains, is not merely a present event, but a present event controlled by a real event of the past—i.e. the dying of Christ: "Bultmann takes over from Heidegger the concept of existence, and uses it to describe the stripping away of illusions and the consequent entry into the authentic human existence. But as far as the historical Christ is concerned, it means no more than the readiness to be

Bultmann's essay, and indeed the whole problem of demythologizing, must now be put to the test from a further angle. What we have to ask is whether the New Testament narratives are affected by mythology less in their objective aspect than in our subjective way of apprehending and describing religious truth. Or, to put it another way, is not mythology an essential element in human thought, and is it not therefore just as valid an approach to reality as, e.g. that of natural science?

It is the particular merit of the HBK memorandum that it has brought this aspect of the problem to the fore, and its very one-sidedness is all to the good. With a stroke of the pen demythologizing has ceased to be an historical problem and has become one of epistemology. It is removed, so to speak, from the sphere of the object to that of the subject. The question is then not whether the New Testament can be emancipated from mythology, but whether human thought can.

This is a veritable Copernican revolution. It is on a level with Kant's discovery that space, time, and causation are not objective categories but a mode of subjective human apprehension. Mythology would then be that form of human apprehension which is peculiarly fitted to deal with religious truth.

All this would mean that mythology could not be dissolved by scientific thinking or the scientific world view. The truth of mythology would still hold good despite all the changes in culture and philosophy, just as the human personality remains the same despite all the changes and chances of human life.

When we remember that Bultmann's starting-point is the tension between mythology and science, it would seem here that we have an entirely new solution to the problem. Both mythology and science are legitimate approaches to the truth. There is no question of the one becoming outmoded by the other in the process of historical development. The two approaches are complementary. "If this be true, mythology, while it would not be the sole approach to truth, would nevertheless be the sole approach to supra-sensual reality, the only way of describing the inner side of things" (HBK). This means that "mythology has

_____

conformed with the death of Christ. But this would be meaningless if the significance of the death of Christ rested only on the interpretation placed upon it by the disciples and were not even in the life of Jesus related as an act to his resurrection" (op. cit., p. 21f.).

a profounder dimension which is beyond the reach of science, since it is concerned with the underlying significance of things and events."[1]

The best presentation of this idea that mythology is the only adequate expression of religious truth is to my mind that of Bachofen. He says: "The symbol [i.e. mythological symbolism] awakens intuition where the language of abstraction can only offer rational explanation. The symbol addresses every side of the human spirit, whereas the language of abstraction is bound to confine itself to a single thought. The symbol strikes a chord in the very depths of the soul, whereas the language of abstraction touches only the surface of the mind like a passing breeze. The one is directed inwards, the other outwards. Only the symbol can combine a wide variety of notions into a single total impression; the language of abstraction, on the other hand, arranges them in succession and presents them to the mind piecemeal, whereas they ought to be presented to the soul at a single glance. Words reduce the infinite to finitude, symbols lead the spirit beyond the bounds of the finite into the infinite world of abiding truth."[2]

It seems to me that these words of Bachofen clarify the purport of the HBK memorandum. Whenever mythology is translated into scientific and rational terms there is an inevitable loss of meaning and consequent superficiality, which shows the inadequacy of the scientific approach to this kind of truth. And if such is the case, then Bultmann's demand that we should replace the mythical view of the world by a scientific one falls to the ground.

It will at once be asked whether the mythical description possesses any objective reality. What lies behind it—an emotion, an existential experience, or an historical revelation? How is justice to be done to the theological concern which lifts the revelation behind the mythology out of the general history of

---

[1] On the relation between mythology, philosophy, and science, cf. J. J. Bachofen, *Der Mythos von Orient und Okzident*, Munich, 1926; Leopold Ziegler, *Ueberlieferung*, Leipzig, 1940; Georg Koepgen, *Die Gnosis des Christentums*, Leipzig, 1940.

[2] Cf. also Alfred Baeumler, "Bachofen, the mythologist of Romanticism", in the work of Bachofen quoted above, p. xc: "Those who are blind to the depths of mythology had better abandon it altogether."

religion? What, for instance, is the difference between the resurrection narratives and the Dionysus myth? The very fact that mythology is only a form makes it even more imperative to establish the qualitative difference between revelation and religion.

This cardinal problem is ignored by the HBK memorandum. Perhaps this is because it limits itself to discussing the points raised by Bultmann, and because its author has not yet realized the immense amount of work which remains to be done even after Bultmann's arguments have been disposed of. This further work concerns the relation between theology and myth in general, and the very different subject matter which myth describes.

The difference between the Biblical and non-Biblical conceptions of myth is indeed implicitly recognized by HBK, for it quotes Alfred Jeremias's definition of Biblical myth: "Myth in the narrower sense . . . is one of the supreme creations of the human spirit. It is the narration of a heavenly process, presented in a definite logical series of motifs reflected symbolically in objective events." Here is an explicit allusion to a "heavenly process" as the real foundation and background of the mythical narrative. This real foundation affects mythological thought rather in the way that Kant's *Ding an sich* affects our capacity for apprehension with its categorical determination. To put it epigrammatically, myth is not the objectivizing of a spook-like experience, but the subjectivizing—the intellectual appropriation —of an objective event of salvation. Here we have the exact equivalent of Jeremias's heavenly process. Myth therefore employs subjective means derived from the human imagination to describe a reality which utterly transcends consciousness, and which possesses an objective validity in its own right, quite apart from its effects on the disciples and witnesses.

Bultmann's conception of myth leaves no room for this transcendental element. This is just the criticism which the HBK memorandum levels against Bultmann, especially in connection with the resurrection narratives. These narratives, for all their mythological colouring, do postulate a real event between God and Christ in a sphere beyond all subjectivity and by no means limited to a more or less spiritual process between God and the disciples. "Bultmann assumes a process between God in Christ on the one hand, and the disciples on the other, but not a process between God and Christ. Yet the one really conditions the other. Hence there is a gap which is only closed by the resurrection of Christ'' (HBK).

The HBK memorandum has thus carried the discussion one important step further than Bultmann. Yet it is to be noted that there can be no theological attitude to the problem of myth which does not take account of what Bultmann says on the subject. Hence we also think it right to advance beyond the criticisms raised by the HBK memorandum and raise a few positive questions for the further discussion of the problem. We shall also try to show the direction the answer may eventually take. But since this is a gigantic task which will demand the co-operation of many theologians, all we can do is to throw out a few suggestions. But those suggestions must be hazarded, if this discussion which has proved so promising hitherto is to be carried further.

II *Important New Tasks in Connection with the Problem of Myth*

It can hardly be disputed that mythology is to be sought not only in its effects in history, but above all in the way men think. It therefore exists in its own right.

Moreover, since mythology is essential to the human mind, there must be a kernel of event behind the mythological façade, or at least there may be. Myth and history are not *a priori* antitheses.

Finally, this means that myth is not to be eliminated, but interpreted. Thus far we agree with Bultmann. But the question is, how is it to be interpreted? Does myth express a timeless philosophy of human life, or is it a real event of salvation history (e.g. the event of the ressurection), an event to which faith knows itself to be related, and to which it bears witness in the language of mythology? We agree with HBK that the second alternative is the right one, for only that can prevent the kerygma from disintegrating into philosophy. All the same, the relation between myth and history requires further consideration.

(a) *The Varieties of Myths*

1. There are myths which contain transcendental truth, and which are therefore absolutely indispensable. Such, for instance, are the myths of the creation, the fall, etc. These are to be dis-

tinguished from legendary embroidery or mythological ballast derived from other religions outside the Bible.

2. There are myths which are pictorial explanations of certain facts in history. The Virgin birth is an example of this sort of myth. It is, as Schlatter has observed, the symbol of the historical fact that Jesus was the Son of God. These myths must be distinguished from straightforward historical narratives, which, though they appear to be mythical, are to be taken as literal history. Many of the miracles belong to this class, and so do the resurrection narratives (though the latter do not fall clearly into one class—what about the empty tomb? To which class does it belong?). When we come down to detail the classification is often uncertain, and there will never be un-animity about the point where the line is to be drawn. But that does not mean that we must give up the attempt trying to draw it.

(b) Translation into a Myth Compatible with the Modern World View?

So far during the discussion it has been generally assumed that mythological thought springs from a particular view of the world. Though mythology is in itself timeless, yet the actual imagery it employs is undoubtedly conditioned by the world view current at the time. The question is therefore whether it is not necessary to discover a new mythical expression for the Biblical truths, an expression which will take account of the change which has come about in our view of the universe. It seems to us imperative that we should hold our ground in face of this question. There would seem to be a great deal in favour of it: if there is to be no demythologizing, let us at least have remythologizing! All the more so since, *pace* Bultmann, whose view of the matter is all too academic, our age is not one of enlightenment. So far from accepting enlightenment as an ideal, it is consciously, and still more unconsciously, searching for a new myth. Would not the modern myths of spirit, existence, or blood, enable us to present the event of Good Friday in an entirely new light?

(c) No Conclusive answer Possible

We cannot avoid raising this question, but the moment it is asked it is seen to be rhetorical. It is so formidable that it defies solution, as we shall see.

1. What man would be bold enough to attempt to produce an authoritative reinterpretation of the whole of the Bible? (For nothing less would suffice.)

2. There are many myths in circulation in the modern world. Several new ones arise in every century, and they vary from country to country. But they have one thing in common. They all imply a monistic, immanentist conception of the universe. They leave no room for the element of transcendence. Their aim is rather to convey an understanding of the visible world around us.[1]

This raises a further question. The form of modern mythology, as we have seen, has the merit of being compatible with the modern world view. But what about its actual content? Can the content be detached from the form? For that content represents immanence as the ultimate truth about the universe. Is it not therefore inherently unsuitable as a vehicle for the Biblical kerygma? If we tried to use it as such a vehicle would not the Biblical material burst through the very form of the modern mythology?[2]

3. There is a third reason why the modern secular myth is a totally unsuitable vehicle for Biblical truth. That mythology is essentially the outcome of a revolt, the revolt of the "vital

---

[1] Although Schleiermacher does not use the term, the classical expression of this aspect of myth is to be found in his *Addresses on Religion*. His immanentism is apparent even in his definitions. Religion, e.g., is contemplation, feeling for the infinite, the universal, etc. His reinterpretation of revelation and miracle as a mode of contemplating the world as it is, is the logical outcome of his immanentism, and typical of the whole of secularized mythology. See especially the Second Address, *On the Nature of Religion*.

[2] Again, this can be illustrated by a comparison of Schleiermacher's *Addresses* with his *Christian Faith*. The *Christian Faith* is an attempt to find a rational basis for the affirmations of Christianity, and it leads him progressively to abandon the mythological form of the *Addresses*. In the *Christian Faith* Schleiermacher's original presuppositions are blown sky-high, and the resultant debris is extremely difficult to survey. Hence the classical controversy as to which is the real Schleiermacher, the Schleiermacher of the *Addresses*, or the Schleiermacher of the *Christian Faith*. This is a barren controversy. The *Christian Faith* is the self-destruction of Schleiermacher's original mythological presuppositions. That is the immediate, unintended but inevitable result of his attempt to fit the Christian dogmas into his original mythological system. This is the clue to the understanding of the structure of Schleiermacher's thought. It is not a matter of a change in Schleiermacher's personal convictions. It is the inexorable consequence of the material with which he is dealing.

gods'', or, to quote idealism, the revolt of "the wisdom of the world". Even the terminology of the modern myths must make an act of repentance if it is to become a suitable vehicle for the kerygma. Now, this is exactly what happened to the concept of the Logos, and this is what made that term acceptable for the Fourth Gospel. But such an act of repentance is impossible for the secular myths. It would involve their self-destruction, as we have seen in the case of Schleiermacher. This is particularly the case with a myth which, with all its other disadvantages is outspokenly pragmatist and propagandist in character, and which ignores the question of truth to such an extent that it no longer exists even in untruth, but in a chilly no-man's-land between God and the devil. It is utterly inconceivable that Biblical imagery should be forced into such a strait-jacket as this. Where this has happened—e.g. in certain modern movements such as German Christianity—the Christian content does not even burst the strait-jacket, but becomes itself demonic.

Our first conclusion, then, is a negative one, and it must be kept in mind throughout the subsequent discussion.

1. It is impossible to translate the Biblical mythology and its associated world view into the language of contemporary myth. In other words, it is impossible to substitute one mythological framework for another.

2. It is impossible to remove the mythology, as Bultmann tries to. In other words, it is impossible to substitute the world view of modern science for the Biblical mythology by what he calls "interpretation". This is because it involves the substitution of an abstract philosophy of existence for a kerygma rooted in history. We seem to be landed in what looks at first sight like an insoluble dilemma; some would call it a state of bankruptcy. There appears to be no way of modernizing Christianity or of making it relevant to the modern world: it is definitely out of date. This *impasse* is not to be evaded or made light of, so let us describe it as brutally as we can.

First, there can be no question of getting behind the mythological form of the kerygma by extracting a non-mythical kernel of truth.

Secondly, we must on the other hand not only take the mythology as it stands (that would be possible, since it is the expression of a permanent mode of thought); we must also take the temporal limitations of the mythology as they stand. We must in contrast to the HBK memorandum assert this dilemma as frankly as we can. And this is where our difficulties really begin. The Church could not afford to ignore the problem of myth. But in facing it she appears to have stirred up a hornet's nest. She believed that this controversy would set her hands free to use her weapons, but now it seems that she has been disarmed by myth itself.

We seek to advance further by asking two questions. First, what is the real meaning of this indisputable dilemma? May there not be a theological reason for it? Secondly, what are the tasks which result from this dilemma?

(d) The Theological Meaning of this Difficulty and the Task it presents.

On 1: Of the Meaning of the Dilemma.

(α) The incarnation meant that Jesus entered into time and space, that he became our brother and comrade,[1] and in so doing exposed himself to the *notitia*[2] of our capacity to apprehend him. This meant that he entered into the particular form in which our powers of apprehension express themselves—i.e. by mythology.

We shall of course have to sketch a distinctively Biblical concept of myth, which is as far removed from a general religious experience of existence[3] as it is from the pragmatism of the secular myth. The pragmatism which characterizes the latter often appears in perilous association with the Christian kerygma, as for instance when it is maintained that for the great majority of mankind the myth must be upheld in its literal concrete form, whether it be true or not, or that the tradition of the Church must be maintained at all costs. Here as always, only the truth will make us free. Any naïve or artificial attempt to bolster up

---

[1] Phil. 2. 7; Rom. 8. 3.

[2] *Notitia* is a term used in dogmatics. It is to be distinguished from *assensus*, and expresses the fact that the earthly manifestation of the Lord is both revelation and concealment. Every manifestation of the Son of Man in time and space is presented to my *notitia* in such a way that he may nevertheless remain concealed: It is then impossible to make the assent of Thomas: "My Lord and my God" (John 20. 29). Despite the *notitia* he is not recognized for what he is.

[3] Cf. e.g. Walter F. Otto, *Die Götter Griechenlands*, Frankfort, 1934.

the Church is bound to reap its own reward. It will leave the Church a prisoner, disarmed and discredited.[1]

The task of theology is rather to work out an interpretation of any given myth which will express the history which lies behind it. Such an interpretation will be distinct from the timeless abstraction of the bare symbol and from the cyclical view of time which characterizes pagan mythology. It may be asked whether myth thus interpreted could be described as myth in any intelligible sense at all, or whether it would not be better to speak with Oscar Cullmann[2] of "prophecy".

There are certain distinctions to be drawn in this connection, and this will prove a difficult and intricate task. For the theologian will never be able to interpret the pagan myths in the same way as the pagan historian of religion does. He can never regard them as pictorial symbols of general truths, existential experiences or emotions. He is bound to see in them a real history between God and man. Not that such a history is the subject or the background of the myth. What I mean is that the creation of the myth is itself the expression of such a history. Here as often Rom. 1. 18ff. provides the classical exposition of the kind of history to which I refer. Behind the portrayal of the gods as crawling, flying, and fourfooted beasts, and behind the more anthropomorphic pictures of the gods, there is concealed a real history between God and man. They represent man's attempt to evade God and to crowd him out of life. Man shows by this a quite definite concern as to what God shall be and what he shall not be. The pagan myth is not so much the expression of a history between God and man as its actual accomplishment. This is true even when it cannot be established so easily and succinctly as is done in Rom. 1. We have here a programme for a theological treatment of comparative religion. The pagan myths may not be the expression of truth (though even this must be only a provisional assertion), but they are certainly an expression of an attitude to the truth, and thus of a real history between God and man. In its mythology a people registers and betrays its relation to the truth.[3]

[1] I am thinking here of such things as Hellbardt's incredible exegesis.
[2] *Christ and Time*, Eng. trans., S.C.M. Press, 1950, p. 94ff.
[3] On the subject of a theological interpretation of comparative religion see further Eckart Peterich, *Theologie der Hellenen*, Leipzig, 1938, esp. p. 21ff.

(β) Mythological thought must be honoured as the crib in which the Lord chose to lie. In this respect it is like the mind of man, which, no less than the body, is the temple of the Holy Ghost (1 Cor. 6. 19), and which is called to think the thoughts of God's revelation after him. Human reason is only a crib, fashioned from the same wood as the cross. Just as human reason may become a whore, so the mythological expression of the truth may become idolatry, and both may lead to the rejection of Christ. But this does not prove that either are not cribs for Christ, and indeed this paradox represents a fundamental theological insight.

How this idea of the crib is to be conceived may be illustrated from the history of the idea of the Logos before it was taken up by the New Testament. It was the destiny of this idea to be used as a vehicle for expressing the fact of the incarnation, and to be such a crib. On this subject the French Thomist Jacques Maritain says in La Philosophie chrétienne (1933): "In order to . . . make the essential supra-philosophical conception of the Logos of one substance with the Father (verbum consubstantiale patri) accessible to mankind, so that it might eventually bear fruit, it was necessary—and this necessity arises from direction in which Christianity itself looks—for a preparatory process in the realm of terminology. This preparation took the form of a long period of meditation on the part of the philosophers on the idea of the Logos."[1] Thus the speculation and the mythology which grew up around the Logos, or rather the insight into the truth which these represent, is taken up and used by revelation as a vehicle, however inadequate, for the event of revelation. In other words, the Logos was destined to become a "crib". It is inadequate, because it is a temporal concept, and the truth which it has to express is a transcendent one. The metaphor of the crib calls attention to this inadequacy, which is further shown by the act of repentance which the Logos concept had to perform, and by the change it underwent when it was taken up by the Child in the crib.[2]

---

[1] Op. cit., German Ed., 1935, p. 69.

[2] It is obvious why Catholic philosophy of religion in particular should take this line. Cf. also E. Peterich, op. cit., p. 179ff. Theodor Haecker, Was ist der Mensch, 1st ed. 1933, p. 28f.

2. *The Positive Meaning of the Temporal Limitation of New Testament Mythology.*

All this has an important bearing on the temporal limitation of the New Testament mythology. This temporal limitation is a hard nut, for the world view which provides the mythological framework of the Biblical narratives cannot be corrected or translated into a modern mythology.

Is there any underlying reason for this temporal limitation, this "antiquarian" character of the Biblical mythology?

Let us first ask why it was that the revelation of God employed the contemporary symbol of the Logos and its associated world view rather than any of our modern "isms"? (We could of course select other symbols, besides that of the Logos). Perhaps it was because the Logos and its associated world view were exceptionally fitted to become vehicles for the revelation of God. At all events, there is no reason why God should not have delayed his purpose for the world until a perfect world view had been developed, and until he could avail himself of the discoveries of Copernicus and Einstein! When St Paul speaks of "the fullness of time", does he refer to salvation history in the narrower sense, to that section of world history which is confined to Israel and the Jews? Or could it be extended to include Greek and Hellenistic thought as a wider preparation for the incarnation, as Maritain suggests? Catholic theology is particularly fond of the idea of "contact" owing to its doctrine of the *analogia entis*, and for that reason it has repeatedly worked out the idea of what Lessing in another connection called "the local and temporal accommodation" of the Logos. Catholic theology can teach us something here. Its suggestions still hold good, even if we cannot agree with the hypothesis of the *analogia entis*, however attractive it may be in this particular connection, and even if we cannot accept the view that the movement from *praeparatio evangelica* in classical thought via the Logos to the Christian revelation is an unbroken line from nature to grace. Despite these reservations, we are ready at this point to pay serious attention to what these Catholic thinkers are saying. Here we come up against the question not only of the positive significance of myth in general, but also of the positive significance of the particular mythology current in New Testament times, with its particular temporal limitations. May it not be that this temporal limitation is something more than an incumbrance upon the gospel to be swallowed as it stands? May it not be that it possesses a positive meaning within the kerygma? May we not go so far as to say that the contemporary myth of New Testament times, with its three-storied universe of heaven, earth, and hell, left open the door for the idea of transcendence? This is what made it peculiarly fitted to express the otherness of God and his intervention in salvation history. For this myth does not assume that the universe is a self-subsistent, finite entity, as does the secular myth. It is for this reason that the secular myth cannot become the vehicle of Biblical truth without disintegrating it.

Does this not, however, mean that the Biblical revelation could be apprehended only because men accepted an erroneous world view which has now been outmoded? Does it not mean that with the change in our world view the Bible itself has become an anachronism? Have we then any cause to rejoice that the old world view left open the door for the idea of transcendence? How can that help us if that world view is now proved to be wrong?

Is then this idea of a self-subsistent, finite universe which has disintegrated the old myth a fate which we must in all honesty submit to?

It is just when we refuse to spare ourselves any intellectual difficulty and any possible objection that we are obliged to make the following points:

It is simply untrue that, as even Bultmann appears to suppose, the idea of a self-subsistent, finite universe is accepted as axiomatic in the modern world. And therefore the modern world view is not necessarily in conflict with the old myth. That idea is no more than working hypothesis in the field of natural science. It is, for instance, necessary in physics to assume the law of the conservation of energy, and that assumption rests upon another—viz., that nature is a closed reservoir of power. When we speak of the self-subsistent finitude of the secular myth we mean something very different from that working hypothesis which, since it is no more than a hypothesis, does at least theoretically leave open the door for the idea of transcendence. We are referring to the step from a working hypothesis as a handmaid of research to an affirmation of faith. This

introduces an entirely new element, which completely transcends natural science, as can be seen, for instance, from the fact
that the affirmations of natural science are intrinsically trans-
subjective in character—that is to say, they are entirely independent of man's subjective understanding of himself. It was to
bring out this difference that the distinction was drawn between
Weltbild and *Weltanschauung*, the former representing a trans-
subjective, scientific fact, and the latter man's subjective
interpretation of himself, an interpretation which is quite
independent of the *Weltbild*.

As soon, however, as the working hypothesis becomes an
affirmation of faith it dominates both man's understanding of
himself and his subjective decisions. Hence we immediately
get immanentist ethics, *Weltanschauung*, religion, philosophy of
history, and so forth.

The proposition of self-subsistent finitude is thus one of
mythology, not of science.

This distinction between the scientific world view and its
extension as a mythological *Weltanschauung* would, logically,
apply to the classical mythology also. And if this be so, we should
be right in saying that both the mythology and the understanding
of human life which it enshrines are not automatically outmoded
with the world view on which they rest. The interpretation of
the universe and man of which it is the record may still claim
to be true. The fact that Aeschylus believed in the Delphic
oracle and we do not does not make the tragic view of life any
less true; it simply compels us to discuss its claim to truth.
Nor is it an accident that there are to-day intelligent people like
Walter F. Otto, who seriously believe in the Greek gods.
They are not at all embarrassed that Hölderlin shared that belief!
But this does not mean that they have abandoned the modern
world view for that of classical antiquity. If they were asked they
would probably admit that there was a special affinity between
the classical world view and Greek religion or the tragic view
of life, whereas the modern world view is so contaminated and
corrupted by idolatry that it cannot provide a basis for the Greek
view of life.

To sum up:

The classical world view leaves open the door for the idea of
transcendence. It is therefore a peculiarly suitable vehicle for

the presentation of the Biblical history of the kingdom of God. We may admit this without the wistful feeling that only classical man could honestly believe in the Gospel, and that we are debarred from accepting it because of the change in our world view. It is not the modern world view which makes Christianity hard to believe, but the *Weltanschauung* of self-subsistent finitude, which, though connected with that world view, does not follow from it. The very naïveté of the classical mythology, on the other hand, which provided the environment for the New Testament, expresses that openness for the idea of transcendence. Our modern world view also does so in theory, but not so naïvely, and only in a highly distorted and obscure way. That is why the classical world view provided the classical "realm of terminology" which served as a seed-bed for revelation. It is as though God chose the psychological moment. For all the differences between Christianity and humanism in the widest sense of the word,[1] we shall have to admit that there is a permanent affinity between them, an affinity which is fundamentally still unimpaired. Every discussion about the "point of contact", about the historical and supra-historical elements in Christianity, about apotheosis and incarnation, has always revolved around this relation between Christianity and classical humanism. Other brands of humanism, such as Enlightenment, scientific humanism, and the various political movements, have proved by contrast ephemeral.

Once more, however, we must stress that there is no unbroken line from the contemporary mythology and philosophy to the New Testament. The Biblical gospel has burst the bonds even of classical mythology, as may be seen from what happened to the idea of the Logos; but it has done so only by first taking that mythology up and using it.

The secular myth, on the other hand, stands so helpless and insensitive before this connection that it interprets it in the opposite way from which it seeks to be interpreted. Even Bultmann cannot be excused of this in many of the more secularized parts of his thought. Wherever in the Christian message a transcendent irruption is all too obvious—i.e. in the miracles—this is attributed to the mythical world view, instead of the

---

[1] I use the word "Christianity" because it is traditional, though I am aware of its vagueness and false associations.

mythical world view being esteemed a particularly suitable vehicle for the expression of certain traits in the revelation.

As we have seen, the mythological element cannot be translated either into a scientific world view or into the modern myth. But the ineradicable temporal limitation is really only a preliminary dilemma, and beneath it is concealed a deeper meaning of salvation history—namely, the attainment of the "fullness of time" in the realm of terminology and myths.

3. Our Response to the Dilemma.

We conclude with the consequences which the mythological setting of the kerygma, as we have described it, will have for our preaching. All we need do, however, is to summarize the results attained so far:

(γ) The mythological element in the kerygma is not, we have shown, the importation into the New Testament of ideas from non-Biblical religions, ideas which could be eliminated or superseded by interpreting the underlying understanding of human life. Rather, the mythological elements represent a permanent aspect of human thinking. If this be true, then it is of the utmost consequence for our preaching to lay bare the background of truth which lies concealed beneath the outer crust of myth. A model of such treatment is to be found in Schlatter's well-known discussion of the Virgin birth, which is also quoted by the HBK memorandum. "The assertion that the Spirit of God created Jesus has an assured basis, even when we recognize the large share which Christian poetic fancy played in interpreting the birth of Jesus" (Christliche Dogma, p. 332). In other words, Schlatter interprets the dogma of the Virgin birth not in the light of its "religious idea"—e.g. as an expression of the overwhelming impact of the personality of Jesus on his contemporaries—but in the light of its background in history and fact. The Virgin birth asserts that the being of Jesus is wholly different from ours: he is from above, we are from beneath. This difference is not one of ideal status, but of real qualitative being. Our chief aim in preaching must be to expose the meaning for redemptive history in all the narratives of the New Testament which are written from a mythological point of view.

(δ) As we saw from the quotation from Bachofen, mythical

symbolism differs from other forms of speech in that it offers an all-embracing view of its object. Now, the object of preaching is to make the gospel message relevant to the individual. It must stress the *hic et nunc*, the *tua res agitur*. In connection with mythology, therefore, our preaching must particularize the all-embracing view for the hearer in his concrete situation. This may be illustrated from the myth of the Fall. As Bachofen's definition suggests, that myth conceals an all-embracing view of the reality we call sin. In our preaching our aim must be to particularize this all-embracing view as the text or the special needs of the hearer demand. Our sermon may concentrate on the whole of mankind and its historical development, or on the particular history of the individual, or even each specific instance of sin—*peccatum actuale*. The text may be used to elucidate the nature of the demonic, of the law, of human responsibility, and so forth. Every conceivable aspect of the reality of sin, which could be made explicit only in an infinite series of theses and experiences, is implicit in the symbolism of the myth of the Fall. It contains both universal history and individual biography; such a combination would be impossible in any form of non-mythological thought. The preacher's task is to split up this combination into non-mythological language, and to place before his hearers whichever aspect is most relevant to their concrete situation.

(ε) In our preaching we must observe the distinction between the various types of myth. These distinctions were noted above (under B II a) and they need only be recapitulated here:

There are myths which are indispensable vehicles for the transcendental realities, and others which are legendary embroidery or accretions from non-Biblical religions. Then there are myths which are pictorial clarifications of some historical fact, and others which are straightforward historical reports, which despite their apparently mythological form are to be regarded as directly historical.

This represents a considerable advance on the terms within which Bultmann has discussed the problem. If we understand him aright, the most remarkable fact about his thesis is that it cannot remain stationary. Either it must advance in the direction of Kamlah, and cease in the end to be Christian, or there must be radical examination of the whole problem of myth from within the Church. By such an examination the Church may finally win a new freedom in the truth (John 8. 36). We began by saying that Bultmann has thrown down a serious challenge to the very foundations of the Church, and our investigations have substantiated this contention. Clearly we must risk the dangers of such an undertaking, even the danger of stirring up the ghosts of heresy.[1] We therefore owe a debt of gratitude to Bultmann.

In examining Bultmann's thesis and his personal orthodoxy[2] care should be maintained to avoid anything like a heresy hunt. This is pioneer work, and there are bound to be casualties on the way. The Church should rather keep in view Bultmann's ultimate objective, which is to secure a firm basis for her own proclamation. He is concerned with the kerygma. We are justified not by the way we travel, but by the Lord to whom we look.

How far can the theologian go without incurring the penalty of excommunication for unorthodoxy? The criterion is never, or very rarely, whether we are travelling on the same road, but whether, as we travel along our different roads, we all look towards the same goal. It is not the road which determines our communion with the Church, but our direction, not the steps we tread, but the end on which our eyes are fixed.

[1] E.g. the dissolution of the historical basis of the kerygma, or the separation of the historical objective genitive, "of Jesus Christ", from the *sola fide*.

[2] As has already been done in various official memoranda, sometimes with very negative conclusions.

FRIEDRICH K. SCHUMANN

CAN THE EVENT OF JESUS CHRIST BE DEMYTHOLOGIZED?

NO subject has caused such a stir in theological circles in recent years as the debate on "New Testament and Mythology". For this subject is not only of immense practical importance; it also raises the most ultimate and profound issues for the academic theologian.

The debate began with Rudolf Bultmann's essay on *New Testament and Mythology*.[1] Let us first give a brief summary of Bultmann's argument. The problem, he says, is that the New Testament presents the events of our redemption in terms of the mythical world view of classical antiquity. This world view entered the New Testament *via* late Jewish apocalyptic and the Gnostic redemption myth and has profoundly affected it on every page. Its principal features are: a three-storied universe consisting of heaven, earth, and underworld; the intervention of natural and supernatural powers in human life; the dominion of evil spirits and Satan over that life and also over the external realm of nature; the imminent end in time of this present world-aeon. The gospel proclaims that "*now* is the time of the End here, for the Son of God has appeared on earth as a pre-existent cosmic being. His death brings deliverance from the bondage of sin and the power of Satan, his resurrection is the defeat of the power of death, his impending return will be the end of this aeon, and the inauguration of the kingdom of God, the judgement of this world and the perfection of the community of believers." All this is undeniably mythological, and Bultmann thinks it is senseless and impracticable to foist this mythical view of the world on modern man, whose thinking is "shaped for good or ill by modern science". If this principle is accepted, then the belief in good and evil spirits must be regarded as

[1] *Vide* p. 1ff.

obsolete, together with the New Testament miracles, at least in their traditional sense, the mythical eschatology with its doctrine of death as the punishment of sin, and the Church's doctrine of a vicarious atonement through the death of Jesus on the cross and the victory over death through his resurrection. Obviously, this involves a serious reduction of the substance of the gospel, and it is not surprising that Bultmann's essay has been widely regarded as a recrudescence of rationalistic liberalism and a further stage in the complete dissolution of the gospel. But this is certainly not Bultmann's intention. He has no desire to erect some modern view of the world as the norm to which the gospel must conform. On the contrary, he seeks to liberate the whole meaning of the gospel and to make it intelligible to modern man in all its fullness. That is why he deems it imperative to release the permanent truth of the gospel from its framework in an obsolete world view—in short, to "demythologize" it.

But this demythologizing is not to be accomplished by selecting certain features of the gospel and subtracting others, for "the world view of mythology must be accepted or rejected in its entirety". It can be done only by what he calls interpretation. This is where Bultmann parts company with the older liberals.[1] If however the New Testament can be emancipated from the world view of mythology only by interpretation, what is to be the source of that interpretation? Bultmann's answer is: Not from any contemporary religious or philosophical conviction derived from outside the gospel. That would be to set up some extraneous authority over the New Testament. No; the interpretation must be derived from the New Testament itself, from the aim which led it to select just these mythological elements. Now, the aim of the New Testament is to offer an existential understanding of the message of Christ. Indeed, the mythological view of the world has also in the last resort a similar existential purpose. The gospel of Jesus Christ is not the communication of factual truths or neutral information which may appeal to us or not. It is the communication of a decisive

---

[1] It should, however, be noted that in their attempt to restate the truth of the gospel rationalism and liberalism also had recourse to interpretation as well as subtraction. Interpretation does not necessarily exclude subtraction. But the crux of the matter is always: from what source is the interpretation derived? See above.

understanding of human existence. And, as Bultmann maintains, the mythological view of the world itself had, fundamentally, this same existential purpose. It too was not the communication of theoretical knowledge about the world, but an attempt to impress on man his personal situation in the universe and his relation to the powers that rule it. If the New Testament is to be interpreted in this sense, Bultmann contends, there is no danger of losing or forfeiting its essential truth. In fact, it is only by such an interpretation that the real meaning of the New Testament can be disclosed and made accessible for those who would otherwise find its mythological elements a stumbling block. (We may note here a point which will be taken up later. We seem to have here two different conceptions of myth used side by side without any attempt to reconcile them. First, we are told that the existential interpretation of the New Testament will cause that mythology to disappear, which seems to imply an antithesis between "mythological" and "existential". Later, myth itself apparently has an existential meaning, and therefore a legitimate place in the New Testament. In that case there would be no need to remove it, but only to pay due attention to the meaning of which it is the sign.)

The New Testament must therefore be interpreted according to the existential understanding of the gospel message: it must begin with the Christian understanding of human life which is disclosed by that message. Now, there are two sides to this understanding. Firstly, it deals with life apart from faith (though always it is disclosed only in the light of faith; cf. the well-known problem of Rom. 7). Life apart from faith is a life of anxiety and fear, of bondage to the past, to corruption, sin, and death. Secondly, it deals with life in faith. This is the true and authentic life of man, a life based on invisible and incalculable reality, a life in the "Spirit". Such a life is made possible by the grace of forgiveness, which brings deliverance from the past and freedom for the future. In short, it means "eschatological existence". Such an interpretation appears to have two advantages: first, it secures the essential truth of the New Testament message, and secondly it emancipates it from myth, and particularly from the eschatology of Jewish apocalyptic and Gnosticism.

Now, this raises a vital question. Is this Christian understanding of human life necessarily bound to the person of Jesus Christ, or can it be detached from him? In the second case, we should have not merely demythologizing, but the actual dissolution of the gospel of Jesus Christ. In the first case, we are bound at once to ask whether this connection with Jesus Christ is a "remnant of mythology". Bultmann has no doubt as far as the New Testament is concerned; there the Christian understanding of human life is inseparably linked to the person of Jesus. But what is the real truth of the matter? According to Bultmann, it would seem to be possible to arrive at an understanding of human life which is unconnected with Christ, and yet goes a certain distance in agreement with the Christian understanding of human life. This is apparently proved by the understanding of human Being as "Fallenness" (*Verfallensein*) in Heidegger and Kamlah.[1] But existentialism and Christianity part company when they come to the question as to how deliverance from this "fallenness" is to be achieved. For the Christian to be "fallen" means to be a prey to sin and death, and our deliverance from that plight is wrought by the death and resurrection of Christ. Evidently it is inseparably linked to the person of Jesus Christ. Does this link then mark the extreme limit of demythologizing? Is there a mythological remnant in the Christian message which must be left at all costs? The crucial question is therefore whether the event of Jesus Christ is itself amenable to demythologizing.

Now, as Bultmann maintains, this particular event is undoubtedly presented by the New Testament as a mythological event. But is that the only way in which it can be presented?— or, as Bultmann asks, "does the New Testament itself demand a restatement of the event of Jesus Christ in non-mythological terms? . . . Now, it is clear from the outset that the event of Christ is of a wholly different order from the cult-myths of Greek or Hellenistic religion. Jesus Christ is certainly presented as the Son of God, a pre-existent divine Being, and therefore to that extent a mythological figure. But he is also a concrete figure of history—Jesus of Nazareth. His life is more than a mythical event; it is a human life which ended in the tragedy of crucifixion. We have here a unique combination of history and myth." Thus the peculiarity of the New Testament is that it speaks in mythological language of an historical figure and of the history of

[1] *Christentum und Selbstbehauptung*, 1940.

that figure. When we ask whether this mythological language can be retained or translated into non-mythological language, we are inevitably confronted with the further question as to the *meaning* of the mythological language in this particular instance. Why is it necessary to transcend the language of history in this peculiar way? Bultmann's answer is this: "This ultimate meaning of the mythological language is that it is an attempt to express the meaning of the historical figure of Jesus . . . viz., what God is saying to each one of us through it." In other words, the mythological language tries to express the significance of Jesus for salvation history. The question is therefore whether this mythological language is the only possible vehicle for conveying the meaning of Jesus for salvation history, or whether the mythology can be surmounted and rendered superfluous without forfeiting the meaning it conveys. This question arises in its acutest form when we consider the proper language for the cross and resurrection of Jesus.

Certainly the "cross" designates an historical event. It is described as "mythological" when its significance—i.e. what at the profoundest level it effected—is portrayed in objective imagery: The pre-existent Son of God is delivered up to the death of the cross, and thereby atonement is wrought for the guilt of mankind, the righteousness of God satisfied and the curse of sin removed. Bultmann, however, contends that all this objective imagery has ceased to be tenable for us to-day. This is due not only to the change in our world view, but also to the intrinsic inadequacy of the mythological language as a medium of expressing the meaning of the cross. The right interpretation, he maintains, is one which raises the historical event to cosmic dimensions (one would have thought that this is just what the objective mythological presentation is trying to do!). "If we see in the cross the judgement of the world—the Kosmos—and the defeat of the rulers of this world (1 Cor. 2. 6ff.), the cross becomes the judgement of ourselves as fallen creatures enslaved to the powers of the 'world'. By giving up Jesus to be crucified, God has set up the cross for us. To believe in the cross of Christ does not mean to concern ourselves with a mythical process wrought outside of us and our world, or with an objective event turned by God to our advantage, but rather to make the cross of Christ our own, to undergo crucifixion with him." This can also be expressed in another way: the cross is to be regarded as the eschatological event; that is to say, it is not an event of the past to be looked back upon, but the eschatological event in and beyond time, for as far as its meaning—that is, its meaning for faith—is concerned, it is an ever-present reality.

But, we ask, what justification have we for attributing such a significance to this particular historical event? Does the historical event itself exhibit this significance? Or, as Bultmann puts it: "Is this significance discernible in the actual event of past history?" If not, then with what justification was that significance attributed to it in the first place? If yes, then the event must itself be more than just an event of past history: it must include within itself as an event of the past this meta-historical, existential significance, and it must be possible to extract that significance from the event itself. Bultmann, however, will not admit these alternatives, and feels obliged to adopt a peculiar way out of his own. He thinks it would certainly be true of "the first preachers" of the gospel. They certainly perceived the meta-historical significance of what they witnessed enacted in their sight and hearing. "For them, but only for them, the cross was a personal experience: it was the cross of one with whom they had lived in personal intercourse. . . . For us this personal connection cannot be reproduced. . . . For us the cross is an event of the past. We cannot recover it as an event in our own lives. All we know of it is derived from historical report." In other words, we should be thrown back upon past history with all its problems. "But", objects Bultmann, "this is not the way in which Jesus Christ is proclaimed to us. The meaning of the cross does not have to be disclosed from an historical reconstruction of his life. Rather, he is proclaimed as the crucified and risen." So in attempting to emancipate the cross from mythology we are thrown back to a similar question with regard to the resurrection.

Bultmann's remark about the inseparable unity of the cross and resurrection is in any case of the utmost practical importance. For in the traditional preaching of the Church that unity has rarely received its due. But it is obvious that it only adds to our difficulties in the present connection. For the resurrection "is not an event of past history" in the sense that the cross is. The cosmic significance of the cross cannot therefore be demonstrated by the resurrection *as an event of past history*. In what sense then do the cross and resurrection form an inseparable unity in which the cosmic, eschatological significance of the cross may be disclosed? The connection between them is not that the resurrection is a miraculous proof of the cosmic, eschatological significance of the cross. The unity between them is of a different order: they "form a single, indivisible 'cosmic' event which brings judgement to the world and opens up for men the possibility of authentic life." "The resurrection is not a mythological event adduced in order to prove the saving efficacy of the cross, but an article of faith just as much as the meaning of the cross itself. . . . Indeed, faith in the resurrection is really the same thing as faith in the saving efficacy of the cross." If that be so, the reference to the resurrection, for all its importance, does not tell us why redemptive significance should be attached to the cross. It does not tell us whether the cross bears that significance in its own right, or only in combination with the resurrection. For Bultmann, apparently, there can be only one answer: "because this is the way in which the cross is proclaimed". Because Christ crucified and risen encounters us only in the word of preaching, therefore faith in this word is "the only real Easter faith", just as this word itself is "part of the eschatological event".

Is our task of emancipating the New Testament complete with this interpretation? "Are there still any surviving traces of mythology?" In view of the very different nuances which Bultmann gives in the course of his essay to such terms as "myth" and "mythological", it is difficult to give any conclusive answer. Here is Bultmann's own answer: "There certainly are for those who regard all language about an act of God or of a decisive eschatological act as mythological." (We may add that if "mythological" means whatever cannot be reconciled with the modern scientific view of the world with its closed system of cause and effect, then an eschatological act of God is either no act at all or else it is mythical in the above sense of that word.) But, thinks Bultmann, that is not mythology in the traditional sense, not the kind of mythology which has become antiquated with the decay of the mythical world view. The difference is not quite clear, for Bultmann had originally defined the mythical world

view as one which left room for extra—and supramundane
interventions, in contrast to the modern world view which
postulates a rigid, closed system of cause and effect. There is
certainly no room in this modern world view for a unique
eschatological act as distinct from that creative action which
may be considered to be present in everything. For such a view
of the world an eschatological act of God can be regarded only
as mythical. What Bultmann means is that the difference between
the mythological language of the New Testament and ecclesiastical dogma on the one hand and his own interpretation on
the other is that the former presents us with a "miraculous,
supernatural event", whereas the right interpretation is one
which suggests "an historical event wrought out in time and
space". Whatever we make of this distinction, one thing is
certain: the idea of a single historical event in time and space
as the judgement pronounced by God over the historical process
in time and space and the radical transformation of its whole
constitution is inconceivable for those who accept the modern
world view, and it would be impossible to make such a notion
intelligible in the terms of such a view. So even Bultmann admits
that this idea must be accepted as the paradox of the New
Testament proclamation—i.e. the paradox "that the eschatological emissary of God is a concrete figure of a particular historical
past, and that his eschatological activity was wrought out in a
human fate, and that therefore it is an event whose eschatological
character does not admit of a secular proof". At the end of
this quotation we have perhaps the clearest indication of what
Bultmann means by the "demythologizing" which he believes
to have effected. "Mythology" in his sense of the word is precisely an attempt to furnish a "secular proof" of the eschatological significance of an event of past history by the use of objective
imagery. So in the last analysis "demythologizing" is for him
identical with the demonstration of the authentically paradoxical
character of the gospel.[1] If however we accept Bultmann's initial
definition of mythology as that which is incompatible with the
modern world view and its closed system of cause and effect,
the very idea of such a paradox would seem to be incurably

---

[1] Cf. the sentence right at the end: "It is just its immunity from proof
which secures the Christian proclamation against the charge of being mythological."

mythological, and the whole endeavour of "demythologizing" would seem, at any rate on this assumption, a questionable procedure. Yet it is just this paradoxical character of the gospel which Bultmann is so firmly resolved to uphold: "All these assertions are of course an 'offence' (σκάνδαλον), and the offence will not be removed by philosophical discussion, but only by faith and obedience. . . .The transcendence of God is not as in myth reduced to immanence. Instead, we have the paradox of a transcendent God present and active in history: 'The Word became flesh'."

It would have been well if those numerous critics who have taken offence at Bultmann's ideas had paid particular attention to the importance of these concluding sentences. Of course, it is in a way not surprising that at first sight much of this looks like a recrudescence of rationalistic liberalism. But the entirely different turn and interpretation Bultmann has given it ought not to have been overlooked. He is not trying to accommodate the gospel to a modern *Weltanschauung*, or to make that *Weltanschauung* a norm to which the gospel must conform. On the contrary, his express intention is to throw into relief the real meaning of the gospel in all its paradox, and so to protect it from those misinterpretations which so easily suggest themselves, but which for that very reason are particularly dangerous. Moreover, he seeks to do this in such a way as to serve the preacher's conscientiousness for truth and maintain the credibility of the gospel in all its seriousness for his hearers. And all this is certainly a legitimate task for theology, and one whose practical importance is not to be underestimated. It extends from the simple narration of the Christmas story with the star and the wise men and the angelic hymn right up to our preaching at Ascensiontide and Pentecost. And in all this the difficulties are not just those of theological debate; they are continually being raised by the ordinary church-goer, and even by children with their insistent inquiries ("What became of the star when it left the wise men? Where did Jesus go to when he ascended? Was it straight up to the third story at the top of the sky, or where was it?").

As theologians we ought not to make light of such questions from the mouths of babes and sucklings. It is just here that we are confronted with the—in the best sense of the word—simple desire for truth on the part of our hearers, and nothing is so damaging to the reputation of the theologian as when his utterances produce the effect of parrot-cries which have ceased to be relevant to the hearer's grasp of truth or reality, and therefore so utterly irrelevant to his daily life. We have therefore every reason to be grateful to Bultmann for opening up afresh a question which confronts every theologian as he pursues his vocation, but which in recent years has been unwarrantably deprived of its sting. Of course, we cannot take Bultmann's essay and the subsequent elucidations he has given so far (see p. 102ff.) as the last word on all the problems he has raised; they are too far-reaching and too complex for that. Moreover, the continuation of the debate in writing has been seriously hampered by the restrictions and delays of wartime. The most valuable contributions so far have been set down only in private correspondence, and have not as yet been published. Even in this place a thorough examination of Bultmann's thesis would greatly exceed the available space. We must therefore content ourselves by calling attention to a few points for further consideration. These will concern not so much the details of Bultmann's argument and his conclusions, as key problems of methodology.

1. Further discussion would seem to be needed on whether the Christian understanding of existence can be detached from the person and figure of Jesus. Bultmann is inclined to the judgement that there exists a substantial agreement between the Christian understanding and a philosophy of existence not orientated upon the event of Christ (Heidegger and others) on the negative side—i.e. the fallenness (*Verfallenheit*) of human life. At this point, therefore, it is arguable that the Christian understanding of existence is detachable from the event of Christ, and so it is only in connection with the overcoming of his fallenness that the question arises. I cannot convince myself that Bultmann is right. He has certainly succeeded in rebutting Thielicke's charge that by starting with the Christian understanding of existence he betrays a subjectivism akin to that of Schleiermacher. He has certainly proved that for him the only basis for a Christian interpretation of human life is in Jesus Christ. But surely this will also apply to the Christian understanding of fallenness. Surely this also is disclosed only in Jesus Christ,

and cannot therefore be identified with the results of a non-Christian analysis of existence. The meaning we attach to fallenness depends on how we answer the question: In relation to what or to whom is man fallen? Surely it is impossible to agree on a formal understanding of fallenness and to part company over the judgement in relation to what human life is fallen. On the contrary, it is on this question that the meaning we attach to fallenness depends. To be fallen to "nothingness" is quite different from being fallen to sin and guilt and being fallen under the wrath of God. It is simply impossible to agree on a formal understanding of human fallenness, and then to diverge, one side believing that human life is fallen to "nothingness", and the other that it is fallen under the wrath of God. The understanding of fallenness in the two cases is not identical.

2. It is clear that Bultmann's thought is orientated quite differently. His guiding conviction is that it is possible to have a formal analysis of human existence which can be detached from every "existential" attitude, from every actual disposition to one's own existence. This is certainly a widespread opinion, and has been from of old. On this view it is held to be possible to make a formal and general statement on the nature—e.g. of death, anxiety, or love—quite apart from one's personal existential attitude to one's own personal death, anxiety, or love. Now, it certainly cannot be denied that mutual discussion about such existential realities is possible between those who hold different existential attitudes, and that for practical purposes there can be provisional agreement on the use of such words as death, anxiety, or love as a basis for further discussion. But to my mind it is quite a different question whether an existentialist analysis can be achieved in complete detachment from the understanding of existence which is presupposed, accepted and applied. At least I am not convinced that such a result has ever been attained. In philosophy as it has long been understood the two things have gone together hand in hand, the analysis of the formal structure of life in the abstract and the making of personal decision in respect of one's own personal existence. Heidegger, for instance, certainly aims at working out a pure existentialist analysis, but in practice certain anterior existential decisions work themselves out all along the line, or at least they are suggested and are not far below the surface. If however such a pure,

formal analysis of existence were possible, it is hard to see how it could be applied without *ipso facto* becoming a norm. In other words, each man's understanding of what love means for him would depend upon his understanding of love in the abstract. Or, to take an example which is crucial for theology, our understanding of what our relation as men to God means for us would depend on our general understanding of man in the abstract. Indeed, it is abundantly clear from this particular example that a pure analysis of existence involves an anterior existential decision (viz., that it is possible to analyse the Being of man without taking into account his relation to God), and is determined throughout by this anterior decision. The results of an existentialist analysis would certainly be very different—or perhaps it would discover its own impossibility—if it set out with the conviction that not only does every man stand in a positive or negative relation to God, but his relation to God is constitutive of his Being. This is exactly what the Bible means when it asserts that man was created in the image of God, and what theology means by its doctrine of the *imago Dei*.

3. Finally, let us at least allude to a further question which at the present is of utmost importance both for our domestic discussion as theologians and also for the controversy between Christians and the opponents of Christianity, and which moreover is the dominant theme of Bultmann's essay. I refer to the meaning of the word "myth". This is of course such a complicated question that we cannot expect to do it justice here. All we can do is to suggest one particular line of thought which may help to elucidate it.

It was at first not easy to see in what sense Bultmann was using the word "myth", and what he really meant by "demythologizing". This ancient word (myth), which appears even in the New Testament (1 Tim. 1. 4; 4. 7; 2. Tim. 4. 4; Tit. 1. 14; 2 Pet. 1. 16), has been used in many different senses especially since the end of the eighteenth century, and thereby has acquired a direct or indirect importance for theology. For example, the French positivists (A. Comte) understood by mythological thought a primitive, pre-scientific interpretation of the universe. For speculative idealism myth was the unfolding of an Idea in an historical process involving persons and events (D. F. Strauss). For romanticism myth was an attempt to interpret the Symbol, which was considered to be by itself unutter-able, the wordless utterance about existence which preceded the myth (so especially J. J. Bachofen). Now Bultmann has come along with his own formula: Myth is "a mode of thought and speech which objectivizes the unworldly so as to make it worldly". What that means becomes clear only when the ques-tion is raised as to the impulse and intention behind this par-ticular mode of thought and speech. Here we are confronted by the problem of the relation between myth and science or scien-tific world view. Now, for Bultmann both myth and science spring from an ultimately existential impulse. In other words, they are both attempts to interpret human existence. Myth seeks to do this by interpreting and bringing influence to bear on encounters with the powers and forces which dominate human life. Science tries to do the same thing indirectly, by taking a detached view of the world in which man finds himself, to apprehend that world as a unity and thus to make it a tool for the use of man. Now, this gives us three possible relations between myth and science. (a) Man may regard his encounter with the powers which dominate his life—death, life, spirit, blood, and so forth—as the decisive factors in his life: science will then be an academic luxury devoid of any existential im-portance. (b) He may regard both the concrete encounter with these powers and the knowledge of the general constitution of the universe as the decisive factors in his life. In that case he will assign an equal importance both to science and to myth, and will attempt a synthesis between them. (c) Science may claim that its knowledge of the universe is such as to entitle it to be the sole and final arbiter of existence and its problems. In that case it must regard itself as able to supersede myth and must "de-mythologize" everything which requires to be taken seriously. The first of these possibilities—which even to-day is not without its representatives—is scarcely relevant for our theological problem. The second possibility will be taken seriously by those who cannot accept the suggestion that the laws of cause and effect and formal structures expressed in a series of concepts are the answer to the riddle of life and death. (Such people, for example, would hold that even the most accurate insight into man's physical and psychic constitution cannot tell us what life and death mean to us personally.) They will therefore maintain that there is existential truth which cannot be expressed in the language of discursive terminology, and which therefore requires an entirely different language, indirect and allusive, but such as cannot be supplanted or explained away. The third possibility will be favoured by those who make their own the anterior existential decision, which—as even Bultmann admits—was imported from Greek thought at the beginning of Western science, and on which that science is largely based even to-day— viz., the existential decision that the individual is no more than a specific instance of a general cosmic law and order which is capable of being expressed in a terminology which is at bottom quite simple and which is detachable from existence. On this view everything which claims to be meaningful and credible must be capable of being expressed in the language of this terminology. And where the influence of myth is still discernible, there is need for "demythologizing".

It does not appear to me that Bultmann favours this third possibility. He surely cannot believe that the ultimate decision about man depends on the possibility of classifying him in a general order of an abstract kind. After all, his aim is to interpret the *gospel*, and the gospel is not an analysis of the formal structure of human life and of the universe, but the proclamation of event and encounter: God is present in Jesus Christ. But in that case the language of proclamation can never be the language of scientific terminology. No mode of human speech hitherto discovered is fitted as it stands as a vehicle for the gospel, for the gospel is something which has never been expressed hitherto. If therefore the gospel is to be made intelligible, it must use a language such as men use when they speak of events with an ultimate existential and cosmic significance. Thus the New Testament—including it would seem even Jesus himself—seizes upon a language which may be called that of "mythology" as the best available means of expressing its subject-matter. It is true that in a certain sense this language presents "unworldly" truths objectively, as if they were "worldly" realities. But it must not be supposed that in adopting this imagery the New Testament does so naïvely, unconsciously or uncritically. It is always aware of the tension between the language used and the reality of which it is the medium. Even the language of Greek mythology—be it never so ancient—is not in the least bit primitive. It too is a language of a higher order, analogous to the language of lyric, which as a matter of fact grew out of it. It is highly indirect, allusive and indefinite as compared with the solid language of objective reality. It is always so to speak transcending itself: it always relies on the ability of the reader to read between the lines. The Greeks who saw the Eumenides of Aeschylus knew that it was not a play about a company of old wives, but they also knew that it was impossible for the playwright to deliver his message in a series of logical or ontological propositions. And on a higher level the same process is repeated in the Bible wherever it makes use of the imagery of mythology. The Bible is certainly aware of what it is doing. It knows that it must risk the impropriety if it is to point at all to the real subject in hand. When the seer in Rev. 19. 11 sees a man sitting on a white horse, he is fully aware that it was not literally a white horse as distinct from a black one. The New Testament is fully aware not only of the indirect character of the imagery it uses but also of the indirect use which it makes of that imagery. It uses that imagery, however, because it is the best available medium for conveying its message. To take an illustration which is particularly apt, as it does not involve any of the central problems of dogmatic theology, in Matt. 18. 10 Jesus says: "I say unto you that in heaven their angels do always behold the face of my Father which is in heaven." Now, he could not have said that in any other language without altering its whole meaning. To "demythologize" that saying by removing the angels would, so far from elucidating the meaning, destroy it completely.

Yet it is just here that we are confronted by an urgent task of theological interpretation, and it is certainly with this that Bultmann is really concerned. Since the language of myth is highly and consciously indirect, its indirect character may easily be overlooked. If it is, the mythological statements are not understood in the light of the meaning which they symbolize, but in the light of their original meaning, which in the end is itself completely misunderstood. The proclamation therefore must not be obscured by the mythological terminology which it employs and which is inseparable from it—and that, despite the modern world view, the whole basis of which has become questionable. But the meaning which this form of expression is intended to convey must be illuminated from the central point of the proclamation, not by disregarding these forms of expression but, if I may be pardoned the metaphor, in continuous dialogue with it. Without such a dialogue, which is the proper task of theological exegesis, the Christian proclamation would inevitably degenerate on the lips of men, as in fact it has degenerated in all forms of Christian folk-religion (superstition). Only the unremitting toil of theologians can prevent this.

By calling God his Father, Jesus is "objectivizing an unworldly reality and making it worldly". In this sense he is using the language of mythology. What we have to do, however, is not to eliminate the mythological expression, for without it we shall never be able to express what Jesus meant by it, but first explore the depth of meaning which this image bears in ordinary human speech and isolate all its features. Then we must confront the meaning which we have thus worked out with what we know so far of the Being and Word of Jesus. By bringing the two things into relation we shall acquire a new apprehension and a deeper understanding of what he means when he speaks of God as his Father. The expression "Father" is not thereby eliminated; all our understanding will repeatedly return to it and go forth from it again, and thus will never be detachable from it. "Demythologizing" cannot consist in the elimination of the "worldly" image here employed, but only in the fact that the "worldly" receives its meaning from the "unworldly".

That is why we shall never succeed in producing a gospel free from mythology even at the end of our efforts. That is so for the elementary reason that the understanding we are looking for can never be formulated and passed on as a conclusive result. In all the work of exegesis and exposition results are possible only in a technical, and not in an absolute, universal sense. The understanding we are seeking is present only in so far as it takes shape in the actual course of our work. That is why theology is never the object of a departmental study which can hand on assured results. Theology is possible only as a stimulus to press on with the work of a life-time. The parish priest is not qualified by taking a theological degree, but only by constantly renewing and deepening his study of theology. To study theology means to desire to live in a progressive understanding of the gospel and to devote one's life ever anew to this understanding.

RUDOLF BULTMANN

BULTMANN REPLIES TO HIS CRITICS

1. *Demythologizing and the Philosophy of Existence*

AS a hermeneutic method, demythologizing has raised the question of the appropriate terminology which exposition should employ. It has thus called attention to a science concerning itself with the systematic development of the understanding of existence which is involved in existence itself—in other words, to the philosophy of existence. The objection that this means subordinating the interpretation of Christianity to a discipline intrinsically alien to it has already been given preliminary attention, but it must now be reconsidered in the light of the particular objection that it is the existentialist interpretation which results in the subordination of the Kerygma to philosophy.

In the first place, it is important to remember that every interpretation is actuated by the framing of specific questions, and without this there could be no interpretation at all. Of course these questions need not be framed explicitly or consciously, but unless they are framed the texts have nothing to say to us. It is self-evident that the framing of the questions must not be allowed to prejudice us about the content of the objects we are asking about. So far from anticipating particular results of our exegesis, it should open our eyes to the precise content of the text.[1]

I think I may take for granted that the right question to frame

---

[1] Cp. my essay on "Das Problem der Hermeneutik". *Zeitschrift für Theol. und Kirche*, 1950, p. 47ff. I am not convinced by H. Diem ("Grundfragen der Hermenentik" in *Theol. Existenz Heute*. N.F. 26, 1951) when he contends that it is wrong to raise the question of hermeneutics at this point, and in particular I think he is evading the issue when he says (p. 20) that the controversy as to whether there is a special theological hermeneutics as well as hermeneutics in general is not very fruitful. It is a controversy which must be settled in the interests of clarity.

with regard to the Bible—at any rate within the Church—is the question of human existence. I am driven to that by the urge to inquire existentially about my own existence. But that is a question which at bottom determines our approach to and interpretation of all historical documents. For the ultimate purpose in the study of history is to realize consciously the possibilities it affords for the understanding of human existence. Of course there is a further reason why I should approach the Bible with such a question, and that is because the Church's proclamation refers me to the Scriptures as the place where I shall hear things about my own existence which vitally concern me, a circumstance which on secularist presuppositions is merely accidental.[1]

The Bible not only shows me, like other historical documents, a possible way of understanding my own existence, a way which I am free to accept or reject: more than that, it assumes the shape of a word which addresses me personally. But that is something which I cannot anticipate or take into account as a systematic principle for my exposition. For, in traditional language, that is the work of the Holy Ghost.

A further objection against the existentialist interpretation is that in order to put the right questions to the text it is necessary to have in advance a vital relation to the subject matter of the text, whereas it is impossible to have such a relation to the revelation of God as it is testified in the Scriptures. This objection is equally untenable. For the fact is that I have such a relationship to the question about God, a truth to which St Augustine gave classical expression in the words: "*Tu nos fecisti ad te, et cor nostrum inquietum est, donec requiescat in te.*" Human life is—consciously or unconsciously—impelled by the question about God.

If faith in the Word of God can only be the work of the Holy Ghost operating through intelligent decision, it follows that the understanding of the text is attainable only in systematic interpretation, and the terminology which directs this understanding can be acquired only from profane reflection, which is the business of the philosophical analysis of existence.

Now, this means subordinating the work of exegesis to that

---

[1] Diem has quite rightly seen this.

of the philosopher. But it would be a fallacy to suppose that exegesis can ever be pursued independently of profane terminology. Every exegete is dependent upon a terminology which has come down to him by tradition, though it is accepted uncritically and without reflection, and every traditional terminology is in one way or another dependent upon a particular philosophy. But it is vital that we should proceed neither uncritically nor without reflection.[1] It is imperative that we should consider the nature and the source of the terminology which directs our exposition. In fact, there is no reason why we should not admit that what we are concerned with is the "right" philosophy.

No reason at all, for I am not suggesting that there is actually a final philosophical system—e.g. idealism, and Hegelianism in particular—or that it is necessary for our exegesis to take over the actual answers that philosophy gives to the existential question of the meaning of my own particular existence. The "right" philosophy is simply one which has worked out an appropriate terminology for the understanding of existence, an understanding involved in human existence itself. Hence it does not pose the problem of existence as an existential question, but asks in existentialist analysis about the meaning of existence in the abstract: for it is aware that the existential problem can be answered only in existence itself.

An objection could be sustained at this point only if the conception of authentic existence propounded by this philosophy implied a material ideal of existence—if, in other words, this philosophy told us *how* we ought to exist. In fact, however, all it says is: You ought to exist, or, if even this is going too far, it shows us what existence means. It tells us that human Being, as distinct from all other Being, means *existing*, a form of Being which assumes complete responsibility for itself. It tells us that our authentic existence is realizable only in existence, which means existing always in the concrete here and now. But it does not claim that existentialist analysis can create the

[1] In the course of the nineteenth century interest in hermeneutics continually diminished, and lectures on hermeneutics disappeared from the lecture lists. Any surviving interest in the subject was confined to specific hermeneutic rules (cp. my essay on the problem of hermeneutics), and ignored the question of terminology and its sources.

existential understanding of the here and now. So far from relieving us of our personal responsibility, it actually lays it upon us.[1]

Clearly, existentialist analysis is founded upon the existential questions of existence, for otherwise it is hard to see how it could know anything about existence. Indeed, its work consists in systematizing the understanding of existence involved in existence itself. It is precisely on this consideration that K. F. Schumann bases his acute criticism[2] that the existentialist analysis implies a decision in favour of a particular understanding of existence.

Schumann is right enough when he says that it is impossible "to have a formal analysis of human existence which can be detached from every 'existentialist' attitude, from every actual disposition to one's own existence", and that "no existential analysis can be achieved in complete detachment from the understanding of existence which is presupposed, accepted, and applied". But this is only to say what I have myself repeatedly emphasized, viz., that existentialist analysis is simply the systematization of the self-understanding of existence involved in existence itself. If such an analysis involves any decision at all, it is the decision to exist; for it distinguishes human Being as existing from the "being to hand" (*Vorhandensein*)[3] of worldly phenomena which may be apprehended in objective thought. So far, however, from excluding the concrete possibilities of existential self-understanding, such a decision actually paves the way for them. This decision is not an act of systematic philosophic thought: rather, it furnishes the philosopher with his premises. Or, if it must be called a philosophical decision, that is an appropriate designation so long as the philosopher's activity is understood as an essential impulse of human Being. Apart from this decision, or, to reduce the whole matter to its simplest terms, apart from the resolve to be a human being, a person who accepts responsibility for his own Being, not a single word of Scripture is intelligible as a word with an existential relevance.

But to deny that philosophic thought can use this basic

[1] Behind all W. Wiesner's objections lies a complete misconception of the object of the existentialist analysis of Being.   [2] *Vide supra*, p. 185f.
[3] *Vide* Heidegger, *Existence and Being*, p. 28f. (Translator.)

decision as the premises for a "purely formal" analysis of existence is to my mind sheer prejudice. How far such an attempt can succeed is of course another question, but in the last resort it is no more relevant than the insight that conclusive knowledge is impossible in any science or philosophy. Any resultant analysis is still open to correction, and here as elsewhere discussion is the *sine qua non* of progress.

Discussion on this subject is possible because every existential self-understanding lies within the possibilities of human existence, and therefore every existentialist analysis based upon an existential self-understanding is generally intelligible. Hence there is sense in trying to work out a formal analysis of existence.

Of course such an analysis does in effect become a "norm"[1] in so far as an attempt is made to make the phenomena of existence intelligible, as for instance to keep to Schumann's own illustration, the phenomenon of love. Yet it is a misconception to suppose that this involves a decision "as to what each man's . . . love means for him".[1] Rather, the reverse is true. Existentialist analysis can only make clear to me that each concrete instance of love can only be understood existentially, and that no man can be deprived of his understanding of his own particular love by any existentialist analysis.

Certainly pure existentialist analysis involves the judgement "that it is possible to analyse the Being of man without taking into account his relation to God".[1] But is there any point in analysing human Being in relation to God if the relation between man and God is possible only as an event in the concrete encounter between man and God? A pure analysis of Being cannot take the relation between man and God into consideration at all, since it disregards the concrete encounters in which existence is realized on each successive occasion. But it is just this procedure which gives that analysis its freedom. If the revelation of God becomes effective only on specific occasions in the "now" of Being (as an eschatological event), and if existentialist analysis points us to the temporality in which we have to exist, an aspect of Being is thereby exposed which faith, but only faith, understands as the relatedness of man to God. So far, however, from being undermined by a formal

1 Schumann, p. 186.

analysis of Being, this understanding is in fact illuminated by it, just as it illuminates the question about the meaning of existence and shows that it is really the question about God.

But are we to call this judgement, that an analysis of Being without reference to God is not only possible but makes sense, an anterior existential decision, as Schumann does? I think we may, though not in Schumann's sense as implying a decision in favour of existence without God. It is an existential decision inasmuch as it is based upon an insight which can only be achieved existentially—namely, that the idea of God cannot be used to sketch out a theory of Being. Yet this judgement cannot be called an anterior decision as though it were made conclusively before embarking upon the analysis. Rather, it accompanies the analysis all through. I may also add that this judgement is an understanding of self which can only be reached existentially, the acknowledgement that when I look into myself I do not find God. It is just this disclaimer which gives the analysis of existence its "neutrality".

2. *The "Act of God"*

Perhaps we may say that behind all the objections raised against demythologizing there lurks a fear that if it were carried to its logical conclusion it would make it impossible for us to speak of an act of God, or if we did it would only be the symbolical description of a subjective experience. For is it not mythology to speak of an act of God as though it were an objective event in which the grace of God encounters man?

In the first place, we must reply that if such language is to have any meaning at all it must denote an act in a real, objective sense, and not just a symbolical or pictorial expression. On the other hand, if the action of God is not to be conceived as a worldly phenomenon capable of being apprehended apart from its existential reference, it can only be spoken of by speaking simultaneously of myself as the person who is existentially concerned. To speak of the act of God means to speak at the same time of my existence. Since human life is lived out in time and space, man's encounter with God can only be a specific event here and now. This event, our being addressed by God here and now, our being questioned, judged, and blessed by him, is what we mean when we speak of an act of God.

Such language is therefore neither symbolical nor pictorial, though it is certainly analogical,[1] for it assumes an analogy between the activity of God and that-of man and between the fellowship of God and man and that of man with man.

The meaning of this language requires further clarification. Mythological thought regards the divine activity, whether in nature or in history, as an interference with the course of nature, history, or the life of the soul, a tearing of it asunder—a miracle, in fact. Thus it objectifies the divine activity and projects it on to the plane of worldly happenings. A miracle—i.e. an act of God—is not visible or ascertainable like worldly events. The only way to preserve the unworldly, transcendental character of the divine activity is to regard it not as an interference in worldly happenings, but something accomplished *in* them in such a way that the closed weft of history as it presents itself to objective observation is left undisturbed. To every other eye than the eye of faith the action of God is hidden. Only the "natural" happening is generally visible and ascertainable. In it is accomplished the hidden act of God.

It is easy to object that this is to transform Christian faith into a pantheistic piety. But pantheism believes in a direct identity of worldly happening with the divine activity, whereas faith asserts their paradoxical identity, which can only be believed on in the concrete here and now and in the teeth of outward appearance. When I am encountered by such an event, I can in faith accept it as the gift of God or as his judgement, although I can also see it within its context in nature or history. In faith I can understand a thought or a resolve as something which is the work of God without necessarily removing it from its place in the chain of cause and effect.

Christian faith is not a *Weltanschauung* like pantheism. Pantheism is an anterior conviction that everything that happens is the work of God, since God is thought to be immanent in the world. Christian faith, on the other hand, believes that God acts upon us and addresses us in the specific here and now. This belief springs from an awareness of being addressed by the grace

[1] On the subject of analogy cp. Erich Frank, *Philosophical Language and Religious Truth*, 1945, pp. 44, 161–4, 179, etc.

of God which confronts us in Jesus Christ. By this grace we are enabled to see that God makes all things work together for good to them that love him (Rom. 8. 28). This kind of faith, however, is not a knowledge possessed once and for all, not a *Weltanschauung*. It can only be an event occurring on specific occasions, and it can remain alive only when the believer is constantly asking himself what God is saying to him here and now. God is generally just as hidden for him as he is for everyone else. But from time to time the believer sees concrete happenings in the light of the word of grace which is addressed to him, and then faith can and ought to apprehend it as the act of God, even if its meaning is still enigmatic. If pantheism can say that any event it likes is the work of the Godhead, quite apart from its meaning in personal encounter, Christian faith can only say that in such-and-such an event God is acting in a hidden way. What God is doing now—it is of course not to be identified *tout court* with the visible occurrence—I may not know as yet, and perhaps I shall never know. But still I must ask what he is trying to say to me through it, even if all he has to say is that I must just grin and bear it.

Similarly, faith in God as Creator is not a piece of knowledge given in advance, in virtue of which every happening may be designated an act of God. Such faith is genuine only when I understand myself here and now existentially to be the creature of God, though it need not necessarily take the form of knowledge consciously acquired as the result of reflection. Faith in the divine omnipotence is not an anterior conviction that there is a Being who can do everything: it can only be attained existentially by submitting to the power of God exercising pressure upon me here and now, and this too need not necessarily be raised to the level of consciousness. The propositions of faith are not abstract truths. Those who have endured the hardships of a Russian prison camp know better than anyone else that you cannot say "*Terra ubique Domini*" as an explicit dogma: it is something which can be uttered only on specific occasions in existential decision.

Hence it is clear that for my existential life, realized as it is in decision in face of encounter, the world is no longer a closed weft of cause and effect. In faith the closed weft presented or produced by objective observation is transcended, though not as in mythological thought. For mythology imagines it to be torn asunder, whereas faith transcends it as a whole when it speaks of the activity of God. In the last resort it is already transcended when I speak of myself, for I myself, my real self, am no more visible or ascertainable than an act of God. When worldly happenings are viewed as a closed series, as not only scientific understanding but even workaday life requires, there is certainly no room for any act of God. But this is just the paradox of faith: it understands an ascertainable event in its context in nature and history as the act of God. Faith cannot dispense with its "nevertheless".

This is the only genuine faith in miracle.[1] The conception of miracles as ascertainable processes is incompatible with the hidden character of God's activity. It surrenders the acts of God to objective observation, and thus makes belief in miracles (or rather superstition) susceptible to the justifiable criticisms of science.

If then it be true that we cannot speak of an act of God without speaking simultaneously of our own existence, if such an act cannot be established apart from its existential reference, if it dispenses with the objectivity attainable by impartial scientific investigation (e.g. by experiment), we inevitably ask whether divine activity has any objective reality at all. Does it exist apart from our own subjective experience? Is not faith reduced to experience pure and simple? Is God no more than an experience in the soul, despite the fact that faith only makes sense when it is directed towards a God with a real existence outside the believer?

This objection rests upon a psychological misconception of what is meant by the existential life of man.[2] When we say that faith alone, the faith which is aware of the divine encounter, can speak of God, and that therefore when the believer speaks of an act of God he is *ipso facto* speaking of himself as well, it by no means follows that God has no real existence apart from the believer or the act of believing. It follows only if faith and

[1] Cp. *Glauben und Verstehen*, pp. 214–28, esp. p. 224f.; W. Herrmann, *Offenbarung und Wunder*, 1908, esp. pp. 33ff. Herrmann rightly observes that faith in prayer, like belief in miracles, transcends the idea of nature.

[2] I might also say "by human subjectivity", provided this is understood in Kierkegaard's sense as "being subject"—i.e., the personal being of man.

experience are interpreted in a psychologizing sense.[1] If human Being is properly understood as historic Being, whose experiences consist of encounters, it is clear that faith, which speaks of its encounter with the acts of God, cannot defend itself against the charge of illusion, for the encounter with God is not objective like a worldly event. Yet there is no need for faith, in the sense of an existential encounter, to refute that charge, and indeed it could not do so without misunderstanding its own meaning.

What encounter means as such may be illustrated from our own life in history. The love of another is an encounter whose essential character depends upon its being an event. For it cannot be apprehended as love by objective observation, but only by myself who am encountered by it.[2] Looked at from the outside, it is certainly not visible as love in the real sense of the word, but only as a phenomenon of spiritual or psychic history which is open to various interpretations. Of course the love with which a man loves me does not depend for its reality upon my understanding or reciprocating it.[3] This is just what we learn when we do reciprocate another's love. Even if we fail to understand it or open our hearts to it, it still evokes a kind of existential reaction. For to fail to understand it, to close our hearts to it, to respond by hatred—all these are still existential reactions. In each case we are no longer the same after the encounter as we were before it, though that does not for a moment alter the fact that it is only in encounter that it can be seen as love.

That God cannot be seen apart from faith does not mean that

[1] When W. Herrmann and A. Schlatter speak of experience, neither of them means a bare psychic phenomenon.

[2] I cannot see why E. Schweizer calls the love awakened by another an "inner-psychic" process. For love can only exist in encounter or mutual relationship. He completely fails to grasp the existential meaning of love when he writes: "Love awakens more in man than does an ideal. It awakens the desire for fellowship, a concern of the I for the Thou, sexuality, or what you will (!). But it is still an inner-psychic process, for the love of the other is only an external stimulus. Admittedly it affects the whole range of our emotional life, and not only the mind, as when we receive instruction, or our enthusiasm, as when we are presented with an ideal."

[3] E. Schweizer, "Zur Interpretation des Kreuzes bei R. Bultmann" (*Festschrift für Maurice Goguel*, 1950).

he does not exist apart from it. That an encounter with the Word of God makes a difference to man, whether he opens his heart to it or not, is a fact which only faith can know, the faith which understands that unbelief is a token of God's judgement.

True faith is not demonstrable in relation to its object. But, as Herrmann taught us long ago, it is just here that its strength lies. For if it were susceptible to proof it would mean that we could know and establish God apart from faith, and that would be placing him on a level with the world of tangible, objective reality.[1] In that realm we are certainly justified in demanding proof.

If faith is man's response to the proclamation of the word of God's grace, a word whose origin and credentials are to be found in the New Testament, must we say that it cannot be proved by the appeal to Scripture? Is not faith simply the hearing of Scripture as the Word of God? That is indeed so, but only when Scripture is understood neither as a compendium of doctrines nor as a document enshrining the beliefs of other people, yet inspiring enough to evoke religious experience in us. It is so only when Scripture is heard as a word addressed personally to ourselves, as kerygma—i.e. when the experience consists in encounter and response to the address. That Scripture is the Word of God is something which happens only in the here and now of encounter; it is not a fact susceptible to objective proof. The Word of God is hidden in Scripture, just like any other act of his.[2]

Nor has God offered a proof of himself in the so-called facts of salvation. For these too are objects of faith, and as facts of salvation are ascertainable and visible to faith alone. Our knowledge of them does not precede our faith or provide a basis for it, as other convictions are based on proven facts. In a sense, of course, they do provide a basis for faith, but only as facts which are themselves apprehended in faith. It is just the

---

[1] This does not of course imply that the idea of God is properly inconceivable apart from faith. The idea of God is an expression of man's search for him, a search which motivates all human existence. *Vide supra*, p. 192, and cp. my essay, "Die Frage der natürlichen Offenbarung" in *Offenbarung und Heilsgeschehen*, pp. 1–26.

[2] Cp. H. Diem's criticism of the view that the Word of God is available in the Bible *ante et extra usum* (ibid., p. 5).

same with human trust and love. These too are not based on any trustworthiness or lovableness in another which could be objectively ascertained, but upon the nature of the other apprehended *in* the love and *in* the trust. There can be no trust and no love without this element of risk. Hence, as Herrmann used to say, the ground and object of faith do not fall apart, but are identical, for the very reason that we cannot say what God is like in himself, but only what he does to us.[1]

If then the activity of God is not visible or open to proof like worldly entities, if the event of redemption is not an ascertainable process, if, we may add, the Spirit granted to the believer is not a phenomenon susceptible to worldly apprehension, if we cannot speak of these things without speaking of our own existence, it follows that faith is a new understanding of existence, and that the activity of God vouchsafes to us a new understanding of self, as Luther said: "*et ita Deus per suum exire nos facit ad nos ipsos introire, et per sui cognitionem infert nobis et nostri cognitionem*".[2]

It is my definition of faith as an understanding of existence which has evoked the most opposition.[3] Is it really so difficult to understand what existential self-understanding means? At any rate it shows a complete failure to understand its meaning when it is objected that my definition reduces the event of revelation to a cause which sets self-understanding in motion, so that it is no longer a fact which interferes and changes reality, like a miracle. All that happens, it is claimed, is consciousness, and the content of the self-understanding is a timeless truth, which once perceived remains true quite apart from the cause which set it in motion and "cranked it up".[4] Is this what Luther meant by "*cognitio nostri*"?

But perhaps I did not express myself clearly enough, and am

---

[1] *Vide supra*, p. 198.

[2] *Schol. ad Rom.* 3. 5, ed. Ficker, p. 67, 21–3.

[3] E.g. H. Thielicke, *Deutsches Pfarrerblatt* 46 (1942), pp. 129ff., *Kerygma and Myth*, p. 146f. No wonder that the declaration of the Provincial Council of the Evangelical Confessional Fellowship in Württemberg (in *Für Arbeit und Besinnung*, 1952, 18–23) echoes this complaint. The only amusing thing about it is that the declaration rules out in advance any chance of clearing up possible misunderstandings.

[4] Thielicke, 148. Cp. also my reply to Thielicke in *Deutsches Pfarrerblatt*, 1943, 3ff.

therefore myself to blame for the confusion which lies at the root of this misunderstanding. Existential self-understanding is being confounded with the existentialist understanding of human Being elaborated by philosophical analysis. The affirmations of the latter are certainly meant to be timeless truths, and in so far as they are adequate, they may pass as such. But existentialist analysis points so to speak beyond itself, by showing (what in itself would be a timeless truth) that existential self-understanding can be appropriated only existentially. In my existential self-understanding I do not learn what existence means in the abstract, but I understand myself in my concrete here and now, in my concrete encounters.[1]

It goes without saying that this existential self-understanding need not be conscious. It permeates and controls imperceptibly all anxiety and resolve, all joy and dread, and is called in question at every encounter. It is something which sustains us even in childhood. For the child understands himself as a child (and therefore those who produced him as his parents) in his life, his trust, his sense of security, in his gratitude, his reverence, and in his obedience. When he is disobedient he forfeits this self-understanding, though never completely, for it makes itself known in a guilty conscience.

This illustration is enough to show that in existential self-understanding there is an understanding not only of self but also of the object of encounter, the person or the environment which is encountered. As a self who exists historically I am not isolated either from my environment or from my own past and future, which are in a special way a part of my environment. If, for instance, my encounter with another's love should vouchsafe to me a new understanding of self, what happens is by no means restricted to consciousness, at least if consciousness is to be taken as a psychic rather than as an existential phenomenon, which is what Thielicke and others wrongly suppose. By understanding myself in this encounter I understand the other in such a way that the whole world appears in a new light, which means that it has in fact become an entirely different world. I acquire a new insight into and a new judgement of my own past and future, which means that they have become my past and future in a new sense. I submit to new

[1] *Vide supra*, p. 199f.

demands and acquire a new readiness for further encounters. Clearly such an understanding cannot be possessed as a timeless truth, for its validity depends upon its being constantly renewed, and upon an understanding of the imperative it involves. We may say with St Paul, *mutatis mutandis*: "If we live by the Spirit, by the Spirit also let us walk" (Gal. 5. 25).

For exactly the same applies to the self-understanding of faith, in which man understands himself anew under the word of encounter. And just as in human contacts the new understanding created by encountering another in love and trust is kept pure only when it permanently retains its connexion with the other who is encountered, so too the self-understanding granted by faith never becomes a possession, but is kept pure only as a response to the repeated encounter of the Word of God, which proclaims the act of God in Christ in such a way as continually to re-present it.[1] "His compassions fail not, they are new every morning." True, but I can only be genuinely aware of it when I perceive it anew every morning, for as a timeless truth it is meaningless. Granted this, however, I can know that I myself am renewed every morning by it, that I am one who allows myself to be renewed by it.[2]

[1] Hence Wiesner ("Anthropologische oder theologische Schriftauslegung?" *Evangelische Theologie*, 1950/51, p. 49ff.) completely misses the point when he charges me with reducing the Biblical understanding of human existence to man's understanding of himself, and therefore secularizing the Christian proclamation (p. 56), and with reducing the redemptive act of God in Christ to the immanence of human existence and its realization in our life in time (ibid., p. 60).

[2] E. Schweizer thinks (op. cit., p. 236) that I am bound to make a theoretical distinction "between an act of faith which sees in the event of the cross the revelation of the love of God, and a second act of faith for which the first act sets us free . . . , an act which consists in a radical change of self-under-standing". No, not at any price! For I cannot imagine how we can see and believe the revelation of God's love without being at the same time set free for a new understanding of self. I simply cannot understand how I can believe that I am really delivered from sin before I "change" my self-understanding (this is what Schweizer actually says, instead of saying "my self-understanding *is changed*"). I am afraid my answer to this must be: "*nondum considerasti quanti ponderis sit peccatum*". The love of God is not a phenomenon whose apprehension leaves a man the same as he was before. Hence even the apprehension itself must be attributed to the operation of the Holy Ghost. No proclamation which possesses "the character of a simple Biblical report of what has happened" can tell a man "that this liberation is a reality antecedent to

Further, my critics have objected that my demythologizing of the New Testament results in the elimination of its eschatology. On the contrary, I am convinced that my interpretation exposes its meaning as never before, at least for those who have given up thinking in terms of mythology. For my restatement of it demonstrates the character of faith as freedom for the future.

Certainly existentialist analysis may assert that freedom for the future is a mark of authentic Being. But is this knowledge sufficient to enable man as he actually is to attain it? It cannot do this any more than it can impart existence as a whole. All it can do is to tell us that if we want to attain authentic existence we must be free for the future. It can only bring home to us the awful reality of this fact by saying that for it—i.e. for philosophical analysis—each man's particular future can in the last resort be defined as "nothingness", and that it can understand freedom for the future solely as "the readiness for dread" (*Angstbereitschaft*), which man has to accept by an act of resolve.

Indeed, faith is identical with this readiness for dread, for faith knows that God encounters us at the very point where the human prospect is nothingness, and only at that point. This is exactly how Luther interprets "Let us rejoice in our tribulations" (Rom. 5. 4): "*Unde cum Dominus habet nomen Salvatoris, adjutoris in tribulationibus, in multis locis, qui noluerit pati, quantum in ipso est, spoliat eum suis propriis titulis et nominibus. Sic enim nullus erit ei homini Jhesus, i.e. Salvator, quia non vult esse damnatus; nullus eius Deus creator, quia non vult esse nihil, cuius ille sit creator*" (Schol. in Rom. 5. 3; ed. Ficker, p. 135, 20ff.). Similarly: ". . . . *quia natura Dei est, prius destruere et annihilare, quicquid in nobis est, antequam sua donet*" (ibid. in 8. 26; p. 203, 4f.). Those "*qui sibi sancti videntur*" are those who "*Deum amore concupiscentiae diligunt, i.e. propter salutem et requiem aeternam aut propter fugam inferni, hoc est non propter Deum, sed propter se ipsos*". With them are contrasted those "*qui vere Deum diligunt amore filiali et amicitiae . . . . Tales enim libere sese offerunt in omnem voluntatem Dei, etiam ad infernum et mortem aeternaliter, si*

---

and transcending all his understanding" (ibid., p. 237f.). For the reality of the deliverance is not something which a report of a happening can display. I hope the ensuing argument will demonstrate Schweizer's failure to recognize the eschatological import of the event of redemption.

Deus vellet tantum, ut sua voluntas plene fiat" (ibid. in 9. 3; p. 217, 18ff.). God *"non potest ostendere virtutem suam in electis, nisi prius ostendat eis infirmitatem eorum et abscondat virtutem eorum ad nihilumque redigat, ut non glorientur in virtute sua propria"* (ibid. in 9. 17; p. 229, 21ff.). *"Deus non salvat nisi peccatores, non erudit nisi stultos et insipientes, non ditat nisi pauperes, non vivificat nisi mortuos"* (ibid. in 10. 19; p. 252, 18ff.).[1] Of course that *"amor filialis et amicitiae"* does not arise through the resolute acceptance of readiness for dread, for *"non est ex natura, sed spiritu sancto solum"* (ibid., p. 217, 28). Readiness for dread is thus the gift of faith, and is identical with freedom from ourselves (= our old self) for ourselves (= our new self), freedom from the fallacy which lies at the root of sin—namely, that we can base our own existence upon our own resolve, and thus attain freedom for the future. As St Paul himself put it: "Death is swallowed up in victory" (1 Cor. 15. 54).

But our critics are still not satisfied. If it is possible to speak of an act of God only in the sense of what he does to me on specific occasions, is this not to deny that he has acted once and for all in Christ on behalf of the whole world? Does it not eliminate the ἐφάπαξ of Rom. 6. 10?[2] Am I really "eliminating the reality of time as a unique fact of the past [sic] from our understanding of the event of redemption in the New Testament sense of the word"?[3]

From what has already been said it should be clear that I am not talking about an idea of God, but am trying to speak of the living God in whose hands our time rests, and who encounters us at specific moments in our time. But since further explanation is required, the answer may be given in a single sentence: God encounters us in His Word—i.e. in a particular word, in the proclamation inaugurated with Jesus Christ. True, God en-

---

[1] Cp. also ibid., p. 206, 10ff.; 216, 18ff.; 245, 4ff. (Man stands in a relation of guilt both towards God and towards his creatures; he who would atone for this guilt *"libens ac volens it in nihilum et mortem et damnationem . . ."*.). Cp. also the quotations from Luther in F. Gogarten, *Die Verkündigung Jesu Christi*, 1948, pp. 306f., 331.

[2] Emil Brunner, *Die christliche Lehre von der Schöpfung (Dogmatik II)*, 1950, p. 314f.; E. Schweizer, op. cit. pp. 231ff.; Schniewind, *supra*, p. 66ff.

[3] Kümmel, *Coniect. Neotest.*, p. 115; "Mythos im Neuen Testament" *Theol. Ztschr.*, 1950, p. 321ff. Cf. A. N. Wilder, *Eschatology and Ethics in the Teaching of Jesus*, 1950, p. 126f.

counters us at all times and in all places, but he cannot be seen everywhere unless his Word comes as well and makes the moment of revelation intelligible to us in its own light, as Luther not infrequently observed. Just as the divine omnipotence and omniscience cannot be realized existentially apart from his word uttered with reference to a particular moment and heard in that moment, so this Word is what it is only in the moment in reference to which it is uttered. It is not a timeless truth, but a definite word addressed at a particular occasion, whose eternal quality lies not in endless endurance but in its actual presence at specific moments. It is the Word of God only in so far as it is a word which happens on specific occasions, and not in virtue of the ideas it contains—e.g. the mercy and grace of God (however true these things may be). It is the Word of God because it confronts me with his mercy and grace. It is only in this way that it is really the *verbum externum*: it is not a possession secured in knowledge, but an address which encounters us ever and again.

This is why it is a word addressed *realiter* to me on a specific occasion, whether it be in the Church's proclamation, or in the Bible mediated through the Church as the Word of God addressed to me, or through the word of my fellow Christian.[1] That is why the living Word of God is never a word of human wisdom but an event encountered in history. The fact that it originates in an historical event provides the credentials for its utterance on each specific occasion. This event is Jesus Christ.

That God has acted in Jesus Christ is, however, not a fact of past history open to historical verification. That Jesus Christ is the Logos of God can never be proved by the objective investigation of the historian.[2] Rather, the fact that the New Testament

[1] It goes without saying that this Word need not necessarily be uttered at the same moment of time in which it becomes a decisive word for me. It is possible for something I heard yesterday or even thirty years ago to become a decisive word for me now; then it begins (or perhaps begins once more) to be a word spoken to me, and is therefore shown to be a word addressed with reference to my present situation.

[2] That is why I cannot share Wilder's concern (op. cit., p. 216f.) that the actual history of Jesus should be verifiable by the historian, or Wiesner's concern that it should at least be relatively ascertainable (op. cit., p. 64f.). If Wiesner imagines that by saying, "It is not the event of redemption because it is the cross of Christ, but it is the cross of Christ because it is the event of redemption", I am turning the whole thing upside down, he obviously does not see that this affirmation about the cross of Christ can never be a statement of fact, but only a confession of faith.

describes the figure and work of Christ in mythological terms is enough to show that if they are the act of redemption they must not be understood in their context of world history. The paradox is just this, that a human figure, Jesus of Nazareth (see esp. John 6. 42), and the destiny of that figure—i.e. a human being and his fate, with a recognizable place in world history, and therefore exposed to the objective observation of the historian and intelligible within their context in world history—are not thus apprehended and understood as what they really are, namely, as the act of God, as *the* eschatological event.

But this is how Jesus Christ is understood in the New Testament (e.g. Gal. 4. 4; John 3. 17–19). The only question is whether this understanding is necessarily bound up with the cosmic eschatology in which the New Testament places it—with the exception of the Fourth Gospel, where the cosmic eschatology has already become picture language, and where the eschatological event is seen in the coming of Jesus as the Word, the Word of God which is continually re-presented in the word of proclamation. But the way for this demythologizing was already paved in the primitive Church with its understanding of itself as the eschatological community, the congregation of the saints. The process was carried a stage further by St Paul with his conception of the believer as a "new creature", since the old is passed away and the new already come (2 Cor. 5. 17). Henceforward faith means to exist eschatologically, to exist in detachment from the world, to have passed over from death unto life (1 Cor. 7. 29–31; John 5. 24; 1 John 4. 14). At the same time eschatological existence is possible only in faith; it is not yet realized in sight (2 Cor. 5. 7.). That is to say, it is not a worldly phenomenon, but is realized in the new self-understanding which faith imparts. Since it is faith in the crucified and risen Christ, this self-understanding is not an autonomous movement of the human will, but the response to the Word of God, which proclaims the manifestation of the grace of God in Jesus Christ. Since he is the Word of God, Christ is *ante et extra me*, not, however, as a fact open to objective verification and chronologically datable before me, but as the *Christus pro me*, who encounters me as the Word. The eschatological event, which Christ is, is consequently realized invariably and solely *in concreto* here and now, where the Word is proclaimed (2 Cor. 6. 2; John 5. 24) and meets with faith or unbelief (2 Cor. 2. 15f.; John 3. 18; 9. 39).

Thus the ἐφάπαξ is understood as never before in its true sense of the "once" of the eschatological event. For it does not mean the datable uniqueness and finality of an event of past history, but teaches us in a high degree of paradox to believe that just such an event of the past is the once-and-for-all eschatological event, which is continually re-enacted in the word of proclamation. This proclamation is a word which addresses me personally, and tells me that the prevenient grace of God has already acted on my behalf, though not in such a way that I can look back upon this act of God as a datable event of the past, but in the sense that God's having acted is present as an eschatological Now.

The Word of God is what it is only in event, and the paradox lies in the fact that this Word is identical with the Word which originated in the apostolic preaching, which has been fixed in Scripture and which is handed on by men in the Church's proclamation;[1] the word of Christ whose contents may also be formulated in a series of abstract propositions. The ἐφάπαξ means that it cannot be the one without being the other, and that the abstract propositions can only become the Word of God when it is proclamation—i.e. when it takes the shape of an event here and now in the *viva vox*—that is the eschatological meaning of the ἐφάπαξ.

The Word of God and the Church are inseparable. The Church is constituted by the Word of God as the congregation of the elect, and the proclamation of the Word is not a statement of abstract truths, but a proclamation which is duly authorized and therefore needs bearers with proper credentials (2 Cor. 5. 18f.). Just as the Word of God becomes his Word

[1] In other words, a man just like myself speaks to me the Word of God: in him the Word of God becomes incarnate. For the incarnation is likewise an eschatological event and not a datable event of the past; it is an event which is continually being re-enacted in the event of the proclamation. I may refer at this point to my essay on "The Christological Confession of the World Council of Churches". *Ev. Theologie*, 1951, p. 1ff. It seems high time that Christology was emancipated from its subordination to an ontology of objective thought and re-stated in a new ontological terminology.

only in event, so the Church is really the Church only when it too becomes an event. For the Church is the eschatological congregation of the saints whose identity with a sociological institution and a phenomenon of the world's history can be asserted only in terms of paradox.[1]

If the challenge of demythologizing was first raised by the conflict between the mythological world-view of the Bible and the modern scientific world view, it at once became evident that the restatement of mythology is a requirement of faith itself. For faith needs to be emancipated from its association with every world view expressed in objective terms, whether it be a mythical or a scientific one. That conflict is a proof that faith has not yet discovered the proper terms in which to express itself, it has not realized that it cannot be logically proven, it has not clearly understood that its basis and its object are identical, it has not clearly apprehended the transcendental and hidden character of the divine activity, and by its failure to perceive its own "Nevertheless" it has tried to project God and his acts into the sphere of objective reality. Starting as it does from the modern world view, and challenging the Biblical mythology and the traditional proclamation of the Church, this new kind of criticism is performing for faith the supreme service of recalling it to a radical consideration of its own nature. It is just this call that our demythologizing seeks to follow.

The invisibility of God excludes every myth which tries to make him and his acts visible. Because of this, however, it also excludes every conception of invisibility and mystery which is formulated in terms of objective thought. God withdraws himself from the objective view: he can only be believed upon in defiance of all outward appearance, just as the justification of the sinner can only be believed upon in defiance of the accusations of the conscience.

Our radical attempt to demythologize the New Testament is

---

[1] A. Wilder appears to have overlooked the paradoxical character of this identity when he criticizes my interpretation for its excessive individualism, on the ground that the acts of God always have "a social and corporate reference" (*Eschatology and Ethics in the Teaching of Jesus*, 1950, p. 65). While the acts of God undoubtedly have this reference, it is hard to see how a "social and corporate" nature can be predicated of an eschatological community.

in fact a perfect parallel to St Paul's and Luther's doctrine of justification by faith alone apart from the works of the Law. Or rather, it carries this doctrine to its logical conclusion in the field of epistemology. Like the doctrine of justification it destroys every false security and every false demand for it on the part of man, whether he seeks it in his good works or in his ascertainable knowledge. The man who wishes to believe in God as his God must realize that he has nothing in his hand on which to base his faith. He is suspended in mid-air, and cannot demand a proof of the Word which addresses him. For the ground and object of faith are identical. Security can be found only by abandoning all security, by being ready, as Luther put it, to plunge into the inner darkness.

Faith in God means faith in justification, a faith which rejects the idea that certain actions can be marked off as conveying sanctification. Faith in God means faith in creation, and this likewise rejects the idea that certain areas of status and event in the world can be marked off as holy. We have learnt from Luther that there are no holy places anywhere in the world. The whole world is profane, though this does not make any difference to the fact that "*Terra ubique Domini*", which is something which can only be believed in contrary to all appearance. It is not priestly consecration which makes the house of God holy, but only the word of proclamation. Similarly, the framework of nature and history is profane, and it is only in the light of the word of proclamation that nature and history become for the believer, contrary to all appearance, the field of the divine activity. It is faith which makes the world profane and restores to it its proper autonomy as the field of man's labours. But it is just for this reason that the believer's relation to the world and to the world view of modern science is the paradoxical relation of ὡς μή.

AUSTIN FARRER

AN ENGLISH APPRECIATION

THE English reader may feel that he has already studied a sufficient variety of personal views on the contemporary German debate. Why should he endure another, and that from a fellow-countryman of his own? Surely this is the sort of thing with which German profundity is more at home than English practicality. Yet, however much the Englishman admires German profundity, he cannot see things altogether with German eyes. Indeed, one effect of reading a book like this is to be reminded how foreign the German religious attitude is to our own. And so some English readers may like to compare their own impressions of the debate with those of an English theologian, and to watch him as he tries to sum up for himself what the German discussion amounts to.

I will first say how the different German papers strike me, and I will begin with Dr Bultmann's initial article. I do not find that it makes much attempt at consistent statement or accurate definition, nor do I suppose that it was designed to do so. It was a direct expression of feeling, a covert sermon to the half-believer, and an open provocation to the theologian. How effectively Bultmann has trailed his coat for his colleagues can be seen from their eloquent reactions; the angle thrown out for the half-believer is more likely to pass unnoticed. Yet surely the instinctive tactics of the apologist give much of its shape to the article. His first move is to disarm prejudice by conceding all the antimythical objections with dramatic recklessness. His second move is to reopen the religious question on neutral and non-mythical ground, the existentialist philosopher's account of the human predicament. He goes on to persuade us that our predicament, as such an account reveals it to us, is a tragedy from which we cannot deliver ourselves, except in so far as we are enabled by an act of God through the Gospel. The divine rescue is a fact encountered by those who are given the faith to make contact with it. It becomes an actual factor in their personal existence, and is guaranteed as not mythical but real by its present actuality. But what is it that receives this guarantee?

Dr Bultmann pours out a stream of covertly mythical descriptions for the saving act. He is bold to use them because he has now got his reader into a state to grasp the reality through the descriptions. He scarcely pauses to justify the apparent reintroduction of a type of language which it was the whole profession of his argument to discard. Now, this may be a good pattern for apologetic persuasion, but it will evidently have to be rewritten to meet academic criticism.

Bultmann professes to be simply giving the Gospel the liberty it intrinsically demands. The real purpose of Dr Schniewind's article is to show us the whole body of the Scriptural truth, in such a way as to press the question, whether Bultmann is not freeing the Gospel from its fetters by amputating its limbs. Dr Schniewind does this very forcibly and pertinently, though of course, to our English minds, very Lutheranly too. When, however, he endeavours to theorize the problem of mythology on his own account, he does not achieve an equal success.

Professor Lohmeyer's papers contribute little to the understanding of Bultmann, whose views (it would be hardly too much to say) he caricatures: pardonably, when we consider that in his original outburst Bultmann had caricatured himself, and that this was the picture which Lohmeyer had before him. But Lohmeyer has his own profound understanding of the mythical problem, and in putting forward positions alternative to Bultmann's he suggests what is of much value in itself, and can serve in a final synthesis to supplement the deficiencies of Bultmann's theory.

The centre of the book, to my mind, is Bultmann's rejoinder to Schniewind. Having seen how his original utterance lays itself open to charges of inconsistency and suspicions of theological nihilism, Bultmann says exactly what he means with beautiful precision. This statement of Bultmann's allows of being construed, like a well-worded legal document.

Dr Schumann's essay is a direct contribution to the clarification of Bultmann's ideas. He writes as a philosophical theologian and offers a criticism both stringent and sympathetic.

Bultmann's final essay is not what its title would appear to make it, a general answer to his critics. That is to be found rather in the rejoinder to Schniewind. It is an apologia on a particular point, the status Bultmann accords to existentialist philosophy in relation to the restatement of Christian theology. It is his philosophical profession of faith, and says less about the special topics of theology.

There, then, is my impression of the part played in the discussion by each of the pieces reproduced in this collection. Though various opinions are mooted, none but Bultmann's receive sustained attention and it is obviously about them that I must attempt to give a judgement. But I shall not plunge straight into Bultmann's thought. I will begin not with Bultmann but with the nature of the question. I will hope to show as I proceed what sort of an answer to it Bultmann offers.

The question is said to arise from the spiritual situation of contemporary society. It is obvious that no general diagnosis of the modern disease is being attempted, for if that were done other remedies might easily be found more urgent and more efficacious than the demythicization of the Gospel. We are simply being called upon to acknowledge that one of the things the modern man cannot take is myth. To judge of Bultmann's argument by its conclusion, "modern man" means for the purposes of the present question a being sufficiently sophisticated to appreciate the existentialist approach which is Bultmann's offered remedy; say one man in five thousand. But these, no doubt, are the leaven that leavens the lump, and many or few, they ought to be catered for.

Without going outside the requirements of the question we may usefully make certain distinctions between the refusals of the modern mind. We will classify them as necessary, accidental, lamentable, and factitious. (1) The established, or virtually established, positions of science and history give rise to *necessary* refusals, as when we refuse to believe that the world was created eight thousand years ago or that the sun stood physically still for Joshua. (2) The things which modern men happen not to pay attention to give rise to *accidental* refusals, in the case (for example) of industrial workers who have a blind eye for imagery based on the procedures of pre-scientific agriculture. (3) Accidental refusals become *lamentable* refusals when they involve the atrophy of a spiritual function, for example, the sense for poetry. (4) *Factitious* refusals are those that arise from a philosophy or attitude which men either embrace or swallow—Communism, physical materialism, or economic utilitarianism.

Now, obviously the sort of respect we pay to these four sorts of refusals is not the same. Our respect for factitious refusals is the respect of the physician for the disease; if he respects the fact it is that he may abolish it. Lamentable refusals are likewise to be cured so far as they admit of cure by the cultivation of the atrophied function. Accidental refusals can be overcome by the imparting of information, but it is often not practicable nor worth our while to attempt it. About necessary refusals nothing can be done or ought to be done. They must be accepted.

If, therefore, men cannot understand a "mythical" language because they are dogmatic materialists, it is a case of factitious error, and the direct target of our attack. If because they have lost their sense for poetical expression and living metaphor, it is lamentable and we ought to sustain and augment whatever rudiments of poetical sense remain. If because the Biblical images draw on unfamiliar fields of experience, it is accidental and must be met largely by the substitution of familiar images, not (if you like to say so) by demythicization but by remythicization. But if it is because of a real conflict with the way in which any decent modern man is bound to think, then indeed it is time to talk about removing the offensive elements from the Biblical story by radical translation into harmless terms.

I take it that the last case is the only case we are considering here. The other cases are important, but they are matters of pastoral tactics, not of theological truth. The question of truth arises only when the modern man we are talking about is ourself just as much as anyone else.

The first sense of myth we have to consider stands for something which no mind, whether modern or ancient, ought to swallow, and that is the taking of poetical symbol for literal fact. Angels above the blue and devils underground fitly frame the setting of man in the spiritual hierarchy, but excavation will not reach the one or aeronautics the other. How far symbol is taken for literal fact in the New Testament is a subtle question. On the whole it is truer to say that the relation of mythical expression to literal belief is left undecided, than to say that it is decided in the sense of literalism. There are undoubted cases of decision in both directions; for example, St Luke did think that the Biblical genealogies gave a tolerable idea of the number of generations from the beginning of the world to his own day;

St John did not think that his description of the Heavenly Jerusalem would or could be executed by angelic hands in gold and precious stones. But the middle cases between the two are the more typical; if we ask with Bultmann, for example, whether spirits good and evil were really thought to be breaths of subtle and potent air physically invading the human person, we run into a mist of ambiguities.

No doubt there is a task of demythicization here which Biblical reflection has begun and theological reflection ought to complete. But that is a platitude. St Augustine was aware of the importance of distinguishing the literal from the symbolic, and the Schoolmen theorized the problem almost *ad nauseam*. When Bultmann suggests that the modern problem can be illustrated from the "three-decker universe" he is surely indulging himself in the pleasures of rhetorical effect. Our actual problems are more subtle. It will suffice to name two of them, the problem of miracle and the problem of transcendence.

The problem of miracle is this. Are alleged historical events like the virginal conception of our Saviour in Mary's womb examples of myth in the sense we have just defined, or are they not? Bultmann appears to beg the question. He writes as though he knew that God never bends physical fact into special conformity with divine intention; the Word never becomes flesh by making physical fact as immediately pliable to his expression as spoken symbols are. Bultmann seems to be convinced that he knows this, but I am not convinced that I know it, and I cannot be made to agree by the authority of the truism that symbolism ought not to be mistaken for physical fact. For it still ought to be taken for physical fact, if and where God has made it into physical fact.

The problem of transcendence is more general. It arises wherever we find ourselves asking to what reality symbolical descriptions refer. The only case which allows of a perfectly simple answer is one in which a non-symbolical description can be alternatively supplied. On the dramatic occasion on which Sherlock Holmes allowed himself the expression "the Napoleon of crime", he was not, indeed, referring to anyone named Napoleon, but he was referring to a person of whom the eminent detective would have been prepared to give an uncannily particular and literal description, down to the microscopic structure of his hair and the size of his boots. But when nothing at all of this kind can be done, philosophical difficulties arise, and they reach their maximum in the case of religious expressions. An angel may be talked of as though he were a luminous and filmy man, but when we have decided that such images are mere parables, then to what are we to refer the parables? Are they parables about a non-luminous and non-filmy not-man? About a conscious and voluntary finite being of indeterminate species? About an impression made in the senses of a visionary by God himself?

But why talk of angels? God cannot be described in literal terms, but only in analogies from the created world. To what sort of reality beyond the analogies do the analogies refer? On this subject the views of Lohmeyer and of Bultmann appear complementary rather than opposite. Lohmeyer considers what the transcendent reality is in its very transcendence of all the comparisons in which our analogical statements place it; Bultmann considers the conditions under which we can either justifiably or meaningfully affirm transcendent reality by means of analogical statements. Lohmeyer says boldly that God and the things of God are simply outside our scope, except in so far as they make themselves known through symbols or parables which they arouse in our minds and which express them figuratively. There is no saying what that is for which the figures stand except in further figures, and so without end. Lohmeyer's position is certainly not an explanation, but the statement of ultimate philosophical paradox. But at least it shows a grasp of the difficulty.

What Bultmann has to say about Lohmeyer's question is of little interest. Sometimes he appears to think that as long as we stick to the existential categories of personal relation we can talk of God literally, as near as makes no difference; if some element of the figurative remains, it may be reduced to mere metaphor, or "cipher"; he sees no reason why the unobservable should have to be expressed in terms of the observable. In another place he casually remarks that of course all theological language is analogical, as a recently published book has shown. It is fair to conclude that he has no taste for this line of inquiry. It is, he might say, an abstract speculative puzzle with no practical bearings. A theologian does not want to know the abstract nature of theological statements, but which statements to make and which not to make. However transcendent divine things may be, we are neither going to be silent about them nor to spin fantasies about them at our own sweet will. We shall make serious affirmations about the invisible, but only in so far as it makes itself visible to us. Well, the invisible as such does not become visible, being by definition the side we do not see, like the back of the moon: but it must show us a visible side. We affirm the invisible side of the medal only when the visible is open to our apprehension, and otherwise not.

We are ourselves talking in metaphors here, and obviously the word "visible" is not literally meant. In the case of the original disciples it would be tolerable to speak literally of a visible side to the medal of which the invisible side was the presence of God, but the case of the disciples is not our case. "Visible" will have to be interpreted to mean "playing a real part in our existence", analogous, let us say, to the part that the friendship of an absent friend can play, when we orientate our life and action towards him and his friendship for us. There is much in the reality of my friend's personal being which transcends my active relation with him, and yet it is on the ground of my active relation with him that I affirm that transcendent and private being of his.

The parable of the two-sided medal is, I think, completely acceptable. That is really the trouble about it: everyone will cheerfully accept it, for it is so ambiguous that all possible differences of doctrine can be covered by it. For where is the theologian who wishes to affirm, anyhow as matters of faith, propositions about transcendent realities which do not determine the character or direction of our present existence in any way? Heaven and Hell? Yes, for we live for Heaven, and to escape Hell; these things should be more real to us than the prizes and dangers of earthly life. Blessed Mary and the Saints? Why yes, for our prayer is undertaken with the support of theirs, our service of God is one piece with theirs.

"Ah, but surely this is to stretch the formula of the two-sided medal too far. The invisible side must be kept no more than a hairbreadth distant from the visible side; faith must not soar, it must modestly affirm an invisible lining to what is actually encountered. If the dictate of conscience and pull of vocation are real factors in our life, let us affirm no more than something authoritative, something which plans for us.'' But obviously the existential affirmations of faith are made in no such spirit. Faith goes to all lengths and affirms that absolute and infinite being is precisely he with whom she has to do. The invisible side of the medal is infinite, the visible stamps its impress on our finite and transitory act, there is no proportion between the sign and the reality signified. And so the formula of the two-sided medal allows any of us to affirm any transcendent reality which he sincerely believes to have a bearing on his spiritual existence or (we ought surely to add) on the spiritual existence of other people whom he takes seriously. No requirement that the "invisible" should be kept in correspondence with the "visible" amounts to anything more than a general exhortation. It tells us to be realistic and sincere in theological affirmation, it does not tell us where or how to draw the line.

Bultmann's chief interest lies in the application of the doctrine of religious belief to the interpretation of the New Testament. He rightly says that the divine in Christ is something transcendent, something affirmed by faith, something we should not affirm unless it came home to us in our present existence. In saying this, he admits a high doctrine of transcendence. For the cross of Christ which in its "visible" side is stamped upon our present existence to crucify our wills, transcends us so far that it reaches in its invisible being all the way back to the Calvary where it crucified him.

Bultmann insists that the divine in Christ can be acknowledged in our present existence only, and never revealed by historical research; and there is a sense in which that is true. The techniques of historical scholarship cannot establish that God lived in man, but only that certain things were done and certain words were said. But of course the work of historical scholarship may bring me face to face with what will awaken faith in me. Suppose I am historically persuaded that Christ preached himself as Son of God in the words of the Gospel, I may believe Christ then and there, and without waiting to hear Dr Bultmann preach him to me from the pulpit. Or again, if I did hear Dr Bultmann proclaiming the faith of the Church, I might not believe him until I had had leisure to search the Scriptures. What turned the scales might be the historical persuasion that the seeds of the Church's faith were not only in the Gospels but in the historical fact behind the Gospels.

There is an ambiguity about "history" into which, perhaps, Dr Bultmann does not fall, but against which his readers need to be warned. "History" is sometimes used to describe a science, and sometimes to describe a sort of statement having a distinctive logical nature. In sense 1 we talk about historical reasoning and historical conclusions based upon it, and only of historical statements in so far as they express historical conclusions. But in sense 2 an historical statement need have no relation to historical method or reason; a clairvoyant makes an historical statement in this sense, if, after stroking the bark of a mulberry tree, he declares it to have been planted by Queen Anne. I may have a high respect for his gift, and may believe him, in which case I believe an historical statement (sense 2) about Queen Anne, but not on historical grounds.

Now it looks (I say no more) as if Dr Bultmann were claiming that nothing but historical grounds (sense 1) can establish an historical belief (sense 2) in our minds. For example, he holds, and we will agree, that the sheer reasoning of scientific history would not oblige us to grant that the narratives of the virginal conception in SS Matthew and Luke, together with the allusions in St John, indicate the actual truth of the event referred to or described. But Bultmann seems to assume that if this is so we cannot believe in the virginal conception as a matter of historical fact (sense 2) on grounds of faith: faith cannot, in his view, extend the area of historical belief, but only add an invisible divine lining to such an area of historical belief as historical reasoning (sense 1) adequately supports. I hold this to be false. What Christians find in Christ through faith inclines them at certain points to accept with regard to him testimony about matter of fact which would be inconclusive if offered with regard to any other man. The Christian who refused to take that step would in my opinion be pedantic and irrational, like a man who required the same guarantees for trusting a friend which he would require for trusting a stranger. Thus it is possible through faith and evidence together, and through neither alone, to believe that Christ really and corporeally rose from the dead, not merely that his death on the cross had a supernatural silver lining significant for our salvation. Obviously the use of faith to confirm evidence makes the most exacting demands on intellectual honesty. We must believe neither without evidence nor against evidence. And so, when Dr Bultmann undermines the testimony to the saving miracles by alleging conflict between the witnesses, I allow the relevance of his argument. What I disagree with is simply his interpretations of the texts he refers to.

A disciple of Dr Bultmann's would no doubt feel that I am travestying his view by substituting my vague figure of the two-sided medal in place of his much more precise existential position. For the existential position will allow deductions about the inadmissibility of the physical and miraculous embodiment of divine action which the formula of the two-sided medal will not. I am, indeed, well aware of that, but I have wished to see how far Dr Bultmann's arguments take us if they are placed on grounds which all reasonable Christians ought to concede. It may be that the real first step of Dr Bultmann's whole plea is the exhortation to embrace existentialism or drown, and that everything else is a mere corollary to that. But in fact many of us are not, and are not going to be, existentialists of the Heidegger school, and so we try to see what Bultmann's position amounts to if we leave the dogmatic existentialism out.

The existentialism which Dr Bultmann admires is of much value for opening the eyes of materialists to inward things. It shows them how to talk in a tolerably hard and exact way about personal interaction, about freedom, responsibility, and decision. It reveals courage and nobility, but also agony and insufficiency: darkness from which a spiritual salvation (if there were one) might deliver us, and some scattered gleams of the glory into which it might, in delivering, translate us. In a word, it reveals *man* in something like the sense the word bears for Christian thought. And so it may prepare the way for the discovery of a sense of need, which is the preliminary to faith. Nor need its contribution end when a man has come to believe. It can still set before his eyes the realm of personal existence to which faith is normally relevant and in which the presence and act of God can normally be looked for by the believer.

In so far as existentialism opens and enlarges vision, what can we do but welcome it? but when it is used to set up arbitrary limits to the scope of our thought we have every reason to suspect and hate it: when, for example, it fixes the narrow

model of personal encounter on the whole form of our relation
with our Creator, or when it sets natural fact in such antithesis
to personal existence that it is handed over wholly to the
unescapable rule of physical regularity. It is, no doubt, a useful
apologetic device to abandon natural fact to the naturalists and
set up shop in the realm of personal existence, for it disarms
the prejudice to which obsession with physical technique gives
rise. But it is not in fact true that nature is set apart from spirit
by the hard-and-fast dichotomy which Kant defined, and the
continuous life of Catholic Christendom testifies to the contrary.
The miracles of the saints never cease: a hundred years ago the
sainted Curé d'Ars multiplied bread and healed the sick and
lived himself by a continuous physical miracle, nor has he lacked
successors since.

Dr Bultmann seems to have no difficulty with the belief that
personal existence can kick off the body and survive: his un-
believing existentialist teachers would hardly follow him there.
To others of us it is vital that we have in physical miracle a token
from God of the power which can adjust spirit and nature to a
new and happier union: as when he bodily raised our Saviour
from the dead.

The criticisms I have ventured to offer bear on the speculative
and doctrinal side of Dr Bultmann's positions. As to the practical
need for the interpretation of the Gospel to people everywhere
in terms they can best understand, I trust that I share his sincere
and Christian concern.

I will add one last remark. There are certain steps in demythicization which, being the elimination of puerile error,
can be got through once for all and not repeated, but there is
another sort of demythicization which never ends in this life
because it belongs to the very form of our religious thought.
When we pray, we must begin by conceiving God in full and
vigorous images, but we must go on to acknowledge the inadequacy of them and to adhere nakedly to the imageless truth
of God. The crucifixion of the images in which God is first
shown to us is a necessity of prayer because it is a necessity of
life. The promise of God's dealing with us through grace can
be set before us in nothing but images, for we have not yet
experienced the reality. When we proceed to live the promises
out, the images are crucified by the reality, slowly and pro-

gressively, never completely, and not always without pain: yet the reality is better than the images. Jesus Christ clothed himself in all the images of messianic promise, and in living them out, crucified them: but the crucified reality is better than the figures of prophecy. This is very God and life eternal, whereby the children of God are delivered from idols.

BIBLIOGRAPHY

English

Cullmann, O. *Christ and Time*. E.T., 1950.

Grobel, Kendrik. *Bultmann's Problem of N.T. Mythology*. *JBL*, 1951.

Henderson, I. *Myth in the New Testament*. 1952

Robinson, J. A. T. *In the End God*, 1950, pp. 25–35, and review by R. H. Fuller in *Theology*, vol. liv, p. 269f.

Schweitzer, W. The Message and the Myths. *Ecumenical Review*. 1950.

Wilder, Amos N. Mythology and the New Testament. A review of Kerygma und Mythos. *JBL*, 1950, p. 113ff.
Eschatology and Ethics in the Teaching of Jesus. 1950.

Wright, G. Ernest. *God Who Acts*, 1952, pp. 116–128.

Non-English

Kerygma und Mythos, Vol. I. In addition to the essays here translated:
Götz Habsmeier: Mythos und Offenbarung.
Ein Briefwechsel von Prof. J. B. Soucek und Götz Habsmeier.
Die Definition des "Mythologischen" bei Bultmann.
Dr. Paul Olivier: Bultmanns Vorverständnis.

Kerygma und Mythos, Vol. II, 1952.
E. Stauffer: Entmythologisierung oder Realtheologie?
H.-W. Bartsch: Die neutestamentliche Theologie in der Entscheidung.
Anmerkungen zu O. Cullmann: Christus und die Zeit.
H. Sauter: Für und Wider die Entmythologisierung des Neuen Testaments.
R. Prenter: Mythos und Evangelium.
F. Buri: Entmythologisierung oder Entkerygmatisierung der Theologie.
K. Barth: Abdruck aus Dogmatik III, 2, pp. 531–7.

Chr. Hartlich und W. Sachs: Kritische Prüfung der Haupteinwände Barths gegen Bultmann.

Chr. Hartlich und W. Sachs: Thielickes Ansätze zur Lösung des Entmythologisierungsproblems.

W. G. Kümmel: Mythische Rede und Heilsgeschehen im Neuen Testament.

A. Oepke: Entmythologisierung des Christentums? Thesen.

R. Bultmann: Zum Problem der Entmythologisierung.

Other non-English works

Althaus, P. Die christliche Wahrheit, Vol. I, 1947, p. 208f.

Bender, D. Erklärung der Landessynode, Baden, 1950.

Beyreuter, Erich. Pietistische Erlebnistheologie, Existentialtheologie von heute. ELK, 1952, No. 1.

Bornkamm, G. Evangelium und Mythos. Zeichen der Zeit, 1/51.

Braun, Herbert. Die Ueberwindung des Liberalismus auf der Ebene des Kritizismus. Verkündigung und Forschung, 1949/50, p. 49ff.

Bultmann, R. Das Problem der Hermeneutik. ZTK, 1950, p. 47ff.

Weissagung und Erfüllung. Ibid., 1949, p. 360ff.

Das Problem des Verhältnisses von Theologie und Verkündigung im Neuen Testament. Festschrift für Maurice Goguel, 1950, p. 32ff.

Das Christologische Bekenntnis des oekumenischen Rates. Ev. T, 1951, p. 1ff.

Das Urchristentum im Rahmen der antiken Religionen, 1949.

Theologie und Glaube. Unterwegs, 1951, p. 273f.

Brunner, E. Dogmatik, Vol. II, 1950, pp. 211ff. and 311ff.

Casalis, G. Le Problème du Mythe. Revue d'Histoire et de Philosophie religieuse, p. 330ff.

Diem, H. Grundfragen der Hermeneutik. TEH, N.F. 26, 1951.

Dinkler, C. Bibelauthorität und Bibelkritik. ZTK, 1950, p. 7off.

Ebeling, G. Die Bedeutung der historisch-kritischen Methode für die Protestantische Theologie. ZTK, 1950, p. 1ff.

Ellwein, E. Fragen zu Bultmanns Interpretation des neutestamentlichen Kerygmas; in E. Kinder, Ein Wort. . .

Fransen, P. Entmythologisierung, Bijdragen, 1950, p. 284ff.

Frey, H. Zum Theologischen Programm Rudolf Bultmanns. *ELK*, 1951, No. 22.

Fuchs, E. 1949, *Ev. T*, p. 447ff.
Das entmythologisierte Glaubensärgernis. *Ev. T.*, 1951/2, p. 289ff.
Warum bedarf der Glaube an Jesus Christus eines Selbstverständnisses? *ZTK*, 1952.
Bultmann, Barth und Kant. *TLZ*, 1950/12.

Gogarten, F. Die Verkündigung Jesu Christi. Grundlagen und Aufgabe. *Die Kirche in der Welt*, 1950.

Gyllenberg, R. Nya testament och var tid. *Via Abodomens fot* 1949.

Herbert, K. *Zur Frage der Entmythologisierung*, 1950.

Hof, Otto. Luthers exegetischer Grundsatz von der *analogia fidei*. *ELK*, 1949, No. 24.

Horstmeier, Marie. *Mythologischer und geistiger Christusglaube*, 1950.

Kamlah, W. Der Mensch in der Profanität. *SG*, 1949.

Kinder, E. *Ein Wort lutherischer Theologie zur Entmythologisierung*, 1952.

Klaas, W. Der moderne Mensch in der Theologie R. Bultmanns. *TS*, 1947.

Künneth, W. Mythos im Neuem Testament. *TZ*, 1950.
Die Stellungnahme der ev.-luth. Kirche zur Theologie Rudolf Bultmanns. *FAB*, 1952, p. 163ff.

Krüger, G. Philosophisches Denken und christlicher Glaube, *SG*, 1948.

Landesbrüderrat der Ev. Bekenntnisgemeinschaft in Würtemberg. Erklärung zur Bultmannschen Theologie. *FAB*. 1952, 18ff.

Lauerer, H. Christozentrische Schriftkritik, *ELK*, 1949, No. 18.
Der Ansatz der luth. Schriftkritik. *ELK*, 1950, No. 19.
Versuch einer luth. Schriftkritik. *ELK*, Nos. 4 and 5.

Leese, K. 13 Thesen zur Entmythologisierung des Christentums. *Freies Christentum*, 1952, p. 71ff.

Lerle, E. *Voraussetzung der nt.lichen Exegese*, 1952.

Merz, G. Bultmanns Standort in der Geschichte der Theologie; in E. Kinder, *Ein Wort.* . .

Michaelis, W. *Was bedeutet die Entmythologisierung des Neuen Testaments?* 1950.

Mundle, W. *Der Glaube an Christus und der historische Zweifel.* 1950. Entmythologisierung und existentiale Interpretation. *ELK*, 1952, p. 161ff.

Neuenschwander, U. *Die Protestantische Theologie der Gegenwart und das Problem der biblischen Mythologie,* 1948.

Nygren, A. Christus und Die Verderbungsmächte in *Viva vox evangelii,* 1952.

Pedersen, T. *Kristendomes afmythologisierung og Forkyndelsen,* 1950. Offenbarung und Schrift. *ELK,* 1949, No. 18.

Prenter, R. *Evangeliets afmythologisierung,* 1946.

Rienicker, F. Stellungnahme zu Bultmanns "Entmythologisierung". *Biblische Studien und Zeitfragen,* 3, 1951.

Schieder, J. Randbemerkungen zu Bultmann, in E. Kinder, *Ein Wort.* . .

Schindelein, F. *Gedanken zu Bultmanns Theologie,* 1950.

Schlink, E. *SG,* 1948.

Schumann, F. K. Verkündigung und Auslegung. *DP,* 1951, p. 121ff.

Schweitzer, W. Das Problem der Biblischen Hermeneutik in der gegenwärtigen Theologie. *TLZ,* 1950/8.

Schweitzer, E. Zur Interpretation des Kreuzes bei R. Bultmann. *Festschrift für Maurice Goguel,* 1950, p. 228ff.

Simmel, Oscar, S.J. Mythos und Neues Testament. *Stimmen der Zeit,* 1952, 7, p. 33ff.

Süss, T. Kritische Gedanken zur Entmythologisierung. *ELK,* 1951, No. 15.

Stählin, G. "Mythos" in *Theol. Wörterbuch zum Neuen Testament,* IV, 1942, p. 769ff.

Steck, K. G. Leugnung der Auferstehung? *Die Stimme der Kirche,* 1949, No. 8, p. 7ff and No. 9, p. 11ff.

Steege, G. *Mythos, Differenzierung, Selbstinterpretation,* 1952.

Steinbach, E. *Mythos und Geschichte,* 1951.

Strathmann, H. Klare Begriffe. *DP.* 1951, p. 157ff.

Tübingen: Für und Wider die Theologie Bultmanns. *Denkschrift der Ev. Theol. Fakultät,* 1952.

Vogel, H. Kerygma und Mythos. *Theologia Viatorum, Jahrbuch der kirchlichen Hochschule Berlin,* 1951, p. 47ff.

Walz, H. H. Das hermeneutische Problem. *FAB,* 1949.

Wiesner, W. Anthropologische oder Theologische Schriftauslegung? *Ev. T,* 1950/1, p. 49ff.

Abbreviations

DP   = *Deutsches Pfarrerblatt.*

ELK   = *Evangelische Lutherische Kirchenzeitung.*

Ev. T = *Evangelische Theologie.*

FAB   = *Für Arbeit und Besinnung.*

JBL   = *Journal of Biblical Literature.*

SG   = *Studium Generale.*

TEH   = *Theologische Existenz Heute.*

TLZ   = *Theologische Literatur Zeitung.*

TZ   = *Theologische Zeitschrift.*

ZTK   = *Zeitschrift für Theologie und Kirche.*

harper 🔥 torchbooks

HUMANITIES AND SOCIAL SCIENCES

American Studies: General

THOMAS C. COCHRAN: The Inner Revolution. *Essays on the Social Sciences in History*   TB/1140
EDWARD S. CORWIN: American Constitutional History. *Essays edited by Alpheus T. Mason and Gerald Garvey* △   TB/1136
CARL N. DEGLER, Ed.: Pivotal Interpretations of American History   TB/1240, TB/1241
A. HUNTER DUPREE: Science in the Federal Government: *A History of Policies and Activities to 1940*   TB/573
A. S. EISENSTADT, Ed.: The Craft of American History: *Recent Essays in American Historical Writing*
Vol. I   TB/1255;   Vol. II   TB/1256
CHARLOTTE P. GILMAN: Women and Economics: *A Study of the Economic Relation between Men and Women as a Factor in Social Evolution.* ‡ *Ed. with an Introduction by Carl N. Degler*   TB/3073
OSCAR HANDLIN, Ed.: This Was America: *As Recorded by European Travelers in the Eighteenth, Nineteenth and Twentieth Centuries. Illus.*   TB/1119
MARCUS LEE HANSEN: The Atlantic Migration: 1607-1860. *Edited by Arthur M. Schlesinger*   TB/1052
MARCUS LEE HANSEN: The Immigrant in American History.   TB/1120
JOHN HIGHAM, Ed.: The Reconstruction of American History ‡   TB/1068
ROBERT H. JACKSON: The Supreme Court in the American System of Government   TB/1106
JOHN F. KENNEDY: A Nation of Immigrants. △ *Illus.*   TB/1118
LEONARD W. LEVY, Ed.: American Constitutional Law: *Historical Essays*   TB/1285
RALPH BARTON PERRY: Puritanism and Democracy   TB/1138
ARNOLD ROSE: The Negro in America   TB/3048
MAURICE R. STEIN: The Eclipse of Community. *An Interpretation of American Studies*   TB/1128
W. LLOYD WARNER and Associates: Democracy in Jonesville: *A Study in Quality and Inequality* ¶   TB/1129
W. LLOYD WARNER: Social Class in America: *The Evaluation of Status*   TB/1013

American Studies: Colonial

BERNARD BAILYN, Ed.: Apologia of Robert Keayne: *Self-Portrait of a Puritan Merchant*   TB/1201
BERNARD BAILYN: The New England Merchants in the Seventeenth Century   TB/1149
JOSEPH CHARLES: The Origins of the American Party System   TB/1049

LAWRENCE HENRY GIPSON: The Coming of the Revolution: 1763-1775. † *Illus.*   TB/3007
LEONARD W. LEVY: Freedom of Speech and Press in Early American History: *Legacy of Suppression*   TB/1109
PERRY MILLER: Errand Into the Wilderness   TB/1139
PERRY MILLER & T. H. JOHNSON, Eds.: The Puritans: *A Sourcebook of Their Writings*
Vol. I   TB/1093;   Vol. II   TB/1094
EDMUND S. MORGAN, Ed.: The Diary of Michael Wigglesworth, 1653-1657: *The Conscience of a Puritan*   TB/1228
EDMUND S. MORGAN: The Puritan Family: *Religion and Domestic Relations in Seventeenth-Century New England*   TB/1227
RICHARD B. MORRIS: Government and Labor in Early America   TB/1244
KENNETH B. MURDOCK: Literature and Theology in Colonial New England   TB/99
WALLACE NOTESTEIN: The English People on the Eve of Colonization: 1603-1630. † *Illus.*   TB/3006
LOUIS B. WRIGHT: The Cultural Life of the American Colonies: 1607-1763. † *Illus.*   TB/3005

American Studies: From the Revolution to 1860

JOHN R. ALDEN: The American Revolution: 1775-1783. † *Illus.*   TB/3011
MAX BELOFF, Ed.: The Debate on the American Revolution, 1761-1783: *A Sourcebook* △   TB/1225
RAY A. BILLINGTON: The Far Western Frontier: 1830-1860. †   TB/3012
W. R. BROCK: An American Crisis: *Congress and Reconstruction, 1865-67* º △   TB/1283
EDMUND BURKE: On the American Revolution: *Selected Speeches and Letters.* ‡ *Edited by Elliott Robert Barkan*   TB/3068
WHITNEY R. CROSS: The Burned-Over District: *The Social and Intellectual History of Enthusiastic Religion in Western New York, 1800-1850* △   TB/1242
GEORGE DANGERFIELD: The Awakening of American Nationalism: 1815-1828. † *Illus.*   TB/3061
CLEMENT EATON: The Freedom-of-Thought Struggle in the Old South. *Revised and Enlarged. Illus.*   TB/1150
CLEMENT EATON: The Growth of Southern Civilization: 1790-1860. † *Illus.*   TB/3040
LOUIS FILLER: The Crusade Against Slavery: 1830-1860. † *Illus.*   TB/3029
DIXON RYAN FOX: The Decline of Aristocracy in the Politics of New York: 1801-1840. ‡ *Edited by Robert V. Remini*   TB/3064
FELIX GILBERT: The Beginnings of American Foreign Policy: *To the Farewell Address*   TB/1200
FRANCIS GRIERSON: The Valley of Shadows: *The Coming of the Civil War in Lincoln's Midwest: A Contemporary Account*   TB/1246

---

† The New American Nation Series, edited by Henry Steele Commager and Richard B. Morris.

‡ American Persectives series, edited by Bernard Wishy and William E. Leuchtenburg.

* The Rise of Modern Europe series, edited by William L. Langer.

¶ Researches in the Social, Cultural, and Behavioral Sciences, edited by Benjamin Nelson.

§ The Library of Religion and Culture, edited by Benjamin Nelson.

Σ Harper Modern Science Series, edited by James R. Newman.

º Not for sale in Canada.

△ Not for sale in the U. K.

MILLARD MEISS: Painting in Florence and Siena after the Black Death: *The Arts, Religion and Society in the Mid-Fourteenth Century. 169 illus.* TB/1148

ERICH NEUMANN: The Archetypal World of Henry Moore. △ *107 illus.* TB/2020

DORA & ERWIN PANOFSKY : Pandora's Box: *The Changing Aspects of a Mythical Symbol. Revised Edition. Illus.* TB/2021

ERWIN PANOFSKY: Studies in Iconology: *Humanistic Themes in the Art of the Renaissance.* △ *180 illustrations* TB/1077

ALEXANDRE PIANKOFF: The Shrines of Tut-Ankh-Amon. *Edited by N. Rambova. 117 illus.* TB/2011

JEAN SEZNEC: The Survival of the Pagan Gods: *The Mythological Tradition and Its Place in Renaissance Humanism and Art. 108 illustrations* TB/2004

OTTO VON SIMSON: The Gothic Cathedral: *Origins of Gothic Architecture and the Medieval Concept of Order.* △ *58 illus.* TB/2018

HEINRICH ZIMMER: Myth and Symbols in Indian Art and Civilization. *70 illustrations* TB/2005

Business, Economics & Economic History

REINHARD BENDIX: Work and Authority in Industry: *Ideologies of Management in the Course of Industrialization* TB/3035

GILBERT BURCK & EDITORS OF FORTUNE: The Computer Age: *And Its Potential for Management* TB/1179

THOMAS C. COCHRAN: The American Business System: *A Historical Perspective, 1900-1955* TB/1080

THOMAS C. COCHRAN: The Inner Revolution: *Essays on the Social Sciences in History* △ TB/1140

THOMAS C. COCHRAN & WILLIAM MILLER: The Age of Enterprise: *A Social History of Industrial America* TB/1054

ROBERT DAHL & CHARLES E. LINDBLOM: Politics, Economics, and Welfare: *Planning and Politico-Economic Systems Resolved into Basic Social Processes* TB/3037

PETER F. DRUCKER: The New Society: *The Anatomy of Industrial Order* △ TB/1082

EDITORS OF FORTUNE: America in the Sixties: *The Economy and the Society* TB/1015

ROBERT L. HEILBRONER: The Great Ascent: *The Struggle for Economic Development in Our Time* TB/3030

FRANK H. KNIGHT: The Economic Organization TB/1214

FRANK H. KNIGHT: Risk, Uncertainty and Profit TB/1215

ABBA P. LERNER: Everybody's Business: *Current Assumptions in Economics and Public Policy* TB/3051

ROBERT GREEN MC CLOSKEY: American Conservatism in the Age of Enterprise, 1865-1910 △ TB/1137

PAUL MANTOUX: The Industrial Revolution in the Eighteenth Century: *The Beginnings of the Modern Factory System in England* ○ △ TB/1079

WILLIAM MILLER, Ed.: Men in Business: *Essays on the Historical Role of the Entrepreneur* TB/1081

RICHARD B. MORRIS: Government and Labor in Early America △ TB/1244

HERBERT SIMON: The Shape of Automation: *For Men and Management* TB/1245

PERRIN STRYKER: The Character of the Executive: *Eleven Studies in Managerial Qualities* TB/1041

PIERRE URI: Partnership for Progress: *A Program for Transatlantic Action* TB/3036

Contemporary Culture

JACQUES BARZUN: The House of Intellect △ TB/1051

CLARK KERR: The Uses of the University TB/1264

JOHN U. NEF: Cultural Foundations of Industrial Civilization △ TB/1024

NATHAN M. PUSEY: The Age of the Scholar: *Observations on Education in a Troubled Decade* TB/1157

PAUL VALÉRY: The Outlook for Intelligence △ TB/2016

RAYMOND WILLIAMS: Culture and Society, 1780-1950 ○ △ TB/1252

RAYMOND WILLIAMS: The Long Revolution.○ △ *Revised Edition* TB/1253

Historiography & Philosophy of History

JACOB BURCKHARDT: On History and Historians. △ *Introduction by H. R. Trevor-Roper* TB/1216

WILHELM DILTHEY: Pattern and Meaning in History: *Thoughts on History and Society.* ○ △ *Edited with an Introduction by H. P. Rickman* TB/1075

J. H. HEXTER: Reappraisals in History: *New Views on History & Society in Early Modern Europe* △ TB/1100

H. STUART HUGHES: History as Art and as Science: *Twin Vistas on the Past* TB/1207

RAYMOND KLIBANSKY & H. J. PATON, Eds.: Philosophy and History: *The Ernst Cassirer Festschrift. Illus.* TB/1115

ARNOLDO MOMIGLIANO: Studies in Historiography ○ △ TB/1288

GEORGE H. NADEL, Ed.: Studies in the Philosophy of History: *Selected Essays from History and Theory* TB/1208

JOSE ORTEGA Y GASSET: The Modern Theme. *Introduction by Jose Ferrater Mora* TB/1038

KARL R. POPPER: The Open Society and Its Enemies △
Vol. I: *The Spell of Plato* TB/1101
Vol. II: *The High Tide of Prophecy: Hegel, Marx and the Aftermath* TB/1102

KARL R. POPPER: The Poverty of Historicism ○ △ TB/1126

G. J. RENIER: History: *Its Purpose and Method* △ TB/1209

W. H. WALSH: Philosophy of History: *An Introduction* △ TB/1020

History: General

L. CARRINGTON GOODRICH: A Short History of the Chinese People. △ *Illus.* TB/3015

DAN N. JACOBS & HANS H. BAERWALD: Chinese Communism: *Selected Documents* TB/3031

BERNARD LEWIS: The Arabs in History △ TB/1029

BERNARD LEWIS: The Middle East and the West ○ △ TB/1274

History: Ancient

A. ANDREWES: The Greek Tyrants △ TB/1103

ADOLF ERMAN, Ed. The Ancient Egyptians: *A Sourcebook of Their Writings. New material and Introduction by William Kelly Simpson* TB/1233

MICHAEL GRANT: Ancient History ○ △ TB/1190

SAMUEL NOAH KRAMER: Sumerian Mythology TB/1055

NAPHTALI LEWIS & MEYER REINHOLD, Eds.: Roman Civilization. Sourcebook I: *The Republic* TB/1231

NAPHTALI LEWIS & MEYER REINHOLD, Eds.: Roman Civilization. Sourcebook II: *The Empire* TB/1232

History: Medieval

P. BOISSONNADE: Life and Work in Medieval Europe: *The Evolution of the Medieval Economy, the 5th to the 15th Century.* ○ △ *Preface by Lynn White, Jr.* TB/1141

HELEN CAM: England before Elizabeth △ TB/1026

NORMAN COHN: The Pursuit of the Millennium: *Revolutionary Messianism in Medieval and Reformation Europe* △ TB/1037

G. G. COULTON: Medieval Village, Manor, and Monastery △ TB/1022

CHRISTOPHER DAWSON, Ed.: Mission to Asia: *Narratives and Letters of the Franciscan Missionaries in Mongolia and China in the 13th and 14 Centuries* △ TB/315

HEINRICH FICHTENAU: The Carolingian Empire: *The Age of Charlemagne* △ TB/1142

F. L. GANSHOF: Feudalism △ TB/1058

DENO GEANAKOPLOS: Byzantine East and Latin West: *Two Worlds of Christendom in the Middle Ages and Renaissance* TB/1265

EDWARD GIBBON: The Triumph of Christendom in the Roman Empire (Chaps. XV-XX of "Decline and Fall," J. B. Bury edition). § △ *Illus.* TB/46

W. O. HASSALL, Ed.: Medieval England: *As Viewed by Contemporaries* △ TB/1205

DENYS HAY: Europe: The Emergence of an Idea △ TB/1275

DENYS HAY: The Medieval Centuries ○ △ TB/1192

J. M. HUSSEY: The Byzantine World △ TB/1057

ROBERT LATOUCHE: The Birth of Western Economy: *Economic Aspects of the Dark Ages.* ○ △ *Intro. by Philip Grierson* TB/1290

FERDINAND LOT: The End of the Ancient World and the Beginnings of the Middle Ages. *Introduction by Glanville Downey* TB/1044

G. MOLLAT: The Popes at Avignon: 1305-1378 △ TB/308

CHARLES PETIT-DUTAILLIS: The Feudal Monarchy in France and England: *From the Tenth to the Thirteenth Century* ○ △ TB/1165

HENRI PIRENNE: Early Democracies in the Low Countries: *Urban Society and Political Conflict in the Middle Ages and the Renaissance. Introduction by John H. Mundy* TB/1110

STEVEN RUNCIMAN: A History of the Crusades. △
Volume I: *The First Crusade and the Foundation of the Kingdom of Jerusalem. Illus.* TB/1143
Volume II: *The Kingdom of Jerusalem and the Frankish East, 1100-1187. Illus.* TB/1243

FERDINAND SCHEVILL: Siena: *The History of a Medieval Commune. Intro. by William M. Bowsky* TB/1164

SULPICIUS SEVERUS et al.: The Western Fathers: *Being the Lives of Martin of Tours, Ambrose, Augustine of Hippo, Honoratus of Arles and Germanus of Auxerre.* △ *Edited and trans. by F. O. Hoare* TB/309

HENRY OSBORN TAYLOR: The Classical Heritage of the Middle Ages. *Foreword and Biblio. by Kenneth M. Setton* TB/1117

F. VAN DER MEER: Augustine The Bishop: *Church and Society at the Dawn of the Middle Ages* △ TB/304

J. M. WALLACE-HADRILL: The Barbarian West: *The Early Middle Ages, A.D. 400-1000* △ TB/1061

History: Renaissance & Reformation

JACOB BURCKHARDT: The Civilization of the Renaissance in Italy. △ *Intro. by Benjamin Nelson & Charles Trinkaus. Illus.* Vol. I TB/40; Vol. II TB/41

JOHN CALVIN & JACOPO SADOLETO: A Reformation Debate. *Edited by John C. Olin* TB/1239

ERNST CASSIRER: The Individual and the Cosmos in Renaissance Philosophy. △ *Translated with an Introduction by Mario Domandi* TB/1097

FEDERICO CHABOD: Machiavelli and the Renaissance △ TB/1193

EDWARD P. CHEYNEY: The Dawn of a New Era, 1250-1453. * *Illus.* TB/3002

G. CONSTANT: The Reformation in England: *The English Schism, Henry VIII, 1509-1547* △ TB/314

R. TREVOR DAVIES: The Golden Century of Spain, 1501-1621 ○ △ TB/1194

G. R. ELTON: Reformation Europe, 1517-1559 ○ △ TB/1270

DESIDERIUS ERASMUS: Christian Humanism and the Reformation: *Selected Writings. Edited and translated by John C. Olin* TB/1166

WALLACE K. FERGUSON et al.: Facets of the Renaissance TB/1098

WALLACE K. FERGUSON et al.: The Renaissance: *Six Essays. Illus.* TB/1084

JOHN NEVILLE FIGGIS: The Divine Right of Kings. *Introduction by G. R. Elton* TB/1191

JOHN NEVILLE FIGGIS: Political Thought from Gerson to Grotius: 1414-1625: *Seven Studies. Introduction by Garrett Mattingly* TB/1032

MYRON P. GILMORE: The World of Humanism, 1453-1517. * *Illus.* TB/3003

FRANCESCO GUICCIARDINI: Maxims and Reflections of a Renaissance Statesman (Ricordi). *Trans. by Mario Domandi. Intro. by Nicolai Rubinstein* TB/1160

J. H. HEXTER: More's Utopia: *The Biography of an Idea. New Epilogue by the Author* TB/1195

HAJO HOLBORN: Ulrich von Hutten and the German Reformation TB/1238

JOHAN HUIZINGA: Erasmus and the Age of Reformation. △ *Illus.* TB/19

JOEL HURSTFIELD, Ed.: The Reformation Crisis △ TB/1267

ULRICH VON HUTTEN et al.: On the Eve of the Reformation: "Letters of Obscure Men." *Introduction by Hajo Holborn* TB/1124

PAUL O. KRISTELLER: Renaissance Thought: *The Classic, Scholastic, and Humanist Strains* TB/1048

PAUL O. KRISTELLER: Renaissance Thought II: *Papers on Humanism and the Arts* TB/1163

NICCOLÒ MACHIAVELLI: History of Florence and of the Affairs of Italy: *from the earliest times to the death of Lorenzo the Magnificent. Introduction by Felix Gilbert* △ TB/1027

ALFRED VON MARTIN: Sociology of the Renaissance. *Introduction by Wallace K. Ferguson* TB/1099

GARRETT MATTINGLY et al.: Renaissance Profiles. △ *Edited by J. H. Plumb* TB/1162

MILLARD MEISS: Painting in Florence and Siena after the Black Death: *The Arts, Religion and Society in the Mid-Fourteenth Century.* △ 169 illus. TB/1148

J. E. NEALE: The Age of Catherine de Medici ○ △ TB/1085

ERWIN PANOFSKY: Studies in Iconology: *Humanistic Themes in the Art of the Renaissance.* △ 180 illustrations TB/1077

J. H. PARRY: The Establishment of the European Hegemony: 1415-1715: *Trade and Exploration in the Age of the Renaissance* △ TB/1045

J. H. PLUMB: The Italian Renaissance: *A Concise Survey of Its History and Culture* △ TB/1161

A. F. POLLARD: Henry VIII. ○ △ *Introduction by A. G. Dickens* TB/1249

A. F. POLLARD: Wolsey. ○ △ *Introduction by A. G. Dickens* TB/1248

CECIL ROTH: The Jews in the Renaissance. *Illus.* TB/834

A. L. ROWSE: The Expansion of Elizabethan England. ○ △ *Illus.* TB/1220

GORDON RUPP: Luther's Progress to the Diet of Worms ○ △ TB/120

FERDINAND SCHEVILL: The Medici. *Illus.* TB/1010

FERDINAND SCHEVILL: Medieval and Renaissance Florence. *Illus.* Volume I: *Medieval Florence* TB/1090
Volume II: *The Coming of Humanism and the Age of the Medici* TB/1091

G. M. TREVELYAN: England in the Age of Wycliffe, 1368-1520 ○ △ TB/1112

VESPASIANO: Renaissance Princes, Popes, and Prelates: *The Vespasiano Memoirs: Lives of Illustrious Men of the XVth Century. Intro. by Myron P. Gilmore* TB/1111

History: Modern European

FREDERICK B. ARTZ: Reaction and Revolution, 1815-1832. * *Illus.* TB/3034

MAX BELOFF: The Age of Absolutism, 1660-1815 △ TB/1062

ROBERT C. BINKLEY: Realism and Nationalism, 1852-1871. * *Illus.* TB/3038

ASA BRIGGS: The Making of Modern England, 1784-1867: *The Age of Improvement* ○ △ TB/1203

CRANE BRINTON: A Decade of Revolution, 1789-1799. * *Illus.* TB/3018

D. W. BROGAN: The Development of Modern France. ○ △
Volume I: *From the Fall of the Empire to the Dreyfus Affair* TB/1184
Volume II: *The Shadow of War, World War I, Between the Two Wars. New Introduction by the Author* TB/1185

J. BRONOWSKI & BRUCE MAZLISH: The Western Intellectual Tradition: *From Leonardo to Hegel* △ TB/3001

GEOFFREY BRUUN: Europe and the French Imperium, 1799-1814. * *Illus.* TB/3033

ALAN BULLOCK: Hitler, A Study in Tyranny. ○ △ *Illus.* TB/1123

4

E. H. CARR: German-Soviet Relations Between the Two World Wars, 1919-1939   TB/1278

E. H. CARR: International Relations Between the Two World Wars, 1919-1939 ° △   TB/1279

E. H. CARR: The Twenty Years' Crisis, 1919-1939: An Introduction to the Study of International Relations ° △   TB/1122

GORDON A. CRAIG: From Bismarck to Adenauer: Aspects of German Statecraft. Revised Edition   TB/1171

WALTER L. DORN: Competition for Empire, 1740-1763. * Illus.   TB/3032

FRANKLIN L. FORD: Robe and Sword: The Regrouping of the French Aristocracy after Louis XIV   TB/1217

CARL J. FRIEDRICH: The Age of the Baroque, 1610-1660. * Illus.   TB/1004

RENÉ FUELOEP-MILLER: The Mind and Face of Bolshevism: An Examination of Cultural Life in Soviet Russia. New Epilogue by the Author   TB/1188

M. DOROTHY GEORGE: London Life in the Eighteenth Century △   TB/1182

LEO GERSHOY: From Despotism to Revolution, 1763-1789. * Illus.   TB/3017

C. C. GILLISPIE: Genesis and Geology: The Decades before Darwin §   TB/51

ALBERT GOODWIN: The French Revolution △   TB/1064

ALBERT GUÉRARD: France in the Classical Age: The Life and Death of an Ideal △   TB/1183

CARLTON J. H. HAYES: A Generation of Materialism, 1871-1900. * Illus.   TB/3039

J. H. HEXTER: Reappraisals in History: New Views on History and Society in Early Modern Europe △
                                                  TB/1100

STANLEY HOFFMANN et al.: In Search of France: The Economy, Society and Political System in the Twentieth Century   TB/1219

A. R. HUMPHREYS: The Augustan World: Society, Thought, & Letters in 18th Century England ° △
                                                  TB/1105

DAN N. JACOBS, Ed.: The New Communist Manifesto and Related Documents. Third edition, revised
                                                  TB/1078

HANS KOHN: The Mind of Germany: The Education of a Nation △   TB/1204

HANS KOHN, Ed.: The Mind of Modern Russia: Historical and Political Thought of Russia's Great Age TB/1065

WALTER LAQUEUR & GEORGE L. MOSSE, Eds.: International Fascism, 1920-1945. ° △ Volume I of Journal of Contemporary History   TB/1276

WALTER LAQUEUR & GEORGE L. MOSSE, Eds.: The Left-Wing Intelligentsia between the Two World Wars. ° △ Volume II of Journal of Contemporary History
                                                  TB/1286

FRANK E. MANUEL: The Prophets of Paris: Turgot, Condorcet, Saint-Simon, Fourier, and Comte   TB/1218

KINGSLEY MARTIN: French Liberal Thought in the Eighteenth Century: A Study of Political Ideas from Bayle to Condorcet   TB/1114

L. B. NAMIER: Facing East: Essays on Germany, the Balkans, and Russia in the 20th Century △   TB/1280

L. B. NAMIER: Personalities and Powers: Selected Essays △   TB/1186

L. B. NAMIER: Vanished Supremacies: Essays on European History, 1812-1918 °   TB/1088

JOHN U. NEF: Western Civilization Since the Renaissance: Peace, War, Industry, and the Arts   TB/1113

FRANZ NEUMANN: Behemoth: The Structure and Practice of National Socialism, 1933-1944   TB/1289

FREDERICK L. NUSSBAUM: The Triumph of Science and Reason, 1660-1685. * Illus.   TB/1105

DAVID OGG: Europe of the Ancien Régime, 1715-1783 ° △
                                                  TB/1271

JOHN PLAMENATZ: German Marxism and Russian Communism. ° △ New Preface by the Author   TB/1189

RAYMOND W. POSTGATE, Ed.: Revolution from 1789 to 1906: Selected Documents   TB/1063

PENFIELD ROBERTS: The Quest for Security, 1715-1740. * Illus.   TB/3016

PRISCILLA ROBERTSON: Revolutions of 1848: A Social History   TB/1025

GEORGE RUDÉ: Revolutionary Europe, 1783-1815 ° △
                                                  TB/1272

LOUIS, DUC DE SAINT-SIMON: Versailles, The Court, and Louis XIV. ° △ Introductory Note by Peter Gay
                                                  TB/1250

ALBERT SOREL: Europe Under the Old Regime. Translated by Francis H. Herrick   TB/1121

N. N. SUKHANOV: The Russian Revolution, 1917: Eyewitness Account. △ Edited by Joel Carmichael
            Vol. I TB/1066; Vol. II TB/1067

A. J. P. TAYLOR: From Napoleon to Lenin: Historical Essays ° △   TB/1268

A. J. P. TAYLOR: The Habsburg Monarchy, 1809-1918: A History of the Austrian Empire and Austria-Hungary ° △   TB/1187

G. M. TREVELYAN: British History in the Nineteenth Century and After: 1782-1919. ° △ Second Edition TB/1251

H. R. TREVOR-ROPER: Historical Essays ° △   TB/1269

ELIZABETH WISKEMANN: Europe of the Dictators, 1919-1945 ° △   TB/1273

JOHN B. WOLF: The Emergence of the Great Powers, 1685-1715. * Illus.   TB/3010

JOHN B. WOLF: France: 1814-1919: The Rise of a Liberal-Democratic Society   TB/3019

Intellectual History & History of Ideas

HERSCHEL BAKER: The Image of Man: A Study of the Idea of Human Dignity in Classical Antiquity, the Middle Ages, and the Renaissance   TB/1047

R. R. BOLGAR: The Classical Heritage and Its Beneficiaries: From the Carolingian Age to the End of the Renaissance △   TB/1125

RANDOLPH S. BOURNE: War and the Intellectuals: Collected Essays, 1915-1919. △ ‡ Edited by Carl Resek
                                                  TB/3043

J. BRONOWSKI & BRUCE MAZLISH: The Western Intellectual Tradition: From Leonardo to Hegel △   TB/3001

ERNST CASSIRER: The Individual and the Cosmos in Renaissance Philosophy. △ Translated with an Introduction by Mario Domandi   TB/1097

NORMAN COHN: The Pursuit of the Millennium: Revolutionary Messianism in Medieval and Reformation Europe △   TB/1037

C. C. GILLISPIE: Genesis and Geology: The Decades before Darwin §   TB/51

G. RACHEL LEVY: Religious Conceptions of the Stone Age and Their Influence upon European Thought. △ Illus. Introduction by Henri Frankfort   TB/106

ARTHUR O. LOVEJOY: The Great Chain of Being: A Study of the History of an Idea   TB/1009

FRANK E. MANUEL: The Prophets of Paris: Turgot, Condorcet, Saint-Simon, Fourier, and Comte   TB/1218

PERRY MILLER & T. H. JOHNSON, Editors: The Puritans: A Sourcebook of Their Writings
            Vol. I TB/1093; Vol. II TB/1094

MILTON C. NAHM: Genius and Creativity: An Essay in the History of Ideas   TB/1196

ROBERT PAYNE: Hubris: A Study of Pride. Foreword by Sir Herbert Read   TB/1031

RALPH BARTON PERRY: The Thought and Character of William James: Briefer Version   TB/1156

GEORG SIMMEL et al.: Essays on Sociology, Philosophy, and Aesthetics. ‖ Edited by Kurt H. Wolff TB/1234

BRUNO SNELL: The Discovery of the Mind: The Greek Origins of European Thought △   TB/1018

PAGET TOYNBEE: Dante Alighieri: His Life and Works. Edited with Intro. by Charles S. Singleton △ TB/1206

ERNEST LEE TUVESON: Millennium and Utopia: A Study in the Background of the Idea of Progress. ‖ New Preface by the Author   TB/1134

PAUL VALÉRY: The Outlook for Intelligence △   TB/2016

PHILIP P. WIENER: Evolution and the Founders of Pragmatism. △ *Foreword by John Dewey*   TB/1212
BASIL WILLEY: Nineteenth Century Studies: *Coleridge to Matthew Arnold* ○ △   TB/1261
BASIL WILLEY: More Nineteenth Century Studies: *A Group of Honest Doubters* ○ △   TB/1262

Literature, Poetry, The Novel & Criticism

JAMES BAIRD: Ishmael: *The Art of Melville in the Contexts of International Primitivism*   TB/1023
JACQUES BARZUN: The House of Intellect △   TB/1051
W. J. BATE: From Classic to Romantic: *Premises of Taste in Eighteenth Century England*   TB/1036
RACHEL BESPALOFF: On the Iliad   TB/2006
R. P. BLACKMUR et al.: Lectures in Criticism. *Introduction by Huntington Cairns*   TB/2003
JAMES BOSWELL: The Life of Dr. Johnson & The Journal of a Tour to the Hebrides with Samuel Johnson LL.D.: Selections. ○ △ *Edited by F. V. Morley. Illus. by Ernest Shepard*   TB/1254
ABRAHAM CAHAN: The Rise of David Levinsky: *a documentary novel of social mobility in early twentieth century America. Intro. by John Higham*   TB/1028
ERNST R. CURTIUS: European Literature and the Latin Middle Ages △   TB/2015
GEORGE ELIOT: Daniel Deronda: *a novel. Introduction by F. R. Leavis*   TB/1039
ADOLF ERMAN, Ed.: The Ancient Egyptians: *A Sourcebook of Their Writings. New Material and Introduction by William Kelly Simpson*   TB/1233
ÉTIENNE GILSON: Dante and Philosophy   TB/1089
ALFRED HARBAGE: As They Liked It: *A Study of Shakespeare's Moral Artistry*   TB/1035
STANLEY R. HOPPER, Ed : Spiritual Problems in Contemporary Literature §   TB/21
A. R. HUMPHREYS: The Augustan World: *Society, Thought and Letters in 18th Century England* ○ △   TB/1105
ALDOUS HUXLEY: Antic Hay & The Giaconda Smile. ○ △ *Introduction by Martin Green*   TB/3503
ALDOUS HUXLEY: Brave New World & Brave New World Revisited. ○ △ *Introduction by Martin Green*   TB/3501
HENRY JAMES: The Tragic Muse: *a novel. Introduction by Leon Edel*   TB/1017
ARNOLD KETTLE: An Introduction to the English Novel. △
Volume I: *Defoe to George Eliot*   TB/1011
Volume II: *Henry James to the Present*   TB/1012
RICHMOND LATTIMORE: The Poetry of Greek Tragedy △   TB/1257
J. B. LEISHMAN: The Monarch of Wit: *An Analytical and Comparative Study of the Poetry of John Donne* ○ △   TB/1258
J. B. LEISHMAN: Themes and Variations in Shakespeare's Sonnets ○ △   TB/1259
ROGER SHERMAN LOOMIS: The Development of Arthurian Romance △   TB/1167
JOHN STUART MILL: On Bentham and Coleridge. △ *Introduction by F. R. Leavis*   TB/1070
KENNETH B. MURDOCK: Literature and Theology in Colonial New England   TB/99
SAMUEL PEPYS: The Diary of Samuel Pepys. ○ *Edited by O. F. Morshead. Illus. by Ernest Shepard*   TB/1007
ST.-JOHN PERSE: Seamarks   TB/2002
V. DE S. PINTO: Crisis in English Poetry, 1880-1940 ○   TB/1260
GEORGE SANTAYANA: Interpretations of Poetry and Religion §   TB/9
C. K. STEAD: The New Poetic: *Yeats to Eliot* △   TB/1263
HEINRICH STRAUMANN: American Literature in the Twentieth Century. △ *Third Edition, Revised*   TB/1168
PAGET TOYNBEE: Dante Alighieri: *His Life and Works. Edited with Intro. by Charles S. Singleton*   TB/1206
DOROTHY VAN GHENT: The English Novel: *Form and Function*   TB/1050
E. B. WHITE: One Man's Meat. *Introduction by Walter Blair*   TB/3505

BASIL WILLEY: Nineteenth Century Studies: *Coleridge t[o] Matthew Arnold*   TB/126[?]
BASIL WILLEY: More Nineteenth Century Studies: *[A] Group of Honest Doubters* ○ △   TB/126[?]
RAYMOND WILLIAMS: Culture and Society, 1780-1950 ○ △   TB/125[?]
RAYMOND WILLIAMS: The Long Revolution. ○ △ *Revise[d] Edition*   TB/125[?]
MORTON DAUWEN ZABEL, Editor: Literary Opinion i[n] America   Vol. I   TB/3013;   Vol. II   TB/301[?]

Myth, Symbol & Folklore

JOSEPH CAMPBELL, Editor: Pagan and Christian Mysteries [?] Illus.   TB/201[?]
MIRCEA ELIADE: Cosmos and History: *The Myth of th[e] Eternal Return* § △   TB/205[0]
MIRCEA ELIADE: Rites and Symbols of Initiation: *Th[e] Mysteries of Birth and Rebirth* § △   TB/123[?]
THEODOR H. GASTER: Thespis: *Ritual, Myth and Drama in the Ancient Near East* △   TB/128[1]
C. G. JUNG & C. KERÉNYI: Essays on a Science of Mythology: *The Myths of the Divine Child and the Divine Maiden* △   TB/201[4]
DORA & ERWIN PANOFSKY : Pandora's Box: *The Changing Aspects of a Mythical Symbol. △ Revised edition Illus.*   TB/202[?]
ERWIN PANOFSKY: Studies in Iconology: *Humanistic Themes in the Art of the Renaissance. △ 180 illustrations*   TB/1077
JEAN SEZNEC: The Survival of the Pagan Gods: *The Mythological Tradition and its Place in Renaissance Humanism and Art. △ 108 illustrations*   TB/2004
HELLMUT WILHELM: Change: *Eight Lectures on the I Ching* △   TB/201[9]
HEINRICH ZIMMER: Myths and Symbols in Indian Art and Civilization. △ *70 illustrations*   TB/2005

Philosophy

G. E. M. ANSCOMBE: An Introduction to Wittgenstein's Tractatus. ○ △ *Second Edition, Revised*   TB/121[0]
HENRI BERGSON: Time and Free Will: *An Essay on the Immediate Data of Consciousness* ○ △   TB/1021
H. J. BLACKHAM: Six Existentialist Thinkers: *Kierkegaard, Nietzsche, Jaspers, Marcel, Heidegger, Sartre* ○ △   TB/1002
CRANE BRINTON: Nietzsche. *New Preface, Bibliography and Epilogue by the Author*   TB/1197
MARTIN BUBER: The Knowledge of Man. △ *Ed. with an Intro. by Maurice Friedman. Trans. by Maurice Friedman and Ronald Gregor Smith*   TB/135
ERNST CASSIRER: The Individual and the Cosmos in Renaissance Philosophy. △ *Translated with an Introduction by Mario Domandi*   TB/1097
ERNST CASSIRER: Rousseau, Kant and Goethe. *Introduction by Peter Gay*   TB/1092
FREDERICK COPLESTON: Medieval Philosophy ○ △   TB/376
F. M. CORNFORD: Principium Sapientiae: *A Study of the Origins of Greek Philosophical Thought. Edited by W. K. C. Guthrie*   TB/1213
F. M. CORNFORD: From Religion to Philosophy: *A Study in the Origins of Western Speculation* §   TB/20
WILFRID DESAN: The Tragic Finale: *An Essay on the Philosophy of Jean-Paul Sartre*   TB/1030
A. P. D'ENTRÈVES: Natural Law: *An Historical Survey* △   TB/1223
MARVIN FARBER: The Aims of Phenomenology: *The Motives, Methods, and Impact of Husserl's Thought*   TB/1291
HERBERT FINGARETTE: The Self in Transformation: *Psychoanalysis, Philosophy and the Life of the Spirit ¶*   TB/1177
PAUL FRIEDLÄNDER: Plato: *An Introduction* △   TB/2017
ÉTIENNE GILSON: Dante and Philosophy   TB/1089
WILLIAM CHASE GREENE: Moira: *Fate, Good, and Evil in Greek Thought*   TB/1104

w. K. C. GUTHRIE: The Greek Philosophers: *From Thales to Aristotle* ° △   TB/1008

F. H. HEINEMANN: Existentialism and the Modern Predicament △   TB/28

ISAAC HUSIK: A History of Medieval Jewish Philosophy JP/3

EDMUND HUSSERL: Phenomenology and the Crisis of Philosophy. *Translated with an Introduction by Quentin Lauer*   TB/1170

IMMANUEL KANT: The Doctrine of Virtue, *being Part II of the Metaphysic of Morals. Trans. with Notes & Intro. by Mary J. Gregor. Foreword by H. J. Paton*   TB/110

IMMANUEL KANT: Groundwork of the Metaphysic of Morals. *Trans. & analyzed by H. J. Paton*   TB/1159

IMMANUEL KANT: Lectures on Ethics. § △ *Introduction by Lewis W. Beck*   TB/105

IMMANUEL KANT: Religion Within the Limits of Reason Alone. § *Intro. by T. M. Greene & J. Silber*   TB/67

QUENTIN LAUER: Phenomenology: *Its Genesis and Prospect*   TB/1169

GABRIEL MARCEL: Being and Having: *An Existential Diary. △ Intro. by James Collins*   TB/310

GEORGE A. MORGAN: What Nietzsche Means   TB/1198

PHILO, SAADYA GAON, & JEHUDA HALEVI: Three Jewish Philosophers. *Ed. by Hans Lewy, Alexander Altmann, & Isaak Heinemann*   TB/813

MICHAEL POLANYI: Personal Knowledge: *Towards a Post-Critical Philosophy* △   TB/1158

WILLARD VAN ORMAN QUINE: Elementary Logic: *Revised Edition*   TB/577

WILLARD VAN ORMAN QUINE: From a Logical Point of View: *Logico-Philosophical Essays*   TB/566

BERTRAND RUSSELL et al.: The Philosophy of Bertrand Russell. *Edited by Paul Arthur Schilpp*
Vol. I TB/1095; Vol. II TB/1096

L. S. STEBBING: A Modern Introduction to Logic △ TB/538

ALFRED NORTH WHITEHEAD: Process and Reality: *An Essay in Cosmology* △   TB/1033

PHILIP P. WIENER: Evolution and the Founders of Pragmatism. *Foreword by John Dewey*   TB/1212

WILHELM WINDELBAND: A History of Philosophy
Vol. I: *Greek, Roman, Medieval*   TB/38
Vol. II: *Renaissance, Enlightenment, Modern*   TB/39

LUDWIG WITTGENSTEIN: The Blue and Brown Books ° TB/1211

Political Science & Government

JEREMY BENTHAM: The Handbook of Political Fallacies: *Introduction by Crane Brinton*   TB/1069

KENNETH E. BOULDING: Conflict and Defense: *A General Theory*   TB/3024

CRANE BRINTON: English Political Thought in the Nineteenth Century   TB/1071

EDWARD S. CORWIN: American Constitutional History: *Essays edited by Alpheus T. Mason and Gerald Garvey*   TB/1136

ROBERT DAHL & CHARLES E. LINDBLOM: Politics, Economics, and Welfare: *Planning and Politico-Economic Systems Resolved into Basic Social Processes* TB/3037

JOHN NEVILLE FIGGIS: The Divine Right of Kings. *Introduction by G. R. Elton*   TB/1191

JOHN NEVILLE FIGGIS: Political Thought from Gerson to Grotius: 1414-1625: *Seven Studies. Introduction by Garrett Mattingly*   TB/1032

F. L. GANSHOF: Feudalism △   TB/1058

G. P. GOOCH: English Democratic Ideas in the Seventeenth Century   TB/1006

J. H. HEXTER: More's Utopia: *The Biography of an Idea. New Epilogue by the Author*   TB/1195

SIDNEY HOOK: Reason, Social Myths and Democracy △ TB/1237

ROBERT H. JACKSON: The Supreme Court in the American System of Government △   TB/1106

DAN N. JACOBS, Ed.: The New Communist Manifesto *and Related Documents. Third Edition, Revised*   TB/1078

DAN N. JACOBS & HANS BAERWALD, Eds.: Chinese Communism: *Selected Documents*   TB/3031

HANS KOHN: Political Ideologies of the 20th Century TB/1277

ROBERT GREEN MC CLOSKEY: American Conservatism in the Age of Enterprise, 1865-1910   TB/1137

KINGSLEY MARTIN: French Liberal Thought in the Eighteenth Century: *Political Ideas from Bayle to Condorcet* △   TB/1114

ROBERTO MICHELS: First Lectures in Political Sociology. *Edited by Alfred de Grazia* ¶ °   TB/1224

JOHN STUART MILL: On Bentham and Coleridge. △ *Introduction by F. R. Leavis*   TB/1070

BARRINGTON MOORE, JR.: Political Power and Social Theory: *Seven Studies* ¶   TB/1221

BARRINGTON MOORE, JR.: Soviet Politics—The Dilemma of Power: *The Role of Ideas in Social Change* ¶ TB/1222

BARRINGTON MOORE, JR.: Terror and Progress—USSR: *Some Sources of Change and Stability in the Soviet Dictatorship* ¶   TB/1266

JOHN B. MORRALL: Political Thought in Medieval Times △   TB/1076

JOHN PLAMENATZ: German Marxism and Russian Communism. ° △ *New Preface by the Author* TB/1189

KARL R. POPPER: The Open Society and Its Enemies △
Vol. I: *The Spell of Plato*   TB/1101
Vol. II: *The High Tide of Prophecy: Hegel, Marx and the Aftermath*   TB/1102

HENRI DE SAINT-SIMON: Social Organization, The Science of Man, and Other Writings. *Edited and Translated by Felix Markham*   TB/1152

JOSEPH A. SCHUMPETER: Capitalism, Socialism and Democracy △   TB/3008

CHARLES H. SHINN: Mining Camps: *A Study in American Frontier Government. ‡ Edited by Rodman W. Paul* TB/3062

PETER WOLL, Ed.: Public Administration and Policy: *Selected Essays*   TB/1284

Psychology

ALFRED ADLER: The Individual Psychology of Alfred Adler. △ *Edited by Heinz L. and Rowena R. Ansbacher* TB/1154

ALFRED ADLER: Problems of Neurosis. *Introduction by Heinz L. Ansbacher*   TB/1145

ANTON T. BOISEN: The Exploration of the Inner World: *A Study of Mental Disorder and Religious Experience* TB/87

ARTHUR BURTON & ROBERT E. HARRIS, Eds.: Clinical Studies of Personality
Vol. I TB/3075; Vol. II TB/3076

HADLEY CANTRIL: The Invasion from Mars: *A Study in the Psychology of Panic* ¶   TB/1282

HERBERT FINGARETTE: The Self in Transformation: *Psychoanalysis, Philosophy and the Life of the Spirit* ¶ TB/1177

SIGMUND FREUD: On Creativity and the Unconscious: *Papers on the Psychology of Art, Literature, Love, Religion.* § △ *Intro. by Benjamin Nelson*   TB/45

C. JUDSON HERRICK: The Evolution of Human Nature TB/545

WILLIAM JAMES: Psychology: *The Briefer Course. Edited with an Intro. by Gordon Allport*   TB/1034

C. G. JUNG: Psychological Reflections △   TB/2001

C. G. JUNG: Symbols of Transformation: *An Analysis of the Prelude to a Case of Schizophrenia. △ Illus.*
Vol. I TB/2009; Vol. II TB/2010

C. G. JUNG & C. KERÉNYI: Essays on a Science of Mythology: *The Myths of the Divine Child and the Divine Maiden*   TB/2014

JOHN T. MC NEILL: A History of the Cure of Souls TB/126

KARL MENNINGER: Theory of Psychoanalytic Technique TB/1144

ERICH NEUMANN: Amor and Psyche: *The Psychic Development of the Feminine* △ TB/2012
ERICH NEUMANN: The Archetypal World of Henry Moore. △ *107 illus.* TB/2020
ERICH NEUMANN: The Origins and History of Consciousness △ Vol. I *Illus.* TB/2007; Vol. II TB/2008
C. P. OBERNDORF: A History of Psychoanalysis in America TB/1147
RALPH BARTON PERRY: The Thought and Character of William James: *Briefer Version* TB/1156
JEAN PIAGET, BÄRBEL INHELDER, & ALINA SZEMINSKA: The Child's Conception of Geometry ○ △ TB/1146
JOHN H. SCHAAR: Escape from Authority: *The Perspectives of Erich Fromm* TB/1155
MUZAFER SHERIF: The Psychology of Social Norms TB/3072

Sociology

JACQUES BARZUN: Race: *A Study in Superstition. Revised Edition* TB/1172
BERNARD BERELSON, Ed.: The Behavioral Sciences Today TB/1127
ABRAHAM CAHAN: The Rise of David Levinsky: *A documentary novel of social mobility in early twentieth century America. Intro. by John Higham* TB/1028
THOMAS C. COCHRAN: The Inner Revolution: *Essays on the Social Sciences in History* TB/1140
ALLISON DAVIS & JOHN DOLLARD: Children of Bondage: *The Personality Development of Negro Youth in the Urban South* ¶ TB/3049
ST. CLAIR DRAKE & HORACE R. CAYTON: Black Metropolis: *A Study of Negro Life in a Northern City.* △ *Revised and Enlarged. Intro. by Everett C. Hughes* Vol. I TB/1086; Vol. II TB/1087
EMILE DURKHEIM et al.: Essays on Sociology and Philosophy: *With Analyses of Durkheim's Life and Work.* ¶ *Edited by Kurt H. Wolff* TB/1151
LEON FESTINGER, HENRY W. RIECKEN & STANLEY SCHACHTER: When Prophecy Fails: *A Social and Psychological Account of a Modern Group that Predicted the Destruction of the World* ¶ TB/1132
ALVIN W. GOULDNER: Wildcat Strike: *A Study in Worker-Management Relationships* ¶ TB/1176
FRANCIS J. GRUND: Aristocracy in America: *Social Class in the Formative Years of the New Nation* △ TB/1001
KURT LEWIN: Field Theory in Social Science: *Selected Theoretical Papers.* ¶ △ *Edited with a Foreword by Dorwin Cartwright* TB/1135
R. M. MAC IVER: Social Causation TB/1153
ROBERT K. MERTON, LEONARD BROOM, LEONARD S. COTTRELL, JR., Editors: Sociology Today: *Problems and Prospects* ¶ Vol. I TB/1173; Vol. II TB/1174
ROBERTO MICHELS: First Lectures in Political Sociology. *Edited by Alfred de Grazia* ¶ ○ TB/1224
BARRINGTON MOORE, JR.: Political Power and Social Theory: *Seven Studies* ¶ TB/1221
BARRINGTON MOORE, JR.: Soviet Politics—The Dilemma of Power: *The Role of Ideas in Social Change* ¶ TB/1222
TALCOTT PARSONS & EDWARD A. SHILS, Editors: Toward a General Theory of Action: *Theoretical Foundations for the Social Sciences* TB/1083
JOHN H. ROHRER & MUNRO S. EDMONDSON, Eds.: The Eighth Generation Grows Up: *Cultures and Personalities of New Orleans Negroes* ¶ TB/3050
ARNOLD ROSE: The Negro in America: *The Condensed Version of Gunnar Myrdal's An American Dilemma* TB/3048
KURT SAMUELSSON: Religion and Economic Action: *A Critique of Max Weber's The Protestant Ethic and the Spirit of Capitalism.* ¶ ○ *Trans. by E. G. French. Ed. with Intro. by D. C. Coleman* TB/1131
PHILIP SELZNICK: TVA and the Grass Roots: *A Study in the Sociology of Formal Organization* TB/1230
GEORG SIMMEL et al.: Essays on Sociology, Philosophy, and Aesthetics. ¶ *Edited by Kurt H. Wolff* TB/1234

HERBERT SIMON: The Shape of Automation: *For Men and Management* △ TB/1245
PITIRIM A. SOROKIN: Contemporary Sociological Theories *Through the First Quarter of the 20th Century* TB/3046
MAURICE R. STEIN: The Eclipse of Community: *An Interpretation of American Studies* TB/1128
FERDINAND TÖNNIES: Community and Society: *Gemeinschaft und Gesellschaft. Translated and edited by Charles P. Loomis* TB/1116
W. LLOYD WARNER & Associates: Democracy in Jonesville: *A Study in Quality and Inequality* TB/1129
W. LLOYD WARNER: Social Class in America: *The Evaluation of Status* TB/1013

RELIGION

Ancient & Classical

J. H. BREASTED: Development of Religion and Thought in Ancient Egypt. *Intro. by John A. Wilson* TB/57
HENRI FRANKFORT: Ancient Egyptian Religion: *An Interpretation* TB/77
G. RACHEL LEVY: Religious Conceptions of the Stone Age *and their Influence upon European Thought.* △ *Illus. Introduction by Henri Frankfort* TB/106
MARTIN P. NILSSON: Greek Folk Religion. *Foreword by Arthur Darby Nock* TB/78
ALEXANDRE PIANKOFF: The Shrines of Tut-Ankh-Amon. △ *Edited by N. Rambova. 117 illus.* TB/2011
ERWIN ROHDE: Psyche: *The Cult of Souls and Belief in Immortality Among the Greeks.* △ *Intro. by W. K. C. Guthrie* Vol. I TB/140; Vol. II TB/141
H. J. ROSE: Religion in Greece and Rome △ TB/55

Biblical Thought & Literature

W. F. ALBRIGHT: The Biblical Period from Abraham to Ezra TB/102
C. K. BARRETT, Ed.: The New Testament Background: *Selected Documents* △ TB/86
C. H. DODD: The Authority of the Bible △ TB/43
M. S. ENSLIN: Christian Beginnings △ TB/5
M. S. ENSLIN: The Literature of the Christian Movement △ TB/6
JOHN GRAY: Archaeology and the Old Testament World. △ *Illus.* TB/127
JAMES MUILENBURG: The Way of Israel: *Biblical Faith and Ethics* △ TB/133
H. H. ROWLEY: The Growth of the Old Testament △ TB/107
GEORGE ADAM SMITH: The Historical Geography of the Holy Land. ○ △ *Revised and reset* TB/138
D. WINTON THOMAS, Ed.: Documents from Old Testament Times △ TB/85

The Judaic Tradition

LEO BAECK: Judaism and Christianity. *Trans. with Intro. by Walter Kaufmann* JP/23
SALO W. BARON: Modern Nationalism and Religion JP/18
MARTIN BUBER: Eclipse of God: *Studies in the Relation Between Religion and Philosophy* △ TB/12
MARTIN BUBER: For the Sake of Heaven TB/801
MARTIN BUBER: Hasidism and Modern Man. △ *Ed. and Trans. by Maurice Friedman* TB/839
MARTIN BUBER: The Knowledge of Man. △ *Edited with an Introduction by Maurice Friedman. Translated by Maurice Friedman and Ronald Gregor Smith* TB/135
MARTIN BUBER: Moses: *The Revelation and the Covenant* △ TB/837
MARTIN BUBER: The Origin and Meaning of Hasidism △ TB/835
MARTIN BUBER: Pointing the Way. △ *Introduction by Maurice S. Friedman* TB/103
MARTIN BUBER: The Prophetic Faith TB/73
MARTIN BUBER: Two Types of Faith: *the interpenetration of Judaism and Christianity* ○ △ TB/75

NATURAL SCIENCES
AND MATHEMATICS

Biological Sciences

LUDWIG VON BERTALANFFY: Problems of Life: An Evaluation of Modern Biological and Scientific Thought △　TB/521

HAROLD F. BLUM: Time's Arrow and Evolution　TB/555

JOHN TYLER BONNER: The Ideas of Biology. Σ △ Illus.
TB/570

A. J. CAIN: Animal Species and their Evolution. △ Illus.
TB/519

WALTER B. CANNON: Bodily Changes in Pain, Hunger, Fear and Rage. Illus.　TB/562

W. E. LE GROS CLARK: The Antecedents of Man: An Introduction to Evolution of the Primates. ○ △ Illus. TB/559

W. H. DOWDESWELL: Animal Ecology. △ Illus.　TB/543

W. H. DOWDESWELL: The Mechanism of Evolution. △ Illus.
TB/527

R. W. GERARD: Unresting Cells. Illus.　TB/541

DAVID LACK: Darwin's Finches. △ Illus.　TB/544

ADOLF PORTMANN: Animals as Social Beings. ○ △ Illus.
TB/572

O. W. RICHARDS: The Social Insects. △ Illus.　TB/542

P. M. SHEPPARD: Natural Selection and Heredity. △ Illus.
TB/528

EDMUND W. SINNOTT: Cell and Psyche: The Biology of Purpose　TB/546

C. H. WADDINGTON: How Animals Develop. △ Illus.
TB/553

C. H. WADDINGTON: The Nature of Life: The Main Problems and Trends in Modern Biology △　TB/580

Chemistry

J. R. PARTINGTON: A Short History of Chemistry. △ Illus.
TB/522

Communication Theory

J. R. PIERCE: Symbols, Signals and Noise: The Nature and Process of Communication △　TB/574

Geography

R. E. COKER: This Great and Wide Sea: An Introduction to Oceanography and Marine Biology. Illus.　TB/551

F. K. HARE: The Restless Atmosphere △　TB/560

History of Science

MARIE BOAS: The Scientific Renaissance, 1450-1630 ○ △
TB/583

W. DAMPIER, Ed.: Readings in the Literature of Science. Illus.　TB/512

A. HUNTER DUPREE: Science in the Federal Government: A History of Policies and Activities to 1940 △ TB/573

ALEXANDRE KOYRÉ: From the Closed World to the Infinite Universe: Copernicus, Kepler, Galileo, Newton, etc. △
TB/31

A. G. VAN MELSEN: From Atomos to Atom: A History of the Concept Atom　TB/517

O. NEUGEBAUER: The Exact Sciences in Antiquity △ TB/552

HANS THIRRING: Energy for Man: From Windmills to Nuclear Power △　TB/556

STEPHEN TOULMIN & JUNE GOODFIELD: The Architecture of Matter: Physics, Chemistry & Physiology of Matter, Both Animate & Inanimate, As it Evolved Since the Beginning of Science ○ △　TB/584

STEPHEN TOULMIN & JUNE GOODFIELD: The Discovery of Time ○ △　TB/585

LANCELOT LAW WHYTE: Essay on Atomism: From Democritus to 1960 △　TB/565

Mathematics

E. W. BETH: The Foundations of Mathematics: A Study in the Philosophy of Science △　TB/581

H. DAVENPORT: The Higher Arithmetic: An Introduction to the Theory of Numbers △　TB/526

H. G. FORDER: Geometry: An Introduction △　TB/548

S. KÖRNER: The Philosophy of Mathematics: An Introduction △　TB/547

D. E. LITTLEWOOD: Skeleton Key of Mathematics: A Simple Account of Complex Algebraic Problems △
TB/525

GEORGE E. OWEN: Fundamentals of Scientific Mathematics　TB/569

WILLARD VAN ORMAN QUINE: Mathematical Logic TB/558

O. G. SUTTON: Mathematics in Action. ○ △ Foreword by James R. Newman. Illus.　TB/518

FREDERICK WAISMANN: Introduction to Mathematical Thinking. Foreword by Karl Menger　TB/511

Philosophy of Science

R. B. BRAITHWAITE: Scientific Explanation　TB/515

J. BRONOWSKI: Science and Human Values. △ Revised and Enlarged Edition　TB/505

ALBERT EINSTEIN et al.: Albert Einstein: Philosopher-Scientist. Edited by Paul A. Schilpp　Vol. I　TB/502
Vol. II　TB/503

WERNER HEISENBERG: Physics and Philosophy: The Revolution in Modern Science △　TB/549

JOHN MAYNARD KEYNES: A Treatise on Probability. ○ △ Introduction by N. R. Hanson　TB/557

KARL R. POPPER: Logic of Scientific Discovery △ TB/576

STEPHEN TOULMIN: Foresight and Understanding: An Enquiry into the Aims of Science. △ Foreword by Jacques Barzun　TB/564

STEPHEN TOULMIN: The Philosophy of Science: An Introduction △　TB/513

G. J. WHITROW: The Natural Philosophy of Time ○ △
TB/563

Physics and Cosmology

JOHN E. ALLEN: Aerodynamics: A Space Age Survey △
TB/582

STEPHEN TOULMIN & JUNE GOODFIELD: The Fabric of the Heavens: The Development of Astronomy and Dynamics. △ Illus.　TB/579

DAVID BOHM: Causality and Chance in Modern Physics. △ Foreword by Louis de Broglie　TB/536

P. W. BRIDGMAN: Nature of Thermodynamics　TB/537

P. W. BRIDGMAN: A Sophisticate's Primer of Relativity △
TB/575

A. C. CROMBIE, Ed.: Turning Point in Physics　TB/535

C. V. DURELL: Readable Relativity. △ Foreword by Freeman J. Dyson　TB/530

ARTHUR EDDINGTON: Space, Time and Gravitation: An Outline of the General Relativity Theory　TB/510

GEORGE GAMOW: Biography of Physics Σ △　TB/567

MAX JAMMER: Concepts of Force: A Study in the Foundation of Dynamics　TB/550

MAX JAMMER: Concepts of Mass in Classical and Modern Physics　TB/571

MAX JAMMER: Concepts of Space: The History of Theories of Space in Physics. Foreword by Albert Einstein　TB/533

G. J. WHITROW: The Structure and Evolution of the Universe: An Introduction to Cosmology. △ Illus. TB/504

11